The Magic of Light

THE MAGIC OF LIGHT

The Craft and Career of Jean Rosenthal,
Pioneer in Lighting for the Modern Stage

Jean Rosenthal and
Lael Wertenbaker

Illustrations by Marion Kinsella

ECHO POINT BOOKS & MEDIA, LLC
Brattleboro, Vermont

Published by Echo Point Books & Media
Brattleboro, Vermont
www.EchoPointBooks.com

All rights reserved.
Neither this work nor any portions thereof may be reproduced, stored in a retrieval system, or transmitted in any capacity without written permission from the publisher.

Copyright © 1972, 2024 by Estate of Jean Rosenthal
              and by Lael Wertenbaker

Excerpts from Mark Blitzstein's reminiscences on *The Cradle Will Rock* are reprinted with permission of the Irving S. Gilmore Music Library, Yale University. Copyright ©1956 Spoken Arts, Inc.

The Magic of Light
ISBN: 978-1-64837-429-6 (casebound)
        978-1-64837-430-2 (paperback)

Title page photo by Jane Purse
Image on page 207 by duncan1890, courtesy of istock

Cover design by Kaitlyn Whitaker

Cover photo by Jane Purse

Preface
by Lael Wertenbaker

Jean Rosenthal, whom I met in 1958, was a small, compact, soft-voiced woman with a heart-shaped face, enormous eyes and a gift for paying total attention to whatever she was doing. We talked then about a book on lighting design, the profession in which she was preeminent and about which I knew very little. It was a mark of her intense professionalism that she wanted a collaborating writer. Writing, she insisted, was not her discipline.

In two concentrated discussions we arrived at an outline and a method for carrying out the project. She would supply the material in her own words, dictated, when she had the time. (I was to find that she had verbal as well as practical command of her field, an easy way with words, a talent for visual phrasing, and an organized way of thinking.) I would edit the material, shape the book. Suzanne Gleaves, my partner on many free-lance projects, would supply any additional research. Marion Kinsella, Jean's on-the-job lighting assistant who was an artist and sculptor the rest of her time, would do the illustrations.

We began bravely, but there was a problem. Jean was one of the most in-demand professionals in the world. When she was designing a show or consulting an architect about a building, she concentrated, disappearing from the rest of her life. I told the publisher: there is a book, and there will be a book — one day.

During the next ten years I spent a lot of odd time with Jean. The book got little further, but the time was well worth spending.

Knowing Jean was rewarding. Her vitality, which refreshed rather than tired you, her profound human courtesy, the provocative originality of her mind, her warmth, which reserved to itself a deep personal privacy and never invaded yours, were characteristics which made her a marvelous friend to have.

To watch her work in the theatre, as I sometimes did, was a study in high talent — genius in my opinion and that of others — controlled by proficiency, knowledge and discipline. The elaborate minutiae of lighting design terrified me. If you took strict care of all that technical detail, how could you fail to lose sight of the creative end? If you kept your attention on the artistic whole, how could you manage not to forget some of the details? I do not understand how she did both, maintaining the while her radiating deep calm — but she did.

The theatre electricians with whom she worked quite literally adored her. I retain a mental image of her onstage, surrounded by Joe and Bill and Jim and George, who almost invariably towered over her, as they listened with something like her own concentration to whatever she said, in that soft, courteous voice. I remarked on their devotion, and Jean grinned. "They used to long to throw wrenches at my head," she said, "for all the extra work I caused them." The devotion grew as these union professionals came to understand and take pride in the results of what she asked them to do ("Would you move that slightly to the left, please, darling?"). They simply gave in. Now she had been in the theatre over thirty years, and I felt that her crews constantly restrained strong impulses to pat her approvingly and fondly on her short, ruffled hair, but Jean, for all her small size and gentle manners, had an impressive dignity.

I also see her when the lights had been focused and colored to her satisfaction, standing in the light, happily dabbling her fingers in it, as if it were a tangible substance, and nodding.

When she talked to the director or the scene designer or the star of a show about what he or she wanted, she closed down her attention to each one so completely that it was as if a narrow, high-walled lane were constructed between them. Her concentration was physically expressed by a kind of focusing with her nose: it would wiggle, and the glasses she wore when she was working would slide back into place and her eyes would turn in, as if physically, to the visions in her head instead of to the exterior scene. And how intently she *listened*.

Jean was open to the thinking, the intentions, of others, so ready and so selfless in serving, as she expressed it, "the creative purposes of other men" that they sometimes forgot her creative integrity. Her invariable courtesy made her seem biddable, but she could, on occasion, display the character of a miniature, gray-headed Italian donkey. When she was sure she was right in terms of the mutually conceived artistic whole, she just stood there, polite and patient, refusing to budge no matter how she was coaxed, bullied or stormed at.

Or she bided her time. Once at Stratford, Connecticut, a rehearsal of *All's Well That Ends Well*, one of Shakespeare's problem plays with disagreeable overtones, came to a halt when the director, John Houseman, bellowed, "Jean! Jean! Where are you? I can't *see*!"

Jean, hidden behind her desk, stood up, and said meekly, "Here I am."

"GIVE ME MORE LIGHT!" ordered John.

Jean murmured into her intercom, and before I could blink, the scene went from dim to bright. "Thank you, boys," said Jean quietly to the electricians, "you've saved us about twenty minutes." Then she settled back, narrowing her eyes at the scene, which was laid in the French king's palace where he lay gravely ill. Studying the effect, she remarked *sotto voce*, "He looks wonderfully healthy, don't you think?"

Me: But what will you do?

Jean: Oh, it's all right. I'll put it back the way it was later.

The rehearsal went on, brightly lit.
"I wish," said Jean wistfully, "I had a pom-e-granate."

Since her intransigence was never based on egotism, but on what was best for the production, she nearly always did win such contests of strong wills. One famous Italian designer, who usually did his own lighting, had bitterly opposed having her. She disagreed with him on how to light one set of his and he flung from the theatre in a temper. When he returned, Jean had completed the lighting her way. He looked at it, squinted, frowned, and sat down beside her. "Darrrrling," he said, "I marry you!"

I worked with Jean once on a script of my own. This was on the sound and light production at Boscobel, in Garrison, New York, for which I wrote the drama she lighted. Sound — as for radio drama — was on tape; the lighting took the place of live actors and movement. She lit that lovely house, interior and exterior, the Hudson River bank and all outdoors in patterns following the sequences drawn from history. There is a chapter on Boscobel in this book, but it does not include the night after night when Jean worked on that immense site until three or four in the morning, ordering a chaos of outlets, cues, a technical empire into a design. It was astonishing to see what a tenth-of-an-inch difference in focusing the light on a single tree could make. It was miraculous to see light from the huge "infranors," which needed twenty minutes to warm up, sweep over the lawn exactly on the word she had chosen for the cue. My part in the venture was over, and the chief contribution I made to those nights was to improve my sense of awe and to do the driving. When Jean was behind the wheel, her gift of concentration on what she was doing wavered alarmingly.

The validity of a book by Jean Rosenthal is obvious. She was a pioneer in the art and craft of lighting design, originating many techniques that have since become commonplace. In her field she is a historic figure, recognized for her particular creative genius. Since her major contributions were in the theatre, which lives on only in faulty memories and dusty work sheets, old programs and insufficient photographs, it seemed essential that the credit line "Lighting by Jean Rosenthal" should have been amplified into this book, a heritage important to students of the theatre, to designers and architects. How she *thought* about lighting — the important thing — will not change with changing techniques.

How she thought about light seems to me to have a value for anybody. This is a subjective conclusion. Being with and working with her, I found that I was gaining a new awareness, a conscious awareness of light, which had nothing to do with "how to." And there is nothing more exciting than an expansion of one's personal consciousness.

Of course I have always responded to light, to its kind and quality. Who does not? If I have fancied myself peculiarly sensitive to gloom or glare, that is a common form of egotism. But, as in listening to music, there are many layers of awareness, of pleasure and pain. Deepening awareness creates fresh intensity. Even those obvious visual pleasures — sunrises and sunsets, sun slanted through woods — have been intensified for me. And to be more aware is to have greater control. I can cope better now with the unhappy moods brought on by troubled or "heavy" light, key up or down the spontaneous euphoria of brilliant days. I do not mean to exaggerate, but increased awareness is growth, and the best teachers of awareness are the masters in any field.

After all the years of delay, this book actually evolved in the harsh, gray light of tragedy. Jean was taken mortally ill in 1968. Whether she knew that she could not live much longer, I do not know. I think not. Her vitality seemed so indestructible. That she was very ill indeed could not be denied, even by one as stubborn as she was. Her affliction by cancer was sudden. The operation was major. After that, she was never well again.

Jean had not been sick before, not really, in all her life. She counted on her robust health, inexhaustible energy, her Herculean working capacity. To be knocked down, to lie about, to suffer such pain, came as a surprise as well as a shock. She regarded her illness with detached interest and admitted that it gave her new comprehension of the normal *condition humaine*. Her impatience was for its restrictions. In the hospital, subject to all the indignities and debilitation of major surgery, as soon as she could sit up she covered her bed or the floor of that hospital room with huge designs and insisted on receiving her working confrères. The doctors gave in, finally admitting that her indomitable energy needed this outlet. Her mind remained clear, although the hours when she could concentrate were foreshortened.

One thing she could do, even when supine and too depleted for visitors, was to talk into her recorder on the subject of lighting. In the morning hours she dictated, at long last, the essential material for this book.

She would choose a subject from our outline for the book and state what she thought about it, one idea at a time. Where she left gaps, she indicated them. We had time, Jean and I, in the hospital and during a period of what resembled recovery on Martha's Vineyard, where she shared a lovely house with Marion Kinsella, to talk over the tapes and how they would be organized into the book. Then she returned to New York — and to work. In April 1969, she went back to the hospital.

For thirty-seven years, from ages twenty to fifty-seven, Jean had lighted Martha Graham's ballets. It was the first work she ever did, and it was fitting that it should be the last. Martha Graham had created a new ballet. Jean insisted on attending rehearsals in a wheelchair, and on designing and lighting the production. On April 20, *Archaic Hours* opened in the Graham repertory at the New York City Center, with "Production and Lighting by Jean Rosenthal." On May 1, Jean died.

To complete this book, to shape it from her material, to keep its integrity, has been labor dedicated to her memory, with love. Any one of those with whom she had worked whom I asked for help gave it, unstintingly. The reader will find quotations from what they said in the margins and an acknowledgment of such sources within the book. We all believe that Jean would have approved of her written legacy, and what she contributed to the art and craft of lighting design will never be lost. All is never lost when a great and talented human being dies.

Contents

One.	The Lighting Designer	1
Two.	About J.R.	9
Three.	Collaboration	27
Four.	The History of Illumination	41
Five.	Lighting the Play	57
Six.	Lighting the Musical	73
Seven.	Lighting the Opera	87
Eight.	Lighting the House	105
Nine.	To Dance in Light	115
	Tools of the Trade	133
	Lighting by Jean Rosenthal	207
	Sources of Marginal Quotations	247
	Index	251

One. The Lighting Designer

MARVIN KONER

The lighting of it affects everything light falls upon:
how you see what you see, how you feel about it,
and how you hear what you are hearing.

I am a lighting designer. The profession is only as old as the years I have spent in it. This is astonishing when you consider the flexibility lighting by electricity had achieved before I was born. I think it simply never occurred to anyone until the 1930s that the lighting of anything should be the exclusive concern of a craftsman, let alone under the artistic aegis of a specialist.

Lighting design, in which I pioneered, is still considered for the most part somewhat less important than interior decoration. That attitude is scarcely justified because light remains primarily important in order for people to see what it falls upon. The lighting of it affects everything light falls upon: how you see what you see, how you feel about it, and how you hear what you are hearing.

"*Affect*" is the key word. Change the "a" to an "e" and you get lighting effects. Effects should be handled with all the care and used with the rarity of fireworks. The most successful and brilliant work a lighting designer does is usually the least noticeable.

The use of light for anything must remain primarily social and logical. A major design feature is that light is a necessity, and you use it as a necessity. The logical, basic function of light, of fixtures, of all artificial light, goes all the way back to the human demand and need for visibility in order to see in the dark.

On that firm basis, and when you have complete technical control of your tools, your medium, you can design lighting for infinite subtlety.

I have been called a "bloody electrician with notions." That is not a bad definition of a lighting designer. In the Tools of the Trade section of this book, the equipment and the manner of using it by which certain of my own designs have been carried out are illustrated. Before getting to that, in a time when equipment is becoming yearly more pliant, I should like to expose as clearly as possible what these "notions" are. Lighting design, the imposing of quality on the scarcely visible air through which objects and people are seen, begins with *thinking* about it.

Writers and painters have always understood how light affects

Jean's lights were never simple. They were complicated because Jeannie considered the most important lighting was lighting air, not scenery or people. The air in one of Jean's shows vibrated with the emotion of whatever the particular scene was about. You can't do that without a lot of equipment so there was always a bit of an argument with the carpenters.

— Lucia Victor

what it falls upon, how you see and how you feel (and how you hear).

All literature is full of light. No novelist who controls the lighting of his lifelike universe is apt to set a tender proposal in a blaze. Or to present tragedy without appropriately shading it. If sad events are fictionally brightly lighted, the light falls subjectively on the scene, merciless and not benign.

Artists *see* the air they see through. Naturalistic painters, seeking the essence of what inspires them, may wait for months to catch the ideal light on a particular landscape. Portrait painters use light to reveal the character in faces. In the twentieth century painters began consciously to create arbitrary sources of light within their canvases, an important step in the direction of abstraction.

Dramatists, dependent on others to carry out their intentions, indicate appropriate light and weather to set their scenes. Shakespeare, whose stage was open to the arbitrary sky, filled his spoken words with subtle light. In the nineteenth century, when "special effects" were added to stage illumination, there were times when Shakspeare's poetic subtleties were lost against lurid, realistic sunsets or deluged by lightning.

In the twentieth century, Eugene O'Neill wrote his stage directions with as much care as his dialogue. For the opening of *Mourning Becomes Electra* he asks for a "luminous mist" and stipulates that "the windows of the lower floor reflect the sun's rays in a *resentful* glare [italics mine]."

What a challenge to designers who refrain from using steam for mist. It requires from us what the light-conscious scene designer Robert Edmond Jones pleaded for: "the artist's approach." Without it, we offer nothing. Yet the humble word "approach" should be kept in mind.

In the past thirty-odd years, during which I have designed the lighting for over three hundred shows, the separate program credit "Lighting by ———" or for those scene designers who prefer to do their own lighting, "Scenery and lighting by ———" has become a standard acknowledgment. It is important to remember that lighting is a contributory art, a high craft serving the creative purposes of other men. We need the artist's approach, but to impose a separate artist's ego through light on the artistic whole becomes destructive.

Only when you know that necessity remains the guiding factor and when the techniques and functions of lighting are under your complete technical control may you adopt even the artist's *approach* safely. The minute you fuss around with light, use it arbitrarily or egotistically, decoratively or in a tricky, arty manner, you get a kind of aggressiveness that is not only unattractive in a show and distracting, but equally annoying in a house or an office.

Why on earth, for example, are so many modern offices lit with downlight? Because it is a pretty design idea and it became the fashion to put a lot of fixtures in the ceiling and turn them on. The fact of the matter is that no office worker can stand downlights. They have headaches. They are always moving their desks around to get out of the

---

The plain truth is that life has become so crowded, so hurried, so commonplace, so ordinary, that we have lost the artist's approach to art. Without this, we are nothing.
— Robert Edmond Jones

The longer you're in the theatre, the more you hate the heroics of individuals and the more you respect people who have a love of the whole. The phrase "love of the whole" occurs repeatedly in Miss Rosenthal's conversation and seems to represent to her a spirit of unstinting cooperation that she not only practices herself but regards as embodying a moral principle of some profundity, by which good may be distinguished from evil in nearly every area of human behavior.
— Winthrop Sargeant

direct light. We have the technical means now to reproduce natural light in most of its shadings and intensities and we live more and more of our lives by artificial light — but most of it is bad light.

There is no excuse for bad light. It is the result of poor thinking and impractical application. You must know what the lighting you choose will *do* before you install it. And that is the reason for a book about a lighting designer.

The first question most people ask you about your profession, if you have succeeded in that profession, is how you got into it in the first place. The second is *who* you are that you got into it in the first place. I have decided to answer those questions — partly at the insistence of my collaborator. So I will talk about myself, about J.R., in terms of how I grew up and became a lighting designer. After that, my professional life has been almost the whole of my life, certainly the whole of what is relevant to this book. Since mine is a collaborative profession, it is relevant to talk also about the people with whom I have collaborated.

Then I should like to do a quick survey of the history of lighting in terms of fixtures, the tools of lighting. This fascinates me. No craftsman or artist has less than a debt and a duty to study the past. I do not believe you can ever do sound work, let alone original work, without an understanding and appreciation of what was done before you. Any man's contribution is merely added to the contributions of his professional ancestors.

There are perfectly sound textbooks on the techniques of stage and architectural lighting. I think this book must be a personal approach to lighting. And the best way to approach the craft is through lighting in the theatre.

All the arts and crafts collaborate in the theatre. You light the stage exclusively with artificial light and can take no advantage of natural light, as films may do. All the conditions of life are reconstructed in the theatre, foreshortened and intensified in "scenes." All emotional states are encompassed. Ranging through drama, entertainment, music and dance, you cover all that lighting may contribute to life.

If Bernard Shaw asks for "a fine spring morning beside a river" in which to introduce the young Joan of Lorraine, you create one, in a physically restricted place, on a stage. Once designed, your moist, country morning air is preset to repeat itself for each performance before yielding to "evening on the Loire" or "a restless, fitful windy night, full of summer lightning." Even so cerebral a playwright as Shaw indicates light to enhance the emotional content of his scenes.

But Bernard Shaw would most certainly have objected if any syllable of his had gotten lost because the lighting of the stage had preempted an audience's attention. The lighting of anything almost never plays a *paramount* role — the lighting designer's business is to be as unobtrusive as he is helpful.

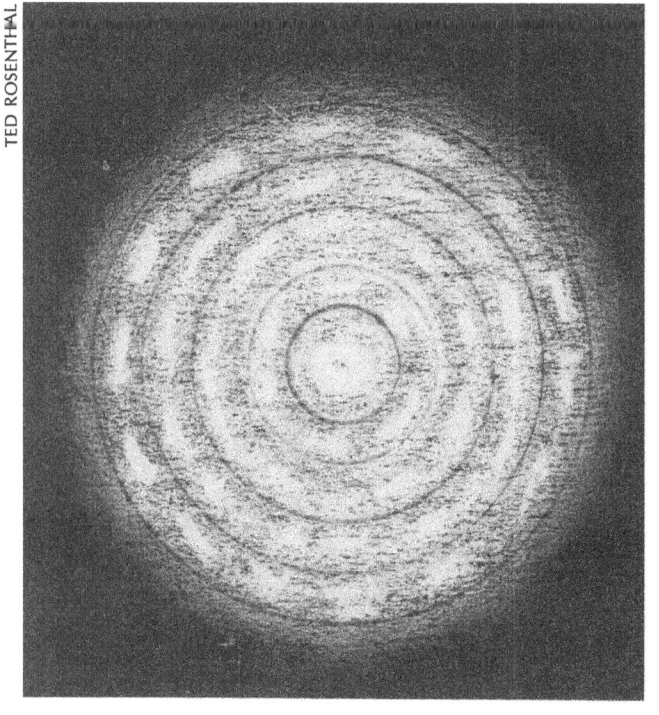

fresnel beam

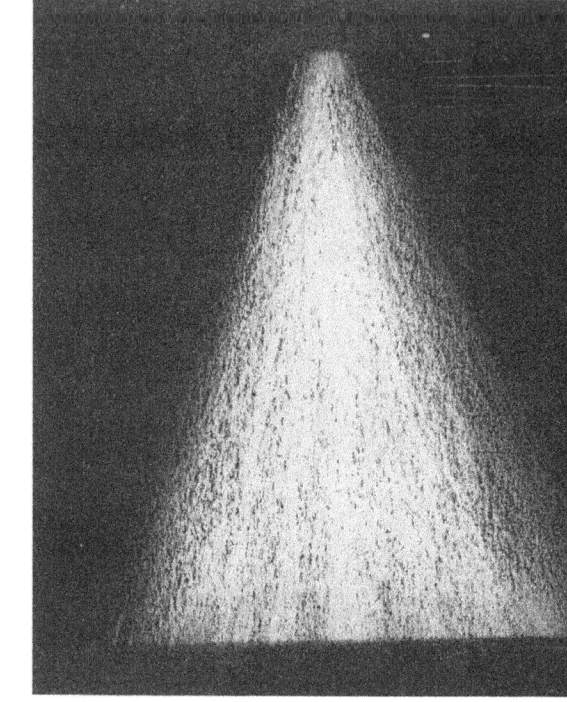

fresnel beam

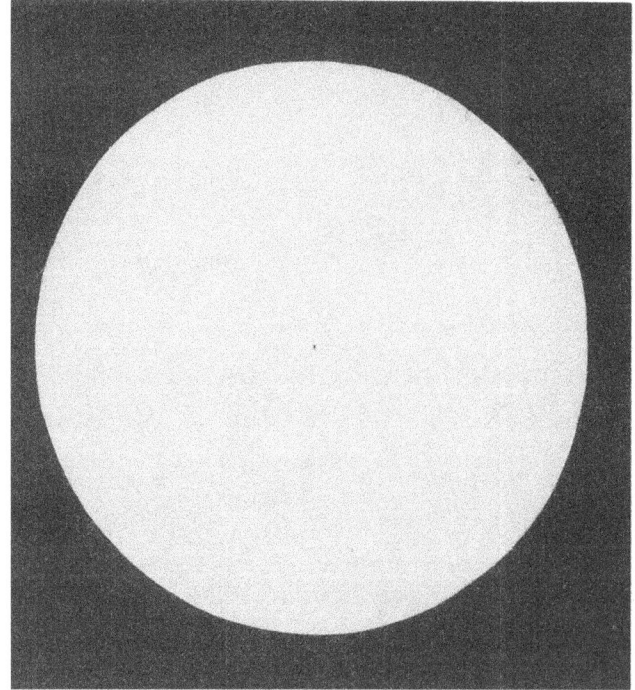

ellipsoidal beam

ellipsoidal beam

beam projector, soft focus

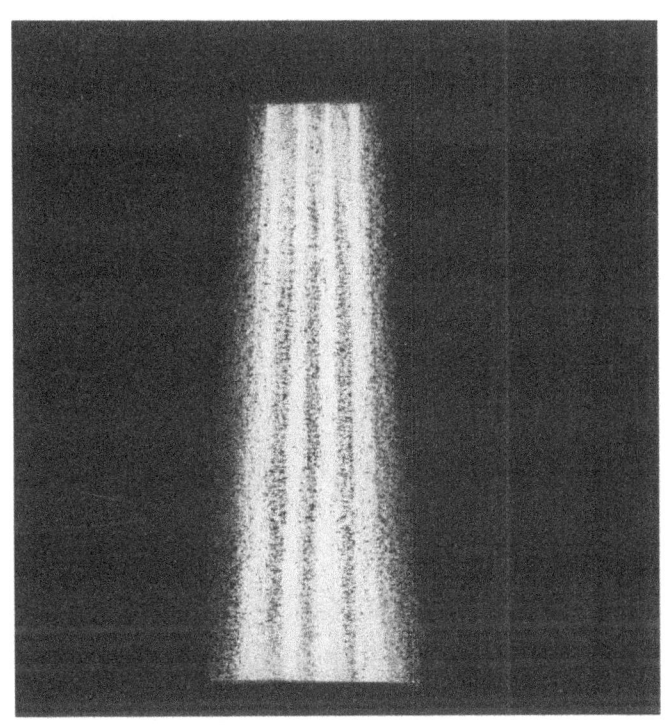

beam projector, hard focus

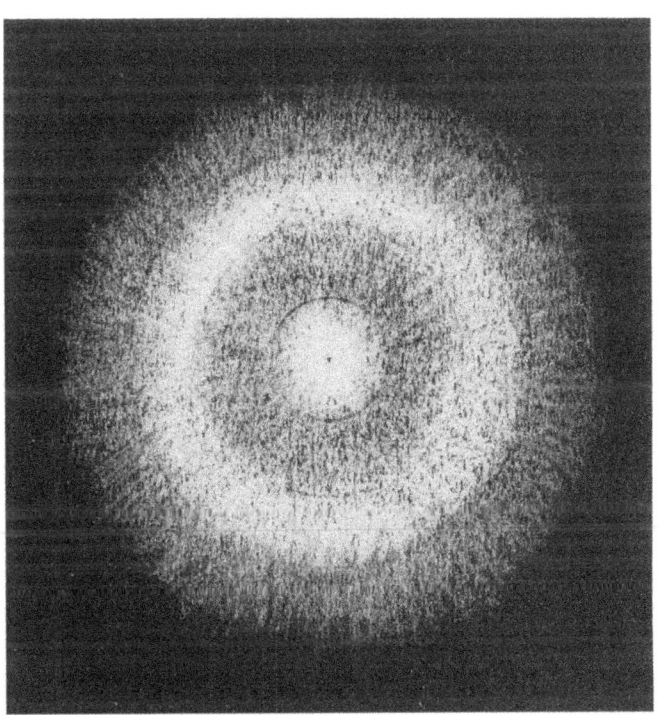

beam projector

HOW LIGHT WORKS
See "Tools of the Trade"

To light a show, any show, demands a mastery of technique — *you must know the tools of your trade* — the acknowledgment that there must *be* a technique, and a method of organizing your ideas. Otherwise you get either a fancy, nervous design that obtrudes itself, or a static, boring mess of light to see the stage by. (The truth is that natural light is never static and that it is only very rarely nervous or sudden.)

I really cannot stand people who go around lighting theatre productions in the disorderly way that many of them do, simply because they do not take the necessary time or face the drudgery of analyzing how each scene or episode should look, visualizing it from a lighting point of view. Pyrotechnics, all too simple to achieve, seldom do more than bring dramatic action to a dead halt, and what I speak of as "European lighting" — a kind of tableau lighting — does little more than make a kind of nineteenth-century picture. I object to scene designers who light their scenery and forget the actors and to directors who light the actors and forget the scenery.

The basic concern in theatre lighting is with the *dramatic intention* of a particular moment. The visibility, or the kind of light, in which you see the actors and the scenery, the place, must have a logic. The logic is based on tying all of these in with the idea of being there, in the scene, in the first place.

Lighting design derives its validity from the answer to the fundamental question *why who* is *where* in the first place. In the answer is the logic of lighting. This logic applies equally to lighting in the theatre or to street lighting or to lighting the interiors of buildings or to the light by which you read a book in a corner.

Two. About J. R.

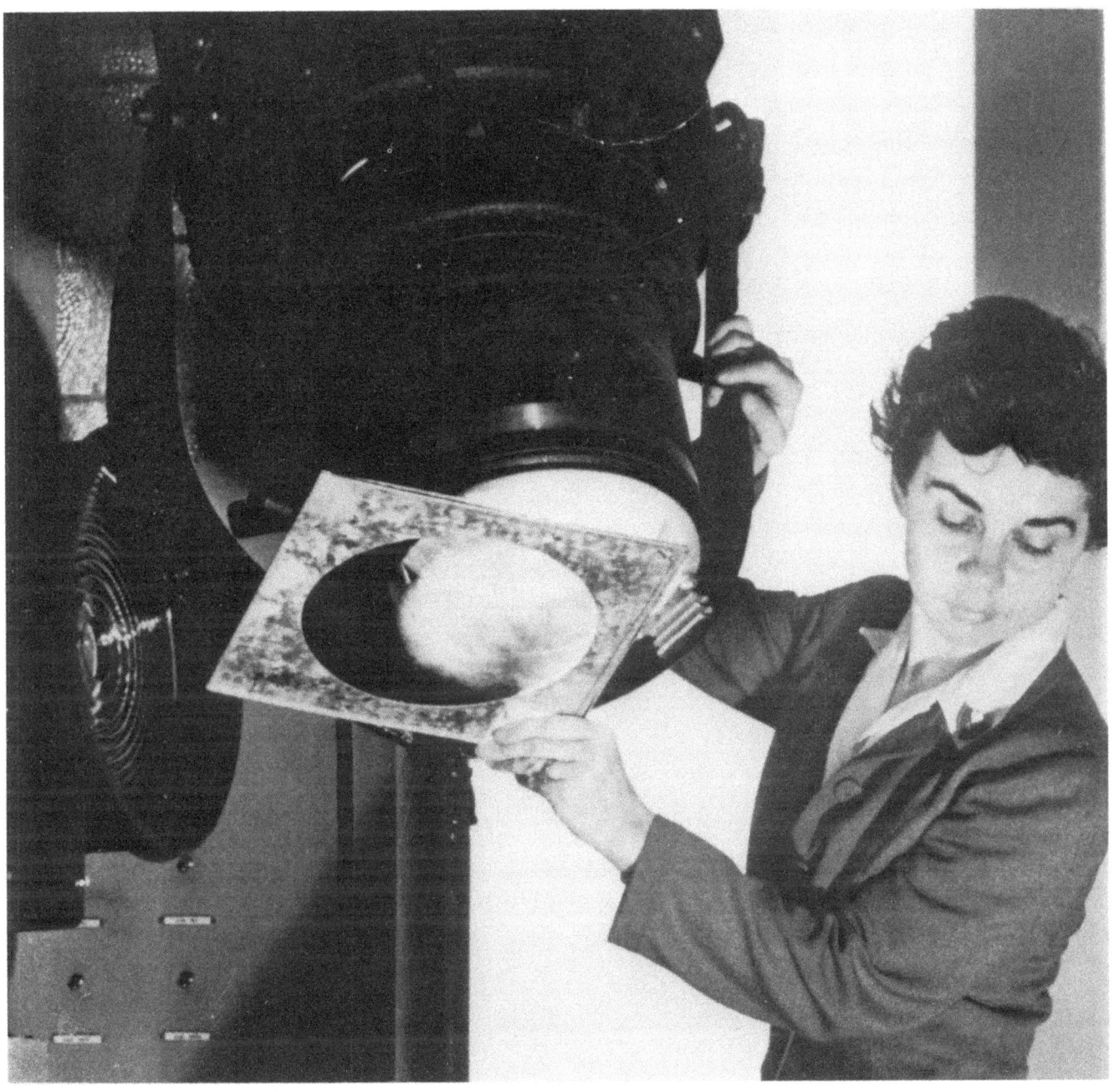

Keeping body and soul together while remaining in
the theatre became one of my favorite investigations.

To talk about my life and self is one way of presenting my credentials, as it were, and of giving some consideration to what sort of person is saying what I have to say. I find, after all, that it is rather fun to think about myself autobiographically. My life has not been that of the solo artist, whose work may speak for itself, but one of constant collaboration with artists, producers, directors, technicians and tools. To think about lighting design or a lighting designer at all is to include a great many other people and a great many other things.

For most of my life, profession and person have not really been separable. At twenty-three I "opened on Broadway" stage managing Leslie Howard's *Hamlet* — a fortuitous opportunity requiring the utmost temerity in the face of chance. More than a quarter of a century later I designed the lighting for Richard Burton's *Hamlet* on Broadway, having, so to speak, worked my way back up to my beginnings.

Professionally and personally I should like to think that I have matured steadily if erratically through my more than half a century. Nonetheless, looking back, I would say that my childhood and the decade of the 1920s and the early 1930s were the years that had the greatest influence on the whole of my life.

My mother, a prejudiced observer if ever there was one, admits that when I was born in New York City on March 16, 1912, I was about as hideous and fragile a specimen as could hope for survival. My birth weight was less than five pounds and for weeks I gained not an ounce. Both my parents were physicians. In despair they took me to a specialist at Mt. Sinai Hospital and demanded what to do with the scrawny, shrunken little thing. On the prescribed Walker-Gordon milk, with an additive, I finally began, I am told, to resemble a human baby rather than a starving animal.

Dr. Pauline Rosenthal, my mother, went back to her practice. The money was needed to support my older brother and me. Cared for by our "one in help," a fat Hungarian cook, I was fed sour cream and bananas, a diet frowned upon at the time when the latest medical practice limited babies to milk for the first year. Her primitive disre-

> Jeannie had the largest, most speaking blue eyes, and they followed me with reproach whenever I left her alone.
> — Dr. Pauline Rosenthal

gard for such a fad may have contributed to the blessing of unusual good health with which I was to be endowed for the rest of my life.

By the time I was six my devoted parents were stuffing me with oatmeal in the mornings. I invariably threw up this hideous substance before I reached the Ethical Culture School in the Bronx from Richmond Hill on Long Island where we then lived. Mine was a family of strong-willed individuals and I suppose, being selfish, I learned then that I could gain my way more easily by being polite and permissive toward others rather than by openly fighting for it. It was a pragmatic approach.

We moved to Jamaica, Long Island. In the evenings our house there was full of friends from Forest Hills and Kew Gardens, most of them younger than my parents. Among others, Dick Rodgers of Rodgers and Hart and Rodgers and Hammerstein, whose father had been a neighbor of ours in Harlem, came with Herb Fields to strum on our rickety piano, constructing tunes with one finger. I remember loving the house, the apple orchard across the Union Turnpike, the Black Stump Road of old, old houses and long hills for winter coasting, but, on the whole, resenting the visitors. I do not remember much about the Ethical Culture School, which I continued to attend, except that at its summer camp I had a chance to ride horses.

My mother believed in the most progressive possible education. When she met William Fincke, she found the educator she sought for her children. Headmaster Fincke was a gentle, tortured man who had served as a chaplain in World War I and afterwards found that he could not in Christian conscience mount another pulpit. His dream of the future, of world peace, was based on children, all children, of every color, creed and level of society, and he founded an academy in which to teach them. Ivan, Jean and Leon Rosenthal were matriculated in Bill Fincke's Manumit School in Pawling, New York. My nickname there was "Sparky" because my pet toy was a wooden horse named Sparkplug from the funny papers.

We scholars chose our own projects and learned what we pleased to under the permissive supervision of a New England poetess, Sarah Cleghorn, and other faculty members distinguished less for pedagogy than for ideals. I was even taught to drive a car by trial and error, without a word of comment or interference. At Manumit the most important thing I learned was how to walk into a chicken house without disturbing the chickens.

One of our class projects was the Shaw play *Arms and the Man*, for which I was stage manager and director, using my prerogatives to cast Ivan in the lead. I never did want to act, but I did love props, scenery and lights.

By the time William Fincke died and Manumit lost its character, the Rosenthals had moved into two floors of an old brownstone on

---

I have spent many sleepless nights over the cruelties we parents practice upon our children, knowing no better. Jean wasted no time protesting, a character trait she developed to an art. She had her own way of dealing with the inevitable. To satisfy an autocratic parent she swallowed her oatmeal without complaint. Later, she quietly disposed of it.
— Dr. Pauline Rosenthal

Manumit School
Pawling, N.Y.
March 4, 1926

Dear Old Things,
. . . I dropped French lessons because I did not feel it was doing me much good, however if you are anioux [sic] for me to learn it I will take it up again if possible. Please write and tell me your disision [sic].

Lots of love,
Sparky
P.S. Could you send me some money.

East Fifteenth Street in Manhattan. Friends' Seminary was just around the corner and we children were enrolled at suitable age levels in spite of our lack of preparation. I managed to get on through the twelfth grade there without distinction except for an athletic trophy or two, in which sports I have forgotten. I think I applied to Swarthmore and other places, but my education had been much too unconventional for college acceptance. What I remember best is that those were stimulating years, although hectic and full of uncertainty, and that the people who were part of them, the people with whom I was in contact, were extraordinary.

I was not raised in a small town but in a vibrant and stimulating city, full of change, full of activity. My parents were fully aware of the importance of taking advantage of such an environment. As a child I saw every play that opened; the opera and symphony were part of my weekly routine. There were the columnists I read, like Heywood Broun and F.P.A.; the dramatic critics, Brooks Atkinson, Percy Hammond, John Mason Brown. The League of Composers was introducing Stravinsky and his colleagues to this country; the Ballets Russes and Pavlova were electrifying audiences. There was the opening of the Museum of Modern Art and the introduction of the great Impressionists. All these were part and parcel of my early days. And the schools I attended reflected the kind of curiosity and imagination my parents wished to instill in their children.

Since colleges would not have me I was sent instead to the Neighborhood Playhouse School of the Theatre, simply to enlarge my horizons. I had shown no predilection for dancing or acting, but since I did not know what I wanted to do it seemed to my parents a good idea — part of a general, overall background. There I met the people who have had the most lasting and dominant influence on my life and way of thinking: Louis Horst, Martha Graham, Laura Elliott, Irene Lewisohn — and of these Martha Graham was certainly the most important. She was a woman of imagination, of total purpose toward what she wished to achieve, and she was busy creating a new language in the dance. I was fortunate enough to grow up with her as it developed. My association with her was really the first I had in terms of lighting design, and it still continues.

I consider myself the luckiest person alive in the theatre. Somehow or other the time and my presence managed to coincide on projects of unbelievable magnitude and interest. After all, what luck to begin with the young Martha Graham!

The Neighborhood Playhouse had been founded in the early twenties by Irene Lewisohn and her sister Alice. They had built it into a distinguished small producing unit. Its most notable productions had been *The Dybbuk* and *The Little Clay Cart*, instantaneous hits with people coming all the way down to Grand Street to see them, my family and me among the crowds.

Manhattan's a wondrous toy,
Just made for a girl and boy.
We'll turn Manhattan into an isle of joy!
— Rodgers and Hart

When she came to me at the Neighborhood Playhouse, Jean was a little, pop-eyed girl, enamoured of the theatre, and she did not know what she wanted to do. Or maybe she did. She wanted to "make theatre."
— Martha Graham

"[Martha Graham's] state of being a woman, virgin-lover-mother-lady-temptress-wanton all at the same time..."
— Leroy Leatherman

Aline Bernstein was the designer. The performers were gifted. Many good solid actors of the 1930s, members of the Theatre Guild companies and successful career actors like Paula Trueman, Dorothy Sands and Albert Carroll, came from there. The Playhouse achieved its early reputation for distinction based on the selection of material performed, the extraordinary designing of Aline Bernstein and the very persuasive directing of the Lewisohn sisters.

I enrolled as a student in 1929, just when the Neighborhood Playhouse moved uptown from the old Henry Street Playhouse to become a school devoted to dramatic education. The curriculum included styles of dance, taught by Louis Horst. I loved this. Louis was a large, shock-haired man, a brilliant musical theorist and an extraordinary teacher, with an acid wit. We all knew, or thought we did, that he was Martha's lover, although we never could figure when she had time to be his mistress. Martha, who taught us to dance, seemed to live most of her life in a change room, with a catchall closet and a hot plate on which she perpetually prepared tea to go with scraps of food. Her intense sensuality and her equally intense spirituality were spent to exhaustion in her dancing. That she had the stark beauty of saint-and-sinner combined in one woman we envied, and we understood why she captivated Louis.

Voice production and speech were taught by Laura Elliott in so inspiring and practical a fashion that none of her students ever after had trouble being clearly heard.

Lyric theatre production was theoretically under the pedagogical direction of Irene Lewisohn. We students, however, were certain that it was her sister Alice who was important, although between the two of them no one was ever quite sure who did what. When we were working Irene gave us very little. She produced one show a year uptown, and that on the grand scale. There were lyric dramas, such as *The White Peacock, Blocks* and *Israel,* with orchestra, mime and dance. The members of the Neighborhood Playhouse dominated the casts, joined by people from outside. I remember one production in which we were supported, in the very lowest ranks of a procession, by the entire university group, which included Henry Fonda, Charles Leatherbee and Myron McCormack. That is an example of the sort of thing that went on and the kind of people involved in such activity.

At our regular classes we students did learn a great deal because our instruction came from such stimulating people. Not what they taught but how they talked about what they taught was pretty compelling.

My receptivity to Playhouse training was limited because I hated performing and I hated dancing. I suspect my subconscious mind of taking the aggressive step which prevented me from dancing when I fell down a flight of stairs and hurt my back. Happily I retired to the sidelines and then moved backstage as technical assistant to Martha Graham, whose personality and purpose fascinated me.

When I left the Neighborhood Playhouse after a year and a half I had begun to know that I had a useful way of seeing things. I saw them in terms of photographic images. It was natural to me to project how a place or a movement or an event should look in my mind's eye.

I have no idea what guided me to Yale. It seems to me that at the time I had never heard of the place. However, I am quite sure my mother knew of the George Pierce Baker Workshop there and in any event I did arrive in New Haven and was interviewed by Mr. Baker. After five minutes, for some reason he decided to take me on in spite of the fact that I had had almost no education at all. For three years I was to work diligently there with quite marvelous people.

George Baker impressed me and I loved his course in the history of the theatre. I gathered from the reactions of the other students that I was the only one who did not already know his stories, but to me they were enchanting. He lectured on the history of the stage as if he had been in each place and had discussed everything with the playwrights. When he reached the late nineteenth century, he actually *had* known them. The "I was there" quality you notice in most people who are totally immersed in their subject always delights me, as I was to be delighted later by the way John Gielgud observes the plays of Shakespeare, as if he had discussed them with the playwright.

To teach scene design there was Donald Oenslager, at his organized best, a man who regards all design work in the theatre as an analysis of style. I still find it curious that an artist whose own work does not inspire me either with its nobility or with its exact rightness for a production should have such an inspiring approach to design. As a teacher he is simply perfect. His system of teaching combines the history of design in each period with the essential social history of the period. When one approached a play after learning from him, one had a technique of approach that encompassed investigating the society of its period, the decorative, musical and artistic aspects of that time. Then one applied oneself to the problem of designing for it. I have used this approach ever since. It has been my pleasure, through my professional years, to meet Donald Oenslager now and then and to find that he has managed to remain the same man. We have never worked together, except once, briefly, on a New York production of *Dear Liar* with Katharine Cornell. As a designer he prefers to have his lighting done under his direct control, which is perfectly valid.

Frank Bevin, a brilliant designer who rarely ventured out of New Haven, taught us costume design. He also investigated with pleasurable thoroughness the historic and decorative background of each period.

In fact, what was happening at Yale then was a teaching of techniques that involved immersion in the whole environment: no play or dance, no music or form was studied or presented in a social vacuum. The men teaching us were, with the exception of Baker, young men active in the theatre outside the university as well as within it. Baker, the older man, really represented the transition from Pinero and Clyde Fitch to the more truly naturalistic theatre.

Each period demands in part its own technique.
— George Pierce Baker

New Haven, 1933

Mother I am getting to be a public character get out the old scrappe book because there are going to be plenty of clippings all about our daughter doing her bit . . . it certainly is swell experience of a kind, although I hope to god I never have to do it again. I am of course devoted to the group I am working with, I praise them to high heaven to their faces without even blushing, I love 'em they've been so good and learned all their lines and come to rehearsals and when the author and I had a fight or rather an argument over a scene that was cut, they horsed it delightfully just to prove my point, so the scene is out, and I loved them for it, aside from that the author and I manage pretty well, we were good friends when he was at school . . .

Your loving Jeannie

> Controlled light is something more than a medium to promote visibility. It affects the appearance of all the elements of the stage and by this power becomes a determining element in the composition of a stage picture.
>
> — Stanley McCandless

> While I don't think Jeannie was totally responsible, she was certainly largely responsible for bringing organization and order into the lighting of shows. It used to be a howling match, with yells and screams between the front and the back of the house. After you lit a show, you knew that you could get back fifty per cent *maximum* of the cues you had instituted. By the time I came back from Hollywood to work in the theatre again, things had been changed. The whole system of writing cues — the whole organization of lights into patterns, was such that you could get exactly what you asked for. That is now true of everybody — Jean's system of organization had been adopted by all her disciples and imitators and by the whole lighting business.
>
> — John Houseman

While I was at Yale the Pinero theatre was moved on — partly by my instructors — into the Philip Barry theatre and all that that implies, into the O'Neill theatre and all that that implies, and before I left there in 1933, the Depression with its economic problems and problems of communication had pushed theatre into another new style. This was in effect the Brechtian theatre, of which Orson Welles was a part and so were those meagre, terse, dry wells of inspiration which resulted in the documentary theatre. With all this maturing at the time, I really could not have been better placed in history. I waltzed through an entire span of dramatic changes in a period of about three years.

Stanley McCandless, the grandfather of us all, was the person with whom I was most involved at Yale. He taught lighting. A man in his middle thirties at the time, he had been a student of architecture who had switched to electrical engineering and at Harvard had become interested in the 47 Workshop with George Pierce Baker. When Baker set up Yale's drama department he invited Mac to come along as professor of lighting. This taciturn Scotsman was quite incapable of expressing his very orderly ideas, although he wrote probably the best book on lighting fundamentals. With his characteristic humility he did not call it "*The* Method for Lighting the Stage" but "*A* Method for Lighting the Stage." I think I loved Mac for that title as much as anything else.

Mac was simply enamored of light. Although he could not communicate about it, somehow or other I learned a lot. Because I knew so little and he knew so much and because I was so interested in lighting by then, I simply listened to every word he said. If I never did learn anything really practical from him, I did learn an orderliness, a way of thinking about lighting, and certainly a way of organizing it. I have come to know since that if you can organize your ideas in the theatre, you have half a chance of putting them over.

Besides being incommunicado, the stumbling block for McCandless was that much as he loved light he did not know how to apply it dramatically. I had an instinct for this and could visualize in such a way that his teaching supplemented this instinctive knowledge and provided the basis for techniques I needed in order to articulate my images. Perhaps that is why we got on so well together. Our relationship, a warm and good one, lasted through many trying circumstances to the time of his death several years ago.

I have always felt that insofar as this country is concerned McCandless was indeed the granddaddy of us all. Not because there were no others before him, but because he did have such a specific and orderly attitude toward lighting and he set up that most important thing: an attitude which demands that there *must be* a technique and a method for organizing your ideas.

By the spring of 1933, when I left Yale for New York, the Depression had settled like a pall over all our lives. To get a job in the theatre at any time is "impossible" — and at that time it was *very* impossible. I had the great good fortune to be economically secure: I could live at home and fail to worry about my next meal while job hunting. Believe me, that was the difference between staying in the theatre or not in those days.

Actually I never did "get a job." I made friends, friends who are still part of my life, among them Martha Graham, with whom I had continued to work — as a privilege — in the summers, and John Houseman, whom I met through friends of my mother. It was Houseman who managed to give me the particular encouragement I needed.

I tied in with a group active in the nonpaying theatre. Then, when the Federal Theatre Project under the WPA (the New Deal's Works Progress Administration) began to employ some of the unemployed in this field, which was nearly everybody, I went onto the One Act Project and began to work very hard.

What extraordinary good fortune to arrive on the scene just at a time when we had the Federal Theatre! I was given opportunities at twenty-one that normally would be extended only if one were at least forty. As technician in charge of the wagon theatres playing in the city parks, I had the strenuous experience of moving shows from place to place each night, setting them up, watching audiences gather on hillsides, tending the performances, taking the shows down again, and moving on.... I could scarcely have been given a more thorough education in the technical problems of touring and making do, all the more valuable because there was no time to be artistic about art.

Then John Houseman was made producer for the leading project under the Federal Theatre: number 891 (which gives you an idea how we had proliferated). He asked for me as a technical assistant, a sort of backstage dog's body.

Orson Welles was 891's director; Abe Feder was in charge of lighting, Nat Carson of design. We had Joe Cotten, Arlene Francis, Bil Baird, Hiram Sherman, Whitford Kane — at least a dozen such talented actors — in the company and Orson was beginning to emerge as a one-man force in the theatre with his own style and special visualization of a dramatic production.

Horse Eats Hat, a high-style farce, was an immediate success in the depressed city. Tickets were so scarce that scalpers hawked them at a premium, which ran the prices up in spite of the federal regulations which made our top ticket eighty-nine cents. (You could sit in the gallery for twenty-three.) We were housed at the Maxine Elliott, a nineteenth-century theatre seating approximately nine hundred. It had the horseshoe shape which promotes intimacy whatever the size, and two high balconies. Even on our salaries of $23.86 a week (no matter what you did) it was satisfying to be with a smash hit.

When John Houseman took a leave of absence from the Federal Theatre to produce Leslie Howard's *Hamlet* he asked me to go along as assistant stage manager in charge of light cues. In those days you sat next to the switchboard with the electrician and relayed cues to him

> That child, Jean Rosenthal, was a genius as an executive! It was a period of exploration ... and all of us had to "express ourselves" in order to fight the *humiliation* of living under the depression, the indignities of unemployment. ... At the Federal Theatre, Jean not only could go into the "chicken coop without disturbing the chickens" as she said she learned to do at progressive school, but she insisted on going into the chicken coop in the first place ... and she was busy discovering how to distribute light against a background, darken certain areas, make things come from longer distances, grow in height ... all taken for granted now.
> — Wendell K. Phillips

Wednesday [1936]

Dearest Ma,

Howard is a lamb . . . but I do think the Englishman as a business man is a riot — he just doesn't know what it's all about. . . . . Mrs. Howard gave me a beautiful compact with a funny little Renoir reproduction on the front of it — she said she thought it looked like me. . . .

Actors are such children — you're put to touch them with sense and kindness and they respond so eagerly they break your heart. . . .

I'd like a chance to put some of this knowledge to the test of reality — I don't know if I can do it with John Houseman, but there are some things that may give me a real chance — to fall on my face or even maybe not . . . and I know deep in my heart that eventually I will get what I am after. . . .

J.R.

from the head stage manager. Leslie Howard's stage manager, Eddie McHugh, had been John Barrymore's stage manager and was an elegant and wonderful man. I remain in his debt. He agreed to take me on.

One of those moments of crisis which make or break theatrical careers occurred when the man who was to install the lighting system — from Century, I think, or Duwico — was felled. John Houseman remembers a burst appendix; I think a ladder collapsed and he broke something. Whichever, we had no time to waste on any private drama in the drama of opening a show. Instantly I became electrical technical director of *Hamlet* as well as second assistant stage manager, duties and titles which I kept throughout the New York run and on tour across the United States.

On the road I recall stretches of forty-eight hours with only one of sleep for the technical director (me) and I remember opening in Boston without the cue sheets for the second assistant stage manager (me) and I remember how kind the Howards were to me during the whole arduous experience.

I loved the company, although like all the rest of us supporting the performers in the theatre I maintained a faint condescension toward the acting profession. At that time I wanted to write plays, design whole productions, and probably to direct. As my ambitions dwindled to what I do best, I have been able to design and mount a number of productions, as well as light them.

When the tour ended I had saved thirty-five dollars in cash and I returned to New York, where I was reinstated with Federal Theatre.

I realize that no one can ever tell the story of the historic opening of *The Cradle Will Rock* as well as the author and composer of the play, Marc Blitzstein, did. His version was reprinted in the *New York Times* as a supplement to his obituary when he died in 1964. That opening was a dramatic highlight in his long, distinguished career.

All our memories of that opening differ somewhat. Wendell Phillips thinks the famous conference took place in the men's room, not the ladies' room, of the Maxine Elliott, but concedes that it could have been in either one, since the peculiar odor — clue to memory — of theatre facilities is universal. John Houseman credits me with "charming the firemen" into moving a piano into the Venice Theatre. I do not remember this, but I have never forgotten the sights and sounds and scents of the garment district of New York City as I rode round and round it on that truck, waiting for Orson majestically to solve everything.

At any rate, Marc has the best right to speak and here is his record of that drama of censorship, emotion and derring-do in 1936:

I wrote both the words and the music of *The Cradle Will Rock* at white heat during five weeks in 1936. Its first paid public performance at the Venice Theatre in June, 1937, provided one of the most curious and, I am informed, spectacular evenings in the history of the American theatre.

It isn't often that the opening of a play in New York is the touch-off for a front page spread in all the next day's papers. The story of *The Cradle*'s opening has taken on a somewhat legendary gloss and blur over the years. There are many embellished and apocryphal versions of it. I'm going to try to tell it now as I remember it — the things I know to be facts and the things that others present told me.

When I played *The Cradle Will Rock* for Orson Welles, he was just twenty-one, but already an extravagantly brilliant and magnetic theatre man. He fell in love with it straight off and made me promise that no matter who should produce it he would do the staging, and I was glad to agree.

Many producers then toyed with the notion of putting it on. All of them dropped it. It was considered "hot stuff" politically, since it dealt with the rising struggle for unionism in America — specifically in the steel industry, at a time when the combine known as "Little Steel" was all over the newspapers with its union problems.

Finally Welles and John Houseman decided to produce the work at the Maxine Elliott Theatre under the auspices of the Federal Theatre Project, which they had joined. That organization was government-subsidized during the Depression days, and everyone, from the charwoman who swept the theatre floor to the most ambitious producer, earned the same, $28.00 a week.

It is not very fashionable these days to refer admiringly to the Federal Theatre Project, and yet it was responsible for a great number of today's writers, stars, directors and stage designers. We had unlimited time to prepare the production, and we had really quite extraordinary talents in every department at our disposal. Rehearsals moved toward a state of perfection rarely attained in any present-day theatre.

But as our opening date began to loom, rumors became rife that *The Cradle* might not be permitted to "rock" publicly at all. One reason given was the unionism subject matter. Another was my secondary theme of liberal prostitution, personified by "the moll," set against the background of prostitution of another kind — the sellout of one's profession, one's talents, one's dignity and integrity, at the hands of big business or the powers that be.

At any rate, on the chance that we might never really open, Welles and Houseman invited to our final dress rehearsal the most elite New York audience imaginable. That rehearsal was the first and the last time the work has ever been fully performed exactly as I wrote it. It seemed a success.

The next day we waited with some impatience for the traditional telegram from Washington authorizing us to go ahead with our premiere. It was not forthcoming. Instead, the Military appeared. The box-office personnel were instructed to turn away ticket buyers and the sets and costumes were placed out of reach. And now the irrepressible energy and lightning drive of Orson Welles revealed themselves.

He called us all — the entire production complement of cast, stage managers, musicians and stagehands — together in the only theatre green room we had. It was actually the ladies' powder room downstairs. I remember an unexplained pink velvet mannequin standing in one corner.

Welles said to us, "We have a production ready; we have a fully paid audience outside." (It was there, many people had come early, in the afternoon, and were standing in front of the theatre. They had heard the rumors and they scented excitement.)

"And," said Welles, "we will have our premiere tonight."

But how and where? The first thing was to find a theatre, but in the meantime there were a dozen other jobs to do. What about the contractual situation of the actors, of the musicians? Could they leave this theatre and perform the work elsewhere? A telephone call to Actors' Equity Union produced the information — which turned out to be false — that the actors could not perform *Cradle* on any other stage under different auspices without losing their status in the project.

Then we were told by the Musicians' Local that moving our orchestra to another theatre pit would set us in competition with regular Broadway musicals and that not only would the men have to be paid Broadway salaries, but we would have to increase the number of musicians instead of reducing it. However, said this informant, if we called ourselves a concert and put our musicians onstage, then we could use as many or as few as we could afford.

So there we were in the position of having a production without a theatre, actors who could not appear onstage and musicians who could appear nowhere else — enough to make the stoutest enthusiast admit defeat and give up, but Welles proceeded to solve problems with an ingenuity, a speed and a daring I can almost not believe as I tell it. To the actors he said, "You may not appear onstage, but there is nothing to prevent you from buying your way into whatever theatre we find, and then why not get up from your seats, as first-class American citizens, and speak your piece when your cue comes."

About the music, Welles, consulting Houseman, decided we could afford only one musician, which would be myself at a piano onstage. I had played and sung the work so often for prospective producers (we used to call it my Essex House run) and I had done so many rehearsals with our actors that I felt quite confident and nothing loath. At once we all began to catch fire.

The ladies' powder room of the Maxine Elliott Theatre became a beehive of activity, an arsenal of planning. Newspaper agencies, reporters and photographers were summoned with the word that something was up. By this time it was six o'clock in the evening. A large crowd had gathered in front of the house, undaunted by Military or box-office pronouncements of "No Show Tonight." Welles wanted to keep them there, so he sent out two of our actors to sing songs from *The Cradle* and entertain them until we could tell them where to go to see the production. And still no theatre.

It was summertime and most empty theatres were in mothballs and would probably not contain a piano anyway. Houseman dispatched little Jean Rosenthal, our production manager, then a pint-sized child just out of college. With a ten-dollar bill in her hand, she was to board and commandeer the first available truck on the street and circle with it around the block while we tried to locate a rentable piano. We found one by phone. Yes, the landlady downstairs said, we could borrow her piano. So Jeannie was shouted the address (for once out of the theatre, you didn't get back in) with instructions to wait, piano in her pocket, until phoned where to deliver it.

We were by now collectively tearing our hair with frustration at the lack of a theatre. And then a little man who had been with us for quite some time sighed and said, "You'll have to take my house, I guess." It was the Venice Theatre, later called the New Century, some twenty blocks away up on Fifty-eighth Street and Seventh Avenue.

Jeannie was phoned and promptly brought an old upright piano to a sleepy caretaker who woke up on cue and managed to get four stalwart neighboring firemen to help lift the instrument onto the new stage. The theatre's address was then announced to the audience outside the Maxine Elliott. And now commenced a parade up Broadway and Seventh Avenue to Fifty-eighth Street, with taxis containing Welles, Houseman, Abe Feder, myself and reporters, all followed by an entire audience on foot, marching to see a show. By the time we reached the Venice our original audience of less than a thousand had doubled as the word spread.

Lehman Engel, our conductor, had rushed home, got his winter overcoat, and returned to smuggle my orchestra score out of one theatre into another. Onstage at the Venice, with the curtains closed, we pulled the front off the piano so that its guts showed, since in so large a house we needed a considerable volume of tone, and Feder arranged a spotlight for it. I could hear an enormous buzz of talk in the theatre and when the curtains opened and I looked, I saw the place was jammed to the rafters. The side aisles were lined with cameramen and reporters. And there was I, alone on a bare stage, perched before the naked piano in my shirtsleeves, it being a hot night. There onstage, I couldn't know which or how many of our actors had elected to take Welles' suggestion or where they were in the audience, but I started, ready to do the whole show myself.

I began singing the "moll's" first song of the play and then I heard the words taken from my mouth by the "moll" herself, seated in a right loge, and clever Feder promptly switched the spot to her. Well, she's here anyway, I thought thankfully. Then occurred a dialogue between the "moll" and a character called "The Gent." Again I heard an actor take my melody and my lines from me, only this time from mid-center in the orchestra.

Flashbulbs began to pop. The audience seethed with excitement. As the play progressed, they turned as at a tennis match, from one actor to another, while Feder caught as many performers as he could with his spotlight and musical conversations took place across the house. The cast had studied the words so thoroughly they could have done it in their sleep, and this was much simpler.

I did about eight parts myself that night. Some of the actors had not wished to take their lives, or rather their living wage, into their hands.

But at one point we all heard an accordion out front joining my piano in the title song. The accordionist from my orchestra had dared to come and bring his instrument.

Not a hitch occurred in the continuity and some wonderful accidents of geography turned up. For example, "Mrs. Mister" was seen handing an imaginary donation from a balcony front box to the "Reverend Salvation" downstairs in mid-aisle. And the play itself held up astonishingly well under this brutal and unpredictable manhandling. At the end of the first act, the poet Archibald MacLeish sprinted backstage to say "a new day had dawned in the theatre, the stagnant and supine audience had been killed forever" and he had to make a speech about it. And so he did, after the final curtain.

Even that moment had its particular theatrical flair. MacLeish wore a Palm Beach suit, and when Welles held up his hand and finally stopped the roaring pandemonium that greeted us, saying, "We will all now sit down, and the one man left standing will be Mr. Archibald MacLeish," there stood the white suit gleaming conspicuously, as we were told we had witnessed a historical event.

Later, critics would give *The Cradle Will Rock* rave reviews and there would be about twenty-five other productions of it in the United States and England. Immediately following that first opening at the Venice, Welles and Houseman were fired from the Federal Theatre. In fact we all got fired.

After some hesitation Orson and John founded the Mercury Theatre; they rented the lovely old Comedie, which was a shambles, changed its name to the Mercury and went into production. They were financed to the tune of six thousand dollars by a man who was a connoisseur of Chinese art and who disapproved of censorship.

I was offered the job as the Mercury Theatre's technical director at the Actors' Equity minimum, which was then forty dollars a week for seniors (by then including me) and twenty-five dollars for juniors. Whether Abe Feder, who had been Project 891's lighting expert, turned the job down or whether Orson did not want him I do not know. Abe, a fanatic about light who talked a streak, went on to become one of the

> I want to take the Light out of the Bottle and put it everywhere. . . . I have no patience with wires or fuse boxes and bulbs. . . . There is more light in [my] Prometheus Fountain than in a dozen fountains in Rome or Paris.
>
> — Abe Feder

> The wonderful days of the Mercury! We were so poor, we had absolutely no money at all, and the whole business of cutting corners and doing things that were not doable. . . . Orson poured his radio earnings into it. . . . Jeannie even inveigled some wonderful night watchman into feeding us heat from a bank across the street when we couldn't pay our heating bills. With four hits in a row, we were very successful, but we were always and constantly and perpetually broke.
>
> — John Houseman

innovators in the lighting design business and a consultant on the lighting of many major buildings and projects as well as working in the theatre. Abe was gadget-happy and opinionated and I recall Orson bellowing at him once to know why a particular and conspicuous light had suddenly appeared on that scene. Abe replied with great heat that it was a NEW one, with a gelatin that he had NEVER TRIED BEFORE. Anyway, I was privileged to move on with those two large, brilliant, independent men, John Houseman and Orson Welles, and to take part in the Mercury experience. They also brought along the actors in whom they had the greatest interest.

The Mercury Theatre's importance was that it represented a group of people who already had a considerable working experience together, involved in real repertory theatre. For all of us, working under the dominant direction of Orson Welles was clear-cut, stimulating and rewarding.

John Houseman, Sam Leve, the scene designer, and I met with Orson to discuss the first production. This was to be Shakespeare's *Julius Caesar,* designed to emphasize its contemporary parallels. Orson dictated clearly and exactly the kind of look he wanted the production to have, a very simple look, based on the Nazi rallies at Nuremberg. The patterns implied in the Nuremberg "festivals" were in terms of platforms, which were the basis of the scenery, and lights which went up or down. The up light was really taken entirely from the effect the Nazis achieved.

One effect, spoken of as stunning and inventive, was a marvelous accident. During a dress rehearsal someone forgot to turn out the bald, overhead work lights — whose sole purpose is to illuminate the grid from which the scenery ropes and pulleys are suspended — and they continued to shine down during the blackout just before the orchard scene. The pattern, crisscrossing the stage, conveyed an impression of ground beneath bare branches. Paradoxically in view of the hard thinking and planning I believe in, accident is often the source of inspiration. Magpie, I use anything that comes along, and I immediately incorporated those work lights in the light plot.

The *Caesar* opened with tremendous éclat. Houseman explained, exactly how I have forgotten, that despite the incidental courtesies of the profession, it was important that Orson be given sole credit for everything. However, it did get around in the profession that Sam had designed the scenery and that I had done the lighting.

For the second production, *Shoemaker's Holiday,* our platforms flipped around with houses on them to simulate a funny little medieval town, and it was as open and friendly a show and as raucous a comedy as the *Caesar* was contemporary in parallel and serious in intent. The two shows played perfectly together and were enormously successful.

Heartbreak House, with Orson as Captain Shotover, was good, too, I think, but somehow managed to have very little life. It closed when the summer doldrums set in. Then everybody went into a great state of eruption and change of plan.

The following season was taken up with *Five Kings*, which was the way, Orson decided, to present Shakespeare's Histories. He put together all of *Henry IV* and *Henry V*, with an introduction from *Richard III* and a codicil from *Henry VI*, and once again was startlingly lucid about what he wanted and how it should look. Jimmy Morcom was the designer, and all of us on the production staff had a fine time working it out, but no excitement ever reached the audience, even through the stars who supplemented the company, like Burgess Meredith as Prince Hal. That really marvelous production was boring — catastrophic from an audience point of view, appalling, really — in spite of extraordinary moments. Its out-of-town tour, cosponsored by the Theatre Guild, was disastrous and it never came back in to New York. At least I learned a great deal about touring heavy shows and about getting along with other managements.

A wild summer interlude was provided by *Too Much Johnson*, a play Orson decided to do half film and half live. The film for it, a farcical piece of exposition, shot in Washington chicken markets and along the banks of the Hudson River palisades, was riotously funny, one of the funniest films I ever saw. It may still be sitting in the lab since nobody had the money to get it out, and the play had to go on without the film. The people who saw the play were pretty confused, but it was summer theatre, which was flopping anyhow, and nobody really cared.

After that, Houseman and Welles went off to Hollywood, where the lighting was all done by the cameramen. My extraordinary employment, in which I had learned to swim by being dumped in deep water, was suspended. They came back in 1941 and produced *Native Son*, which was, I think, one of the great productions of the American theatre. Once again Orson was very clear about how it should look and with Paul Green, the author, very clear about what it should say. It had no ending, which was disturbing, and Orson hired a leading player who was not an actor but a boxer, which made for complications, but still it ranks very high indeed as a successful statement in terms of Orson's system of visualizing an environment.

I think the Mercury Theatre made so much sense to me and I was so sorry when it broke up because it was an *organization*, which is necessary for repertory. I function best in this area. The orderly use of rehearsal and performance time, the limitations repertory imposes, have an unhurried tension, a design, which makes every moment count. No time is wasted in having hysterics. You can only work if you plan your work, thinking it out in advance. And I like the order imposed because every night is an opening night and no night is really a failure.

I still worked for Martha Graham, and I began an association with Lincoln Kirstein and his Ballet Society which was to last eighteen years, but this was during the days when devotees of the dance were not very numerous. (Ballet still does not *pay*, but it does sell out.) Keeping body and soul together while remaining in the theatre became one of my favorite investigations.

> Jeannie was fantastic. She went through all the agony of *Five Kings,* installing a huge revolving stage without enough money to buy the motor to drive it. . . . She was not only very good at lighting and an extremely able technical expert, but she kept up the morale when too much was being asked of human beings, particularly of the electricians. Jean kept up their spirits, kept the whole thing going. We could not have survived at the Mercury without the particular combination of talents she brought to us.
> — John Houseman

The theatre was a tough place in which to get started or to earn a living in when you had. In 1940, while still sporadically engaged with Orson Welles as well as with ballet, I opened a little firm called Theatre Production Service. It was a mail-order house for theatrical supplies, a market already competed for by Cleon Throckmorton and Scrim Plywood. I offered a complete design service, for shows and for theatres, so that I could plan my customers' needs as well as supply them. Joining me in the enterprise were two able, talented women graduates of the Yale Drama Workshop, Helen Marcy and Eleanor Wise.

Our offices were two rooms over the lovely old Empire Theatre at Fortieth and Broadway. From the first the TPS catalogue, if I do say so myself, was a masterpiece of clarity and practicality and we did pretty well until the nation went to war. After that you could not get materials for much of anything without government priorities. Helen went to work days for Eaves Costume Company as a stock clerk and I took a job nights drafting in a shipyard. Eleanor (Ellie) manned the office full time.

When the old Mercury's John Houseman and George Coulouris drifted back east from Hollywood, I had a flurry of work as a producer, in technical charge of *Richard III* and other shows. TPS handled all the contracts, supplied the physical properties and all that. But still, in order to stay alive and continue to pay the rent we had to do business with the government.

Our contract to put together special service recreation kits for the army was, like many war efforts, as supremely wasteful to the taxpayer as it was necessary to us. The kit was designed by an ignoramus and made up of a very specific assortment of doubtful items: a certain number of yards of theatre muslin, a certain number of rolls of crepe paper, so many pounds of clout nails, so many packages of Rit or Tintex fabric dyes, so many cans of latex paste . . . This collection had to be exquisitely packed according to government specifications so that the kits could be pushed off boats and floated ashore in the Pacific. On weekends we hired flocks of high school kids to assemble these items, wrap them in waterproof liners and seal them with wax. We rented two rooms in a building next door to the Empire, half a floor down, with a pass door between so that we could all wiggle our way through.

There was no profit per se. Government money took three months to arrive. During the interval you had to resort to usurers, who knew you had to have the money in order to operate and also that you would get the money in the end. It was all nicely calculated to keep you broke and afloat. But there was legitimate profit for us in the inefficient planning. Muslin, for instance, came in bolts. After cutting each bolt to the Army's immutable orders, we had one hundred yards left over for our own use.

On government waste we survived and even hired another staff member, Nan Porcher. She was to run the "grocery business" end of TPS and we made her swear to have NOTHING TO DO WITH THE THEATRE. On her first rush delivery job, at Lewisohn Stadium, she was hauled in the stage door to serve as emergency assistant stage manager that night. Later she became my invaluable stage manager for ballet and opera.

Over the years TPS has never made much, but it has involved a great many other people and really kept me alive, interested and active in a curious profession where people tend to rot six months of the year. Also it has provided me, through the years, with a much-needed sense of organized professional continuity.

My professional home was always "on Broadway," although for most of my career I have been associated with the special kind of theatre that only periodically invades Broadway — lyric rather than commercial theatre. I was on Broadway from the beginning because the theatres were there, physically. The Mercury succeeded on Broadway, all the way through *Native Son*, which was squarely on Forty-fourth Street in what was then the St. James Theatre. The Ballet Society became the New York City Ballet at the City Center on Fifty-fifth Street, well within the area included under "Broadway." Gian Carlo Menotti's engaging little operas opened on Broadway. Martha Graham's breakthrough into popular recognition and success happened one night at the Martin Beck Theatre on Forty-fifth Street. TPS, although its business was mail-order, moved from the Empire Theatre only as far as West Forty-sixth Street. (In 1969 it was forced downtown by high rents and the need for more space to East Ninth Street.) In 1957 I did begin to concentrate on the classic sort of show identified with Broadway, including three musicals that year, one of which was *West Side Story*. Broadway is an idea, a domain and an enterprise, with its own identity within which I had an identity. During the decade 1958-1968 the development of an extremely active off-Broadway theatre and an extremely active regional theatre has compounded the theatrical scene, but Broadway still represents the standard by which excellence in the theatre is judged. And that is where I was and am.

From Broadway, I have traveled on tour all over this great country and its major cities, around Europe and its great cities. I also know Broadway's tryout towns well, the museums and restaurants, hotels and haunts, as well as the theatres of Philadelphia, Boston, and New Haven and half a dozen others.

For five years, between 1953 and 1957, I spent a great deal of time in nearby Stratford, Connecticut, in technical charge of the Shakespeare Festivals, until John Houseman left as director, and I left.

A second career, as a consultant on lighting systems for theatre buildings and other buildings where offbeat lighting was called for took me farther afield psychologically than did touring — whether I was working on the Los Angeles Music Center, Canada's national theatres, the Pan American building at Kennedy Airport, or the Juilliard School of Music and Drama at Lincoln Center.

Fortunately I can work anywhere — and do — out of a briefcase designed to carry tightly rolled plans, layouts, architect's drawings, blue-

---

I tried to get the Graham management to cut down on paper — the free tickets they gave out to fill the house — for that recital. I can't tell you why — the advance sale was light. But something was in the air. And that night, the hordes came. No audience is so ruthless as those who have decided to see a dance recital. They fought each other like tigers to get at the box-office window when the last seats began to go. After the "Standing Room Only" and then the SOLD OUT signs went up, we had to call the mounted cops to clear the lobby and the street.

— Dora Chamberlain

prints. I can create an office with invisible walls in a plane seat (I *do* travel first class, for elbowroom), in airport alcoves, in hotel rooms, in any corner of any theatre. My mind is a bit like a camera, its inward eye registering a series of constant visual images. Now and then I stop when one is right and print it, to file. From these files, I can always recall a print. Words to me are like captions for these images.

It is not easy to communicate about light, in captions to pictures you cannot make anyone else see quite the way you do. On Broadway, a common vocabulary has been adopted — terms such as *quality* of light, *pattern, color washes, downlight* and *backlight* convey accepted meanings. When I leave the island of Manhattan and the inner island that is Broadway, it becomes harder to communicate. Perhaps that is the reason I am there and that I have a sense that being in Manhattan is *restful*.

I live there, too, downtown on the East Side. I never moved far. My succession of apartments have been on East Seventeenth Street, on Irving Place, between Eighteenth and Nineteenth, and on Twenty-sixth Street, east of Park Avenue. Sometimes I have lived alone and sometimes shared my apartment. Of necessity I learned to cook and then to love cooking as domestic recreation and an art.

The need to be close to nature came very late to me, child of city streets and woman of the metropolitan theatre. When it came, it hit me hard. Because I loved the sea, I thought of its shores and somehow, quite naturally, landed on another island to make a second home. Once I settled on Martha's Vineyard, it seemed as much mine as Manhattan is.

I love Martha's Vineyard and insist, as all its dwellers do, that its air is the softest and its light the most delicate in the world. I walk the island's undulating roads and through the low-growing woods and on the sand or pebble beaches with the pride of ownership. New York, like London and Paris, is a walkers' city, which most other cities are not, so my legs (not my best feature, by the way — they are stubby) were used to walking, but I had forgotten the pleasure of breathing deep with each step.

To get to Martha's Vineyard one must make the utmost effort — fly by small, weather-sensitive planes or end up a trek by car or bus with an hour's ride across to the island on those small, inelegant ferries. But it is worth the effort, even for the shortest intervals. I have even rediscovered dawn, which I had not seen in years except for occasions when I had been up all night.

For the first time, on the Vineyard, I have had the time — for time seems to stretch itself as I do, within its cradle of seas — to consider and sum up my lifetime in light.

I became very fond of those rather fat little legs. (Jean could stand on a stage fourteen hours a day.) They had great charm. They weren't fat, they were *sturdy*.

— Oliver Smith

Three. Collaboration

RADFORD BASCOME

Collaboration flourishes when there is an understanding on the part of each member of the team that the others involved are to be respected and their authority fully recognized. The motions of carrying out the collaboration, the different techniques each group will require because of the personalities involved, make collaboration a hope, not always an achievement.

Collaboration is a beautiful word, or was until debased by the Nazis. Its true meaning is working together toward a common end. Lighting design is a collaborative profession in which the lighting designer collaborates with backgrounds, things, purposes and people. In the theatre the lighting designer's collaboration is with all these at once. No one can say the light in a play "gave a good performance." It *can* be said that it enhanced the performance given by others. So it is pretty important with *what* the lighting designer collaborates — and with *whom*.

You cannot collaborate by yourself, except by simply doing what you are told to do. You can try to make your colleagues think you are doing what they think they told you to, or you can yell your head off in a display of more temperament than your temperamental associates. Or you can be reasonable — and stubborn. Friendship is not involved. I do not mean that you cannot be friends with your collaborators. But I do find that most of my friends come from among my associates in organized repertory. Collaborating talents in repertory, organized for continuing effort, have time to attain, at the very least, a comfortable respect for each other. For some reason, in the dramatic theatre in the United States, repertory has seldom succeeded for long. Not in my working lifetime. For the most part, in Broadway's commercial theatre you make contacts, not friendships. These contacts can be thrilling and rewarding, but the associations do not imply friendship at all. Collaboration on each single entity is based on a kind of instantaneous response to the people with whom you work. For the length of its endurance, this can be a perfectly lovely relationship, but when the association ends, you return to your home base and they return to theirs.

I think I have been pretty much of a loner through all these associations. I really have only one or two colleagues in the lighting business, since we are all pretty arbitrary. Working with directors — often by nature arbitrary men — in the brief, intense association of putting on a show, I have been constantly stimulated by them. Trying to find out what their image was, what they were searching for, I have found that it does not take much to trigger the basic images of a production.

Sometimes I think this is because I respond so readily in visual terms. At others, I think it is because the material we deal with is not very profound. On their part, directors have known they could count on me to do my level best. The luckiest part of my association with a creative craft that so often suffers from too much imposition of one person's ideas upon another's is that I have almost always been hired not out of friendship but because a director liked my work and wanted me to do it.

My involvement in the theatre has been within the span of what has been known, pretty caustically at first, as the directors' theatre. This is fairly short by historical standards.

Before the seventeenth century, the European theatre, from which ours derived, was itinerant and the members of its troupes were as anonymous as gypsies. Not until Shakespeare's time and Molière's time did the *person* emerge — the actor as a person, the manager as a person. With these playwrights plays began to have the kind of productions we now know.

There were properties and scenery and lighting and all sorts of means and schemes to foster the illusion that the audience was not in the theatre but somewhere else — up a tree, in a room, or wherever, anywhere but the place it sat in. Somebody had to be in charge of all that.

The nineteenth century saw the actor-managers' theatre create this illusion in terms of extreme romantic realism. As all theatre production in this country began to center in New York, the producers' theatre took over what had been the actor-managers' theatre. Men like Arthur Hopkins and David Belasco produced their shows, directed them, hired designers and with the designers lit their productions. Reality became more specific. On the stage, a faucet dripped real water and rain was wet, running along pipes with little holes in them. As little as possible was left to the imagination.

The producers spent their own money, kept their own profits, met their losses, created their stars, dominated their industry. The "road," radiating out of New York as the nation's railroads radiated out of Chicago, was operated by syndicates: the Shuberts, the Klaws and the Erlangers.

A play was produced and tried out in towns near New York, ran for a limited time on Broadway, and was sent on the road for an extended tour. Show business was a fairly well-organized, orderly and settled entertainment industry, full, of course, of the labor-management injustices of the time. The artist always faces these injustices when he brings art to commercial use, but in those days at least a certain regularity of theatrical employment existed. Then came the terrible days beginning in 1929.

In the 1930s Broadway began to assume its overwhelming importance to American theatre. The objective of all productions became the New York run and production *teams* became part of the organization of the theatre. Producers collected and dispersed invested money and handed over artistic control to another group of men: the directors. This was the theatre of Orson Welles, of Elia Kazan, of Harold Clurman and Lee Strasberg (directors of the Group Theatre).

Their area of authority was concentrated and they were held responsible for the success or failure of enterprises financed by other people. Failures outnumbered successes and fear of failure increased, or seemed to, the arbitrariness of directorial dictatorships. This led to some pretty interesting struggles on the part of their collaborating talents to retain their own identities. In fact, the preservation of personal identity seems to be the hard-core problem of the artist today. Why, I am not quite sure. Perhaps it is only part of what is now generally labeled a "crisis of identity" in a world where interdependence has become a prime condition of existence.

In discussing collaboration in the theatre during the present era, one must begin with those dominant figures, the directors.

I hesitate to talk about people as individuals — including myself — partly, I suppose, because I am so much a technician. Technicians relate to things, and our reactions to people may often be in terms of how *they* relate to *our* things. To the extent to which we are artists, we may also be intuitive about people as well as things. If I do *see* other people very clearly, perhaps I comprehend them through this visual clarity, but I hesitate to claim that I do, although, of course, I think I do. I can only present my collaborators as I saw and comprehended them, working with them.

Orson Welles related to every single thing about a production. He was really in the older tradition of actor-managers and he had a great deal to do with creating the directors' theatre. Orson was, and is, visually monumental and his dominance was, I must say, pretty overwhelming. At the Mercury, no one else had any identity for him at all. You were production material. If he liked you, the association could be pretty pleasant. If not, it was injurious. As a director, he approached other talents as he did his Gargantuan meals — with a voracious appetite. Your contributions to his feast he either spat out or set aside untouched, or he ate them up, assimilated them, with a gusto which was extraordinarily flattering.

The initial stages of anything with Orson were immensely entertaining, which carried everything along. I have come since to suspect that he was born bored and that much of his overabundance of energy has been spent in alleviating that boredom. He never counted the cost of anything to himself or to anyone else.

I do not think that Orson made the utmost use of his collaborators' talents, although he often inspired their achievements. He did make the utmost use of his own talents in the beginning, but perhaps his lack of respect for others accounts in some measure for the ultimate dissipation of his own multiple talents. I suppose this is unimportant, since his genius did mark the theatre and the cinema for all time.

Since those days in the Mercury, I have collaborated with many a directorial talent: with the cannibalistic genius of Balanchine in ballet, under the persuasive omnipotence of Tyrone Guthrie. "Gadge" Kazan flourished his whip, like a ringmaster's, openly; Garson Kanin carried his behind his back, held in one of his velvet gloves. The Lunts permitted someone else to "direct," while keeping every element of the collaboration under their capable control. Jerome Robbins, an immensely creative choreographer, was one man in dance repertory and quite another in musical comedy, where his dominance tended to be crushing.

The ideal of the "happy creative whole" Martha Graham strives for is very rare in the commercial theatre with its hit-or-flop syndrome and the frantic, sometimes hysterical, search for opening-night perfection. One director who has it is the young Mike Nichols, whose commercial successes have followed each other in phenomenal succession.

Mike is likely to choose his associates, from those available, for the important reason that they enjoy each other. Toward his technical staff and his cast his attitude is that he and they are going to have a great time. So far they have. Although Mike has not (yet) tested his quality on anything more profound than deft comedy, his attitude toward his collaborators remains as warm and respectful as it was in his early partnership with Elaine May when they performed as comics. Nobody could write an article, much less a book, claiming that Mike had undermined his integrity as an artist.

The director is in charge and it is his failure or his success. That makes the responsibility of the designers subject to his. But the designers, by a kind of logical arithmetic, partly economy and partly because there are fewer designers than there are directors, have usually done more shows than the director has. You have already made more mistakes than he has. You know that what seems like an original production idea may really be only a revival of discarded and forgotten errors of the past.

Working with those of us who had much longer experience in the theatre than his own, Mike exhibited a flattering deference toward that experience. He was not hung up on his own originality. He did get his own way, essentially, but with the unfailing courtesy and consideration that made it seem to be — and often was — your way, too. If Mike has yet to learn from failure, because he has had none, success has not swelled his witty head.

It has been my good fortune to work, over the years, with many very talented people. Besides my first mentors, Martha Graham, John Houseman and Orson Welles, madmen and geniuses in ballet — like Lincoln Kirstein, George Balanchine and Jerome Robbins — contributed in extraordinary measure to my education.

In the big-time commercial theatre, I have been associated with tremendous talents. Among producers, still theoretically at the top of the theatrical hierarchy, that strange impresario David Merrick has returned a measure of artistic control to the producer's role. Arnold

---

[*Luv* is] suavely lit by Jean Rosenthal so that a night scene manages to look both atmospheric and cheerful.
— Harold Clurman

[During the filming of *Catch 22*]: On the set they all perform like a rep company, with no upstaging, no prima donna antics or tacit reverence for Mike Nichols.
— Newsweek

Saint Subber is one producer who understands the technical aspects of his productions. The "names" that last are almost always justified by talent: names in music like Leonard Bernstein, in design like Oliver Smith and Boris Aronson, in direction like Franco Zefferelli.

Cinema stars may survive without anything more than "star quality" and careful direction plus expert cutting rather than talent. Stage stars, never. Consider the longevity of careers like those of Katharine Cornell, Judy Garland, Alfred Lunt, John Gielgud, Zero Mostel.

Beautiful stage actresses are a special problem to the lighting designer. They survive their youth on talent, but they are obligated to remain beautiful. (In the days before there were lighting designers, Maude Adams, that most delicate of beauties, became so fascinated with lighting that when she retired she moved to Schenectady and worked to develop lighting equipment in the laboratories there.) Most pretty actresses are light-conscious, but not light-*wise*. They tend to flutter toward the hot spot, moths to flame, regardless of what happens when they do, often wearing base makeup which absorbs light and tends to make their faces invisible. To match makeup properly, to light it well, is one of the interesting studies in lighting design. Also to choose the colors that suit the beauty. The black hair and alabaster skin of Lynn Fontanne take neutral colors; lavender tones make her coolly beautiful. (She understood this very well.) Gwen Verdon's red hair is made entrancing and delicate by pink or straw colors. The raven complexion of Anna Magnani can stand powerful, Toulouse-Lautrec poster colors. The easiest coloring to light is the brunette with her definitive hairline framing her face; the most dangerous color to use on anyone is gray, which makes hair and skin run together muddily. If hair is not its own color, the best light to pick is one that suits the skin tones. Too many actresses are under the impression that pink lighting always prettifies.

Sometimes it does. Pink is good for Mary Martin — she is a pink-tinted lady. But what you really light for Mary is her ineffable grace and vitality. Onstage, Mary is always in motion. Thus the lighting for her can be full of motion, "happening" on cue. Mary is quicksilver, and you treat her as quicksilver, light glancing from her shining surface.

Part of Lynn Fontanne's glamour, on the contrary, comes from her ability to be absolutely and beautifully still. Her magical voice could create, out of her physical languor and her physical beauty, humor, radiance, sexuality, intelligence — and the desire on the part of every woman in the audience to be Lynn Fontanne.

Lighting Lynn was a meticulous affair. There was a special session to focus on her. She would come to it in a duster, her hair in a knot on top of her head, with no makeup. If you made her look good that way, she would be ravishing in costume and makeup. The director (after she and Alfred Lunt left the Theatre Guild, they took Bretaigne Windust with them as their director) would sit in one corner, the stage manager in another. Alfred moved around constantly, while Lynn went through every one of her lines. In each position the lights were focused

---

Jean had great respect for Lynn's lighting instinct. Lynn would point to a spot that was doing the harm and Jean would go into fits of laughter, saying only one other actress could do that — Jane Cowl.
— Alfred Lunt

I am embarrassed to admit that I do not know the name or number of the pink gelatin that Jean found which did project "me" best. Sometimes Jean had one of the pink gelatins in the front spot, sometimes two. At other times pink in one while the second spot was white. . . . After all Jean was, yes, a craftswoman, a technical expert, but she was equally an artist — she used lights instead of oils.
— Mary Martin

Jean Rosenthal was by far the most expert in stage lighting we had ever known. Every play she did for us, she did to perfection. Furthermore she took less time than most others. . . . This is pretty fulsome praise, isn't it; but she was truly remarkable.
— Alfred Lunt

and never changed after that. You could not do cues for Lynn, but you could count on her. She moved onstage as if her feet were wheels, on invisible rails, and she was always exactly where she had planned to be. It was this meticulousness, applied to every aspect of the show, that made Lunt-Fontanne productions so dependably perfect.

It is a pleasure to collaborate with stars who use lighting as part of their performances. Angela Lansbury did and so did Maria Callas. Part of the reward of working on *Night of the Iguana* was that Margaret Leighton and Bette Davis (no longer beautiful by then, but fantastically skilled) understood how to play into the lighting.

The lighting designer is privileged to collaborate with everybody in a show — and is often criticized by everybody. The producer: "There's not enough light!" The director: "There's too much light!" The scene designer: "I don't like what's happening in that part of the set." It is important to keep *your* central idea (and your counsel along with your temper). If your *closest* collaborator, the scene designer, respects and recognizes your area of authority, you will be able to return to that central idea and to prevent anything from happening that will wreck the inner disciplines of your design.

Some designers argue that all the scenic aspects of a production should be under a single control. Jo Mielziner is one; Donald Oenslager another. This is perfectly valid. I have enjoyed it myself when I have carried out the entire scenic design. But nothing is more rewarding than to collaborate truly with an artist who respects what you have to offer the collaboration.

Easel artists can do marvels in scene design when they accept the practical limitations of designing for the stage, accepting the craft as well as the art. Most professional scene designers are able craftsmen — otherwise they could not last in the competition. (Sets are rarely criticized in reviews, but I *have* seen sets that overpowered and killed plays — perhaps better dead?) Only a few are artists. Robert Edmond Jones was an artist. Oliver Smith and Boris Aronson are artists.

I think both these men are pleased when they are asked to work with me. I think our separate talents have the special harmony that contributes to a creative whole. They are gifted and complex, which does not make it easy. (Oliver's floor plans get more difficult and complicated all the time.) But I like a challenge — not for its own sake, but when the challenge is so worth meeting, within a collaboration.

Design in the theatre is the creation of atmosphere. It is either representational atmosphere, such as in the naturalistic theatre of accurately placed suns and moons, or it is the abstract arrangement of an environment that creates an atmosphere right for the dramatic intention of the play — even if it is so ludicrous a place as the inside of a typewriter, as in *archy and mehitabel*, or a pile of garbage pails, as in *Endgame*. A set may contribute immeasurably to extending the emotional and physical limitations of the stage. And the lighting designer is

---

In a way, Jean almost directed that play [*Night of the Iguana*]. Her lighting patterns affected where people stood, where they moved, and their reactions. Leighton and Davis are very sensitive to light . . . many actors and actresses are not.

— Oliver Smith

I liked working with Jean so much I used to make it part of my contract whenever I could. I consider her a great artist.

She enjoyed finding solutions. If she ever came to a designer and said, "I cannot do this," he had better listen.

— Oliver Smith

I resented Jean when I first met her — and ended up refusing to do a show without her if she could be had. It was not like working with a technician or craftsman — it was working with a theatre *person*. Her shows carried her own signature.

— Boris Aronson

the set designer's closest collaborator — whether working with a set such as the one Oliver Smith designed for *Becket*, a marvelous Gothic spider web, or one such as the one he designed for *The Odd Couple*, which he wanted to look like a terrible old cigar box — and it did. You carry out his intentions, just as you both carry out the intentions of the play.

Collaboration does not flourish under the do-it-yourself attitude of the old actor-managers or of certain directors. It flourishes when there is an understanding on the part of each member of the team that the others involved are to be respected and their authority fully recognized. The motions of carrying out the collaboration, the different techniques that each group will require because of the personalities involved, make collaboration a hope, not always an achievement.

When I began my career the theatre had accepted women as stars, set designers, stage managers and even directors, but not in the technical field. In the long years since the time when women's roles were even played by boys, that had remained a closed male world.

To overcome rude prejudice, I used courtesy, on which my mother had insisted since my birth. I also cultivated a careful impersonality, which disregarded sex, in spite of the "dears" and "darlings" used between the sexes as part and parcel of social usage in the theatre world. My only real weapon, though, in the battle for acceptance, was knowledge. I did know my stuff, and I knew that the technicians knew theirs. I honored, truly, their knowledge and their prerogatives. And gradually they came around — from stagehands to directors — to honor mine.

It was easier with Americans. They give greater credit where it is due to technical ability. I remember one radar expert in World War II, from the Deep South with a deep prejudice against blacks. He was asked if he would work peaceably under a black officer in his field. "Sure," he said, "if the son of a bitch knows radar!"

My first experience lighting European productions was during the war and *was* war. I came to the conclusion that European men might love women, but did not like them or respect them, and that European women did not like or respect other women either. Also, whatever they were doing, Europeans clung to the traditional way of doing it, backed by centuries of self-approval.

In 1944 I was hired as lighting director for the Marquis de Cuevas ballet, which he was bringing over from Paris where there was no ballet because of the war. It was an international European company.

To house the company, an old theatre on Columbus Circle, empty for sixteen years, was bought from the estate of William Randolph Hearst. It had been used exclusively for the showing of Marion Davies films, and the only good thing left in it was the central box, suspended over the balcony, from which Mr. Hearst could watch Miss Davies. We kept that private box for the Marquis de Cuevas and gutted the rest of the house.

I never really had to tell Jean what I was trying to do. She would look at the plans, get the point, and use it as an inner core. She worked just as hard on *The Odd Couple* as on *Becket*.

— Oliver Smith

Jean's quality of tranquil impersonality was not real. It was self-protective. She had a hard time in the theatre. There was constant and long-term and even violent opposition to her from the electricians because she was a woman, in the beginning a child, and show business is death on women, especially in the technical end. She had to weather it, so she cultivated a great invulnerability, along with her courtesy, to deal with this.

— John Houseman

Jean taught me a great deal about working with people. We never did a thing against the unions — if I wanted to have a chair on the stage, I would ask if I could have one. "Not if you ask like *that*, Martha. . . ." They always called me Martha and Jean taught me how to ask. She would say, always through the microphone, so that no one else overheard, "Joe, that light on 31 isn't working very well. What's the matter with it?" They loved her because she always gave them honor. I believe there are failures in the theatre where directors or producers do not give honor to technical people. Without it, they are nothing. With it, they will do anything for you.

— Martha Graham

For the reconstruction, I got Willy Nolan, of Nolan Brothers scenery builders. When there was anything tough to be done technically, I always got Willy. Until his death we collaborated. I think we had fallen in love, a little, when I was "that girl at the Mercury." Willy was a roughneck, an uneducated, large, round Irishman who had started life as a stage carpenter and who knew everything there was to know about making things work, from winches to stage floors, steel girders, rigging. He understood backstage in his bones, and his relation with *things* was personal and profound. Materials were human to him. When a designer would ask for the wrong material, Willy would say, "It don't want to do that!" And "it" didn't — and wouldn't. Willy was always right. Given his own way, he could accomplish anything for you with his friends the materials.

Willy understood about star traps for the nineteenth-century ballets, in which dancers were always appearing or disappearing in flashes of smoke or whatever. When he got through, there wasn't an inch of the stage — with movable beams — you could not put a trap in. Willy also rigged my lighting system my way, which was based on all I had learned from lighting the Martha Graham and the Lincoln Kirstein ballet repertory companies. I had already toured the system for Lincoln, through South America, before he went off to war. I knew that the system would work under all conditions and how to make it work. But it did give, basically, a new look to ballet, and when the designers and choreographers arrived from Europe, I was in trouble.

They did not accept the idea of lighting design anyway and they had always seen their ballets lit just one way: that is, the first ten feet of the stage was pretty well lit and after that you got flat, nineteenth-century lighting, without mood. You could use color — go blue for *Swan Lake* or pink for *Les Biches* — and if ghosts came on, you might have some green specials, but only in a restricted area. Ninety-nine percent of the quality had to come within those first ten feet. The system of lighting was based on the standard equipment available in every European opera house, which was based on the gaslight era, and was inflexible.

My lighting was in depth and they did not like it. Their culturally conditioned eyes object to change. Lordly, autocratic people like Massine and Madame Nijinska threatened to throw me out of the theatre. Madame Nijinska, during a rehearsal of her *Bolero*, did.

I was not the only problem in that financially disastrous venture. There was no communication among the fascinating designers (one of whom was Salvador Dali) about the actual size of the stage or the repertory schedule. The fact that no two shows could occupy the stage space at the same time had been ignored. We got through because one does, and I had my way for the most part because there wasn't time to fire me and start over. But the only time I laughed during the whole season was when Eleanor Wise telephoned from the TPS office to report that Madame Dali had asked when Miss Rosenthal had "her assignation with my husband."

After the war, Madeleine O'Shea, a partner in TPS and my "house philosopher" — a marvelous woman who taught acting as her regular profession and taught me a great deal about the theatre — told me I must *go* to Europe. I listened to her about this as about everything else and I took my accumulated pennies and went to Europe. Mostly on that trip I just looked. I think I was the most indefatigable museum-haunter in history. My debt to Europe is as great as my inheritance — my father was German, my mother Rumanian. I understood after that trip why Europeans clung so to tradition. They had so much that was marvelous to cling to.

Later, Ballet Society, which became the New York City Ballet, sent me to Europe many times. These times were doubly rewarding, not only because of the amusement, and the pleasure, of bringing work to Europe, and the exchange of ideas, but also for the very special experience of working in the great theatres of Europe — not only in terms of the way the crews operated and the theatre was organized, but in terms of the architecture of the structures themselves. It was a way of gaining an enormous amount of information almost impossible to acquire any other way.

All this was grist to my mill — since my real interest is the theatre as a whole, visually, with a specialized use of the visual in terms of lighting and a kind of space designing.

My second career, as a lighting consultant, brought me into collaboration with architects and faculty members. Even though most of this work was within a theatre framework, in buildings which were theatres or in university dramatic departments, the collaborations were very different from those within the theatre itself. For one thing, both architects and professors are more inclined to be romantic about the theatre than theatre professionals are.

Architects, in my opinion, are generally by nature dreamy and impractical. They are trained in practicality but are always ignoring practical considerations. (Sometimes I got the impression that they had all read *The Fountainhead* too young.) I literally found myself explaining once that an office building, although it houses three thousand people, does not need as many toilets per occupant as a theatre, where everybody is trying to get in during one fifteen-minute intermission. As for lighting, most architects think about their buildings and not about the uses made of these buildings by people. Although they consult with specialists in various fields, they hate to pay attention to them.

For theatres, I really did work out a kind of standard approach. I would say to the architects, let's forget that this building is for the arts. Let's consider it as a factory in which certain things must be produced — in this case, plays. Then, of course, the height of the stagehouse must be sufficient for scenery to fly out. The steel in the grid must be able to carry so much live weight. The loading door must be designed to let scenery of a certain size through. Once the romance was out of it, the job was easier to do. And an exciting new architectural concept

> It is hectic and dangerous to lead the life of a consultant. . . . I think I can divide the groups concerned with a theatre building into the client, the architect and the vendor. These forces are all applied to the consultant, and if he or she has humor, judgment, and the ability to sort out the essential aims of each of the people involved, then I think the consultant serves a proper purpose. Most of us operating as consultants are really not so in the architectural use of the word at all. We are advisors. We are experts because of our passion for the theatre, and in terms of our experience. And we will do anything to communicate this information to anybody who asks us for it.
> — From a speech by J.R.

could be treated as a practical challenge rather than an innovation for its own sake.

I do *like* working with architects. I love buildings and I do know about stresses and materials and all that, so I can talk their language. Also an architect's blueprint is as clear and beautifully readable to me as the pages of a primer. Although I cannot draw and have often been bored with the inevitable "chalk-talks" architects give, I am happy conferring over blueprints.

I think perhaps the most successful and practical building on which I have collaborated and in which I take pride is the Los Angeles Music Center. For the Chandler Pavilion they wanted to hire a man committed to a laboratory grid system which had not yet been solved. I persuaded them to hire Willy Nolan. The big pavilion is currently perhaps the only modern theatre that works equally well for the modern things and for all the old-fashioned things.

When I was hired as a consultant I had what the word implies: a body of experience in my field and a recognized authority on my subject. Entering the academic world as a consultant, as an expert on theatre lighting, I found my experience invalidated to some extent because it had been on Broadway. In the universities Broadway was held in strong contempt. At first I thought this might be the business of people who wanted to be on Broadway and could not make it. I think this is not very important. What is important is why they are in the university theatres and not on Broadway.

People in universities really aren't very knowledgeable about the theatre in New York. They regard it as a sort of total Establishment, without regard to the brevity of its history in this condition. I concluded, trying to figure it out, that their reactions were really based on the problem of being academicians in the first place.

Whether he is an instructor, full professor or whatever, your academician really functions on only two levels: either he is teaching or he is being taught. He is hostile toward the people he is willing to learn from, although he concedes enormous respect to another academic degree, which certifies in his terms that someone knows more about a subject than he does. He has no means of identifying with the expert who comes from the workaday world or with the attitude of those whose working experience has taught them that a discourse or discussion is *not* a teacher-student relationship but is a sharing of ideas in the hope that two ideas are better than one.

I began with Martha Graham, whose idea of "the happy creative whole" was the standard she set and I adopted. That basic idea, that kind of collaboration, has been part of the condition in which I have been able — much of the time — to live. The fine disciplines and longer associations of repertory theatre provided the best possible schooling for the improvised disciplines of commercial theatre. You can nearly always recognize the quality of artists trained through repertory or alternating in repertory. (That may account for the higher standard of acting among the British.) There is more willingness to subordinate the individual performance for the sake of the whole. There is no loss in this of ego or identity.

Lighting, my primary concern, *must be* subordinated. It is only valuable to the extent to which it contributes to and never dominates any scene. Yet it has its separate identity and its vital contributory importance.

In the effort to formulate what I think I am about as a producing craft artist, I find I have not emitted many wisdoms nor dropped many pearls. I am rather a dull girl, with a natural response based on images. If I read history I absorb no facts, but I *see* what I am reading about. (The battle is plain.) Music creates visual images for me, and that glade, or house, or abstraction, or cloud is perfectly clear. In leaving the subject of the craftsman to talk about the craft, I feel more at ease.

Light is quite tactile to me. It has shape and dimension. It has an edge. It has quality and it is an entity. It is the one miracle of creation without which, to me, the others would be meaningless.

I have always objected to the usual reading of the great line from Genesis, especially from the pulpit. It is read: "God said, let there be light, and there WAS light." It should be read: "God said, let there be light, and there was LIGHT!"

Four. The History of Illumination

When we gain in wisdom we say we are enlightened.

Previous page: Theatrical design by Giacomo Torelli

Scholars have surmised that man first acknowledged the existence of his soul by worshipping his sources of light, the sun and the moon. With his discovery that he could control fire man began to master his environment, and with firelight the history of artificial illumination — of controlled light — begins. When we gain in wisdom we still say we are "enlightened."

Early man left evidence that he could light the darkness of his caves and paint on their walls what he saw outside of them. We may and do suppose that the most singular human ability, that of self-dramatization, developed at the same time. Prehistoric ritual, tale-telling, comic recital — the forerunners of legend, of abstracting what he had learned, of tragedy, in which man envisioned his own death, of entertainment at his own expense — must have acquired aspects of mystery and theatricality when the flickering lights of fires and torches revealed the moving shadows of priest or performer.

From recorded time on, I am sure the best way to study lighting, all lighting, is in terms of theatre. Like light itself, all theatrical productions are temporary, annihilated at the moment they end. A drama must be rekindled, re-created, reconsidered each time it is played.

Pre-Christian drama reached its unsurpassed heights under the pellucid and dependable light from the skies of Greece. Natural light, I think, was for the first time consciously used in — or rather organized into — theatrical production by the Greek playwrights. Study Greek drama and you follow dramatically the sun as it moves from east to west over the long arc of the day. The plays are clearly constructed on the basis of the daily rhythms of light, and the Greek amphitheatres were carefully calculated and sited to take full advantage of the artifice of natural light.

The Romans, copying from the Greeks, proved that you really cannot steal ideas. Their theatres were replicas of the Greek ones, but sited far less well, just as their statues, with exactly the same dimensions, seem without bones. According to such records as remain, though, the Romans were lavish with bringing out torches when it got too dark to see. I like the kind of matter-of-fact logic of "If it's dark, let's get on some light, one way or another."

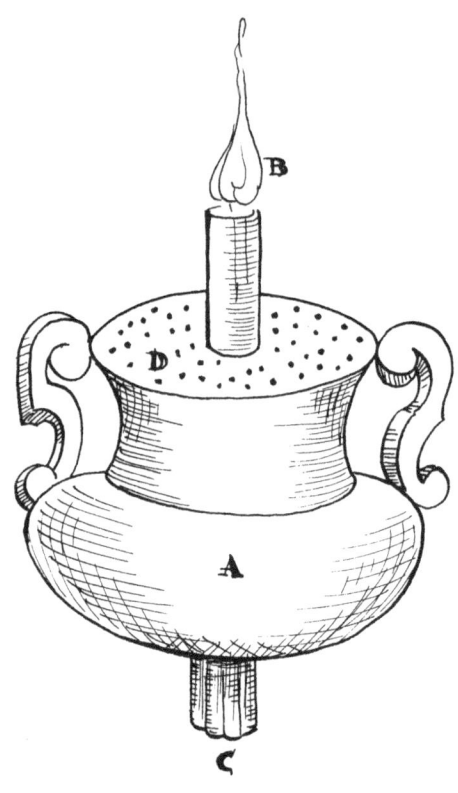

A Method of showing a Hell.

"Let A be the pot in which we pass the piece of torch BC, long enough to let B come out of the top and C remain below the pot. When the time comes to use it, some one must hold part C in his hands, the torch having been lighted at B. When we want the flame to be thrown on the stage, the pot will be rapidly lifted, and the resin will come out of the holes which were made in the paper D, and catching fire will result in a big flame. Thus, the other men will do the same thing from time to time while the trap is opened."

— *Nicola Sabbattini (1574–1654)*

Until the Renaissance, we can only guess at how much artificial light was used theatrically, although we have a great deal of evidence on the early use of scenic artifice. As far back as 400 B.C. there were "effects" — such as lightning flashes painted on three sides of a prism-like structure which was rapidly revolved. (Perhaps the best-informed reconstruction of pre-Christian theatre has been done by Mary Renault in *The Mask of Apollo*.) Medieval plays were pageants — the long mystery plays had "crowds" of as many as five hundred people. They were also apt to be road shows, moved on from place to place. Although they stressed a lighted heaven and a flaming hell, nobody knows whether these actually burned.

From the 1500s and 1600s we have a great number of surviving records. In fact the Renaissance left such a strong imprint on later theatre that seventeen-century principles of how to light the stage remained in force well into the twentieth century. For three hundred years the positioning of light sources for indoor theatre production was so widely accepted a convention that no improvement was considered necessary. Torches, oil lamps and candles were replaced by gas, and gas by electricity, with virtually no alteration in lighting principles and basic layouts.

Periods and centuries, though, really divide even less neatly in the matter of lighting and lighting design than for other subjects. The best way to cover this subject is quite simply to consider lighting fixtures.

The earliest movable lights developed from the blazing brand snatched from the fire: soaking sticks of wood in pitch increased the burning time. Torches became, in due course, fixed lights. When Tiberius ruled in Rome five hundred slaves bearing torches conducted the audience home after a spectacle, and for festive occasions, the great Roman feasts and gatherings, stationary light was provided by enormous numbers of fixed torches. These were held by slaves or placed on columns, singly or inclusters. In effect, these torches, as well as being the first street lights, were the first floor lamps and the first chandeliers. Candles of sorts, long in use, improved in medieval times, and torches moved outside, called for as soon as it was dark. Cervantes describes a farce in the courtyard of a ducal palace lit by about a hundred torches set in sconces. The religious mystery plays, which toured Europe for five hundred years, often began before daylight and lasted until well after dark. Torchbearers came "on" after sunset, but where they stood was never defined. Cresset lights — torches made of ropes wreathed, pitched and placed in small, open iron cages — were invented by the Romans and much used for the medieval theatre. Cressets are mentioned in the dramatic literature of past centuries, but rather in passing.

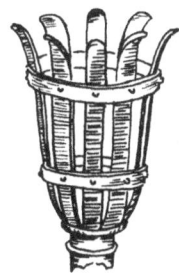
fifteenth-century cresset — an iron basket for holding a blazing pine knot

There is no concrete evidence defining the use of stage lighting in Shakespeare's day, but the playwright does bring on torches to indicate that it is night. Romeo demands a torch, and says that he will bear it. Whether these were borne lighted or symbolically unlit is for guessing at. Long before Shakespeare's time, extensive use of candles had added to the hazards of light-by-fire those of asphyxiation and odor. Candles gave a more efficient light than oil lamps, which were more efficient than torches, so if torches were actually used and lit indoors it was only because they were cheaper and more dramatic. You cannot beat the chiaroscuro of a great flaming smoking torch, casting more shadow than light.

Roman floats, Greek and Hebrew and Egyptian floats — those little clay pots in which they put a bit of oil and then lighted it — made particularly good stationary light. Wick and cage and handle were added to make a lantern to carry.

The lamp, surmised to exist thirty thousand years back in the Stone Age, was prevalent by the time of the Lascaux Cave paintings, fifteen thousand years ago. In those caves hundreds of stone lamps were discovered. Fabricated lamps, other than skulls, hollowed stones and seashells, seem to have been used the world over from 3500 to 2500 B.C. In Athens, archaeologists dug up over ten thousand lamps from the third through fifth centuries B.C., which argues for their common household use, and ancient Rome is known to have had a flourishing pottery lamp industry. Even slaves there used snail shells with tow wicks and vegetable oil, while patricians had their lamps worked in bronze. The Erectheum on the Acropolis had a rare gold one, sculpted by Callimachus, which burned without refilling for a whole year; and

open-flame oil lamps

in the late myth of Cupid and Psyche, Psyche carries an oil lamp, from which a drop of hot oil falls on Cupid and awakens him — a theatrical touch.

floating wick on olive oil

Candles competed with lamps from the first century A.D. on so successfully that the famous 1911 *Encyclopaedia Britannica*, in an extensive article on artificial light, dismisses the entire subject of lamps, from prehistoric times through the 1780s, in three sentences. The first sentence acknowledges that oil lamps were the primary source of indoor light for thousands of years. The second lists the varieties of oil used. And the third states: "Up to the latter half of the eighteenth century lamps were shallow vessels into which a short length of wick dipped; the flame was smoky and discharged acrid vapours, giving the minimum of light with the maximum of smell."

Lamplight and candlelight remained a luxury for centuries partly because what they burned could also be eaten. When food was lacking, the poor ate the oil for their lamps and consumed candle tallow, which was even more nourishing. Tallow — cheaper than wax — may be graded in quality, but even the best gave off a lot of heat. Tallow candles burned brightly enough to see by close up, but the light diminished rapidly over any area. Besides stinking, one candle used up as much oxygen as two men — so the authorities calculated — and polluted the air.

tallow candle

Also the use of candles required enormous labor. Even those of the finest quality needed constant snuffing. Snuffing was an art: in order not to lose your tallow or wax at an uneconomical and smoky rate, you had to clip the wick without putting the candle out — which then required relighting, a wasteful process. In order to use candles in the theatre you had to have snuff boys. A snuff boy might walk onstage in the middle of the most dramatic scene. He was supposed to be ignored, but if he was especially skillful he was apt to get a round of applause.

Snuffers, those early scissorlike clippers for cutting the wicks were expensive; douters and extinguishers for snuffing *out*, less so. Rush-

snuffer

douter

extinguisher

lights, the simplest form of candle, made from prepared pith dipped in any sort of tallow, did not need snuffing as they burned in a nearly horizontal position — but they burned fast and greasy drops followed the paths of their flames.

Small wonder rushlights were unpopular, though cheap, and candles were in regular use only by the rich, who had money for wax ones and servants to tend them. Even in royal households the use of candles was sparing. In the *Delectable History of Fortnum and Mason* there is a note that after William Mason became footman to Queen Anne in 1707 he went into the used-candle business, becoming, in fact, a candle grocer in his spare time. The royal family had its personal candlesticks refilled every night. Mason, the footman, as his special perquisite repossessed the used ones — which he sold to the ladies of the court, who would otherwise often have had to blunder about in the dark.

With torches and lamps and candles all burning merrily, smokily and smellily, one can return to theatrical lighting — in which lavish use was made of all three.

If I could transmigrate backwards and meet some of my professional ancestors, I would choose the Italians of the period from the 1550s through the 1650s. I wrote my thesis at Yale on the commedia dell'arte and for a while I taught the subject at the Neighborhood Playhouse. I have always been particularly impressed by those marvelously inventive thinkers about the theatre Serlio, Sabbattini and Furttenbach the Elder — whose treatises appear in translation in a book called *The Renaissance Stage*, edited by Barnard Hewitt — and by Leone Hebreo de' Sommi (or de' Somi or di Sommi) whose book *Dialogues on Stage Affairs*, written in the 1550s and preserved in manuscript at the library in Parma, was translated by Allardyce Nicoll, professor of English language and literature at the University of London. Thanks to Nicoll, whose lectures I attended at Yale during his brief tenure there, I was able early on to read that perceptive and exciting discourse on lighting. De' Sommi is the man whom the *Oxford Companion to the Theatre* credits with first using reflectors — small mirrors fixed to the back of the wings of the stage — and with creating footlights — or "floats," as footlights are still called in England — of wicks in oil.

De' Sommi was a designer and architect, and his "dialogues" purport to be among various theatre workers. Herewith his lovely dialogue on light as carried on by "Santino," "Veridico" and "Massimiano" in trio:

SANTINO: What is the use and origin of those lights on the rooftops of houses on the stage? They do not seem to me to aid the perspective, and for purposes of illumination there are torches enough.

VERIDICO: I think I have said and repeated the fact that comedies are presented for the purpose of enjoyment and of alleviating gloomy thoughts; for that reason . . . the actor must be bidden to speak his lines in a happy and bright manner. Now, granted that the author gives us a pleasant, charming plot and that the actor interprets it in a joyous spirit, surely it is necessary that the architect on his part should represent gladness and joy and since both modern and ancient custom is and has been to light fires

> Marry, sir, she's the kitchen wench, and all grease; and I know not what use to put her to, but to make a lamp of her, and run from her by her own light. I warrant her rags, and the tallow in them, will burn a Poland winter.
> — *Comedy of Errors* III. ii

and torches in the streets, on housetops, and on towers as a sign of gladness, therefore this is the origin of the convention —

SANTINO: These lights, then, could not be used in tragedy?

VERIDICO: Perhaps . . . since generally tragedies open in happiness it will not be unfitting to arouse the mind as much as possible to this happiness. Once I had to produce a tragedy. The stage was brightly illuminated through all that part of the action in which the episodes were happy: as soon as the first unhappy incident occurred — the unexpected death of a queen — while the chorus was in exclamation that the sun could suffer to see such misery, I contrived . . . that at the very instant most of the stage lights not used for the perspective were darkened or extinguished.

MASSIMIANO: Will you please tell us now why your lights are mostly shaded with transparent or colored glass?

VERIDICO: That was the invention of those who realized what few pay attention to — namely, that a brilliant light striking on the eye irritates the person looking at it for long. As the spectator has to turn his eyes always upon the stage to see the actions passing now on this side and now on that, this invention was established to minimize the annoyance by the shading of the lights.

In nature, a man standing in the shadow sees much better whatever is brightly lit at a distance, than does one who stands in an illuminated position: for the sight moves with less hesitation and with greater concord to the object, or, as the peripatetics think, the object comes more harmoniously to the apprehension of the eye. Hence I place the fewest possible lights in the auditorium, while at the same time I endeavor to illuminate the stage brightly.

In that hundred years (1550–1650) the major design elements of the eighteenth- and nineteenth-century theatre were developed: auditorium design, stage sets with wings and flats, the proscenium arch. It was this arch, framing the stage as paintings were framed, which made the happy absorption with perspective displayed by Italian painters applicable in the theatre. The theatre men of that century also developed the curtain, the musicians' pit and balconies. Lighting plans, including footlights, sidelights, downlights, colored lights, dimming and darkening lights and even spotlights, were conceived and carried out with amazing ingenuity.

At first, Renaissance "theatres" — like those of the Middle Ages — were temporary structures, built for touring and put up and taken down as structural units. Concern with acoustics, when the theatres were put up in courtyards, created the colonnade to go behind tiered seats. (It is possible that there were already complaints that actors no longer knew how to throw their voices as they had in the "old days" — the secrets of those astonishing Greek amphitheatre acoustics had been lost.) These seats, rising along the colonnades, were the forerunners of balconies.

On medieval stages cloths might cover the opening of a mansion, or even a whole front of a mansion, but were not used to introduce the stage to a waiting audience. Almost as soon as secular drama was played in Renaissance courts, curtains were drawn over single scenes and a little later, indoors, the falling curtain, disappearing into the pit, began to cover the whole proscenium arch. "A great cloth hung in front extending from the ceiling to the floor," wrote Furttenbach the Elder in Paris in 1632, ". . . will keep the audience in an impatient desire to see what it is hiding."

Rising curtains — like doors on hinges — were used inside the stage as early as 1515, but many writers make no mention of any that went up instead of down.

In his famous *Practica* or "how-to" on theatrical devices, Nicola Sabbattini, born in 1574, offers specifics on everything a producer needed to know, from "How to Paint the Heavens," and "How to Locate the Vanishing Point," through "How to Light the Lamps."

Your method of lighting the lamps, said Sabbattini, "must be practical and safe lest the haste cause disorder and harm and still greater delay." One way to light an auditorium was by making a fuse, or braid, with a flaxen wick on an iron wire dipped in coal oil or *aqua vitae*. This wire followed around the tops of all the candles in the chandeliers, fixed in at least three places to the master wire holding the chandeliers. Experienced men could set fire to the end of each candle taper. But this did not really appeal to Sabbattini as the most practical because either the flames went out before reaching the candle ends, or burning pieces of flax fell down causing "general confusion." He preferred to soak the top of each candle in coal oil, put a "reliable and experienced man" with two thin poles near each chandelier, wire a candle for lighting to the top of one pole, and on the other fix a sponge soaked in water in case a candle began to drip on people below. This method taxed the patience of the audience longer but was safer, unless you could arrange to have your chandeliers let down, be lighted, and then hoisted up again.

What should be lighted he defines with all the detail of a master handbook. On the stage, where the lighting of fixtures is less of a problem, use oil lamps, in good quantity, of good quality, invisible to the spectators. Set them in front of the heavens on the inner side of the stage — in such a way as not to interfere with scene changing, or, he warns you, you will ruin your reputation as a stage director. Lamps — or torches, which he prefers — are distributed over the stage and should be fixed with plaster to the floor, passing through the stage floor by means of holes, and *well* fixed so that when the stage is shaken they do not tumble or flicker. (Keep water in containers ready at hand above the beams or the "heavens" and below the stage.)

It was the practice to place oil lanterns stage front, behind a parapet made higher than the stage for this purpose. Sabbattini warns that there may be more harm than gain by this because the large wicks necessary for illumination often give off dense smoke, creating a veil between spectators and scene besides creating a very bad smell.

He ends his discourse on lighting with a piece of wisdom which Belasco relearned in the twentieth century: although one can see the costumes of the actors and dancers better by bright frontlights in low

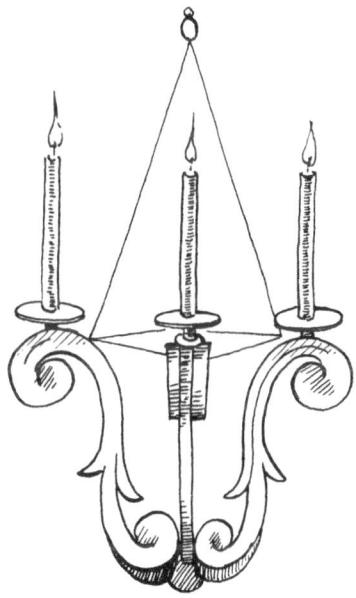

Italian Renaissance theatre chandelier

positions, "their faces seem so pale and wan that they look as if they had just had a bad fever."

In fact Sabbattini's basic principles concerning illumination of the stage, briefly set forth by him, with the insistence that you *begin* with the light and not the scenery, set a standard scarcely surpassed and often forgotten over three hundred years.

Both Sabbattini and Joseph Furttenbach the Elder, a German architect who studied in Florence, gave much more thought and space to the theatre machines, of which the impresarios right on through the nineteenth century remained so fond, than they did to lighting. How they loved flying machines for floating angels, trapdoors, and machines for making lifelike seas billow on stage, with ships upon them. Dolphins and marine monsters spouted water, rivers "flowed," storms were stupendous, and there were clouds, clouds, clouds.

Furttenbach, only cursorily interested in illumination, nevertheless developed a system of black metal covers let down from a single cord located in the "heavens" for turning day into night by blacking out all the lights at once while leaving them lit, and his "Four Methods of Lighting" details the use of oil lamps, mica reflectors with lanterns, leaning lights and standard light boxes. In his most explicit original design, he combines machine with illumination in the *parisol*.

A "homely device," the Italian *parisol* struck him as an ideal fixture for creating a burning bush. Covered with black leather, he explains, the *parisol* was used in Italy as a roof over the traveler's head to protect him from sun or rain. It could open three feet in diameter "like a peacock fan" and then be closed for carrying. For his purpose, the *parisol*'s twelve leather panels were gilded and painted in figured golden streams. Then he poked the closed *parisol* through a hole one foot square about four feet off the floor of the stage. A man concealed behind the wall pushed and pulled the knob that turned it from side to side. Two perspective lanterns on the inner stage lit the *parisol* from below and the whole thing seemed like a burning bush, burning without being consumed.

Sebastiano Serlio, a painter before he became an architect, is the one who went in the most fervently for color — flames burning behind translucent containers of color. Sapphire blue was to him the most beautiful for stage use, and he gives a recipe for making it, adding saffron for emerald. Ruby he creates from light and dark red wines; topaz from white wines; while pure water filtered through felt makes the best counterfeit of diamond. The glass containers with these liquid colors are to be placed on a board with lamps on a pierced board above them, one lamp to be lit behind each container.

So there we are — with the tableau lighting of scenes raised to an art which could only be elaborated upon in the extravagant nineteenth-century theatre.

Floats or footlights had been used in Italy long since, but when

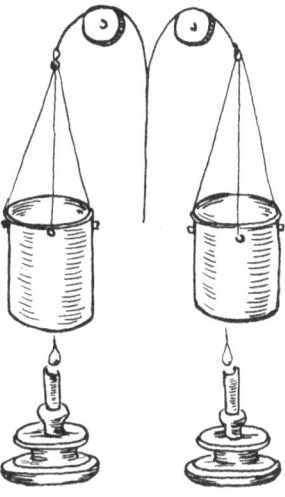

seventeenth-century theatre blackout system

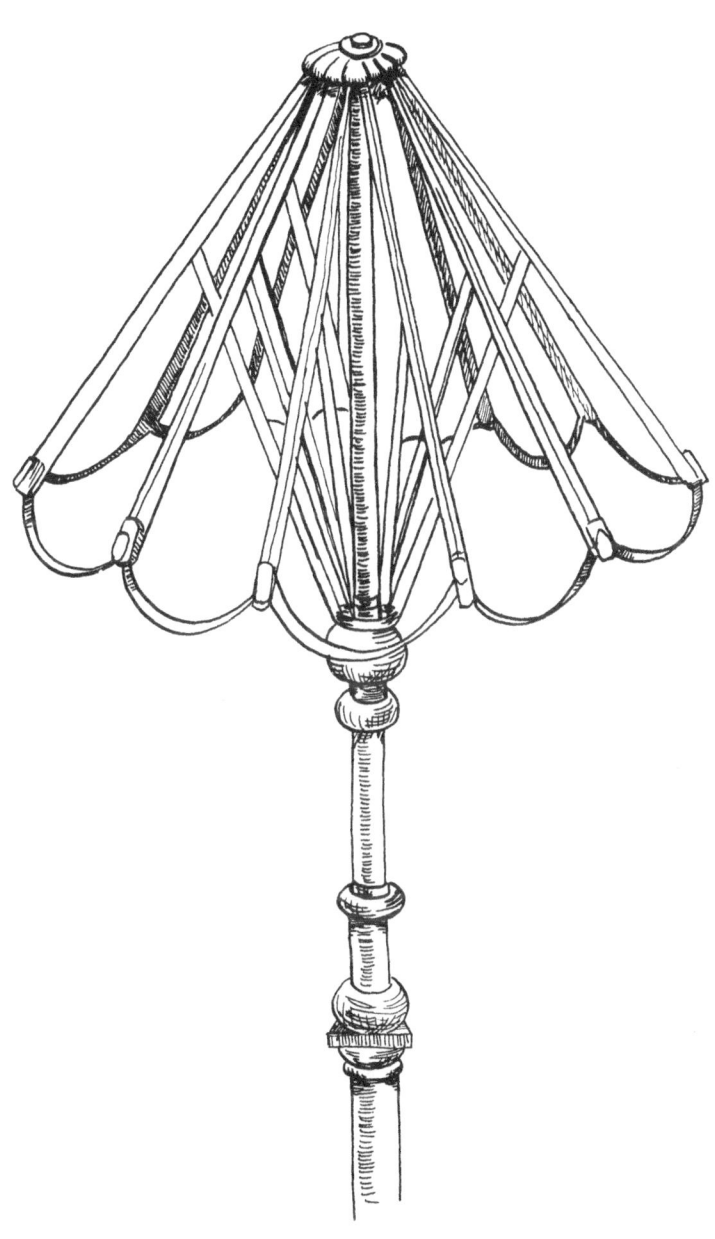

an Italian *parisol*: gilded and painted like streams of flame, used to suggest a burning bush

a reflector for a candle made by applying gold tinsel and mica to white-painted tin

David Garrick in 1775 placed a row of candles masked by metal hoods below and in front of the stage it was considered an innovation.

Next came the Argand lamp, in 1783, and the use of camphor, kerosene and other higher-grade illuminants, bringing brighter and more efficient light into the theatre. The gas chimney enclosing the lighted flame came along to provide the most important scientific advance in lighting fixtures in four thousand years. These lamps took over — hanging in clusters from the ceiling, projected from walls, balconies and boxes, used as footlights, borderlights and wing lights.

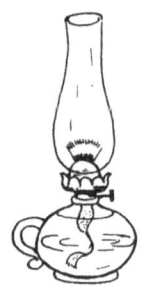

kerosene lamp with an adjustable wick
(invented in France in 1783)

In 1743 the list of theatre properties at Covent Garden in London had included "6 douters, 8 lighting sticks, 9 single blinds with 48 tinn candlesticks, the border bell and 12 candlesticks for thunder, 5 tinn blinds for stage lamps, 115 three-corner tinn lamps, 192 tinn candlesticks and 14 lamp posts for stage out of use." When Covent Garden burned down in 1808, the rebuilt house was lighted by glass chandeliers in front of each circle — 270 wax candles was the nightly supply — while 300 patent lamps lighted the stage and scenery.

But gaslight was already on the way. The Chinese had probably first used it, piping natural gas in bamboo tubes from salt mines. As early as 1664 the Reverend Dr. John Clayton collected some coal gas in bladders, and a century later Jean Pierre Minckelers, professor at Louvain University, lighted his lecture room with gas. A thermo-gas lamp was patented in 1799, and in 1802 "Bengal lights" — open burners — were

an open-flame gas burner
(invented in Scotland in 1782)

an incandescent mantel used with a
gas burner (invented in Germany in 1890)

introduced by one William Murdock. The year 1806 saw the earliest theatrical use of gas when F. A. Wintzler, a German, lighted the Lyceum Theatre in London. America had the first complete gas lighting system, at the Chestnut Street Opera House in Philadelphia, but gas was so expensive that it was not generally used before 1850. By 1886 the Elsbach mantle had increased efficiency many times, and the old conventional borders, foots, wings and bunch lights were converted to gas.

Now you could control lighting from a central location. The switchboard was born in the "gas tables" used first at the Lyceum in London and the Boston Theatre in America. A master valve located near the prompter controlled the whole layout. Dimmer valves and flash buttons (to give quick bursts of flame) were developed and used, and darkening the auditorium during a performance — recommended by de' Sommi — became practical. In some ways gaslight was all too practical, since managers became ever more fascinated with effects for their own sake.

Henry Irving, one of the great actor-managers of the gaslit era, played around with lighting in his grand manner. He used individual lights to illuminate objects and experimented with color through arrangements of silks or screens in front of lights. When limelight came along he used it for follow spots — those concentrated white lights that pursue a single character about the stage in his own personal illumination.

"Realism" of an excessively romantic sort took over. Henry Irving had Lady Macbeth carried out with her red hair streaming in torchlight, and Macbeth, in the final scene, took a torch from behind a pillar and hurled it blazing to the ground. Sir Herbert Beerbohm-Tree as Nero was drawn across the stage in a chariot by live, stage-trained horses, and he burned Rome with crumpling houses, crashing temples and shooting flames. Introducing his Macbeth, Beerbohm-Tree had such a roar of wind, rattle of hail and blinding flashes of lightning that when Macbeth appeared on the heath against a dazzling background of stormy skies, the audience burst into applause. "Emerging from the theatre into a thunderstorm after one of these stage-quaking exhibitions," wrote Hesketh Pearson in his book on the last actor-managers, ". . . one had to admit that Nature put up a pretty feeble imitation of what several barrels of stones and a few sheets of tin could do in His Majesty's theatre."

English critical writings of the time illustrate how the theatre turned everything it produced into action-laden melodrama, essentially unrealistic. When the actor-managers presented Shakespeare they reinterpreted and reoriented his plays so that the action was heightened and the lyricism, poetry and intellectual aspects of his writings were either omitted entirely or mumbled in the dark so that they would not impede the melodramatic line.

Victorian stage lighting, except for "effects," was strictly for visibility and to illuminate the scenery. The Victorians painted that scenery to incorporate *motivated* light meticulously. A window would be painted and the light coming through the window would be painted in.

The visual technique was that stars and leading players performed on the apron, or in the downstage area. The upstage area was used to create locale. Stage sets were over-scale, almost operatic in scale, and within the huge, romantic scenery, dimly lit and carefully painted, the extras or crowds or courtiers would be assembled.

The innovation of the time was the light known as limelight. Lime was the basis of the light source and it gave a brilliant white glow with sharp edges. Operated from the side of the stage or from a perch, it was used to accent the leading players.

It all had its element of danger. Gas footlights occasionally set fire

> In the present days of scenic display, when even no poor ghost can walk undisturbed by scientific satellites, limelights, mirrors, and the like, the scene-painter is a far more important person than the Tragedian.
> — Thos. Wm. Robertson, 1850s

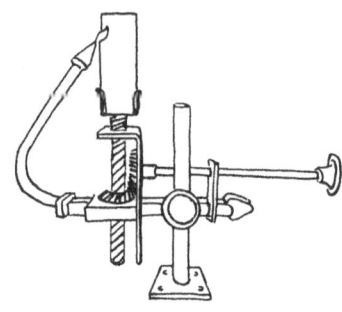

"limelight": a block of lime heated to incandescence by an oxy-hydrogen blowpipe

Edison's first electric light, 1879

to performers, especially dancers in their inflammable tulle. Theatre fires were started by the spirit wads on long poles used for lighting the gas jets. But in its day, which lasted, at least on the streets of Paris, until after World War II, gas did give a lovely light.

In 1882 a congress of theatre managers issued a report recommending all-electrified theatres. Electricity had become practical.

The electrical engineer was a magician. He could do anything. "Effects" became even more stupendous. Stages were raised and lowered as lights went up and down on electric dimmer controls. Colors were no longer a matter of wines in water or laboriously ground sal ammoniac, or created by running painted reels of silk in front of lamps. You could color the bulbs themselves or slip gelatin slides in front of them.

The spectacle perhaps reached its happy vulgar height — using the word in its pejorative sense, because that sort of thing does not appeal to me, and also in the Latin sense of "appeal to the masses" — at the old Hippodrome in New York, perhaps best remembered for its onstage chariot race in *Ben Hur*. Wagnerian opera, especially in Germany, commanded effects as overpowering as the music. For Wagner's grand mythology, romantic realism was raised to even grander proportions. Now that man was *really* able to imitate nature, he was more than ever inclined to outdo it.

A soberer realism invaded the drama through Ibsen, Strindberg and the others. Producers, especially David Belasco, began to think in terms not of romantic realism but of *ultra*-realism, in the scenery, properties and lighting of their stages. Belasco once spent five thousand dollars on a sunset for *The Girl of the Golden West*, and then scrapped it because it was "not Californian." Later he sold it to the producers of *Salomy Jane*.

The electrified theatre was burdened with gaslight traditions. Posi-

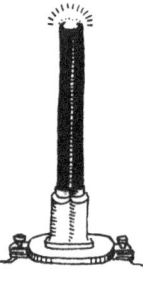

Jablochkoff candle
(arc light)

the electric arc invented in 1808
by Sir Humphrey Davy, used on the stage
since the early 1840's

tions for lighting remained the same and lighting was limited to flood-lighting in borders and footlights and to spots and arcs elsewhere. Spotlights — casting the pools of light which are the true beginning of modern lighting design — could be hung in relatively few and severely regimented places. The layout for scenery seldom reserved physical room for lighting equipment. It was primitive — but so were the expectations of the audiences. Comedies were bright; dramas were uncheerful. Day was yellow; night blue. Effects were naïve (storms, fires, clouds) and ranged from those as corny as the ones in *East Lynne,* to the refined and mysterious, as in *The Return of Peter Grimm.*

In the latter Belasco did away at long last with footlights, a move long since advocated by such disparate people as Sir Henry Irving and August Strindberg. Wrote Belasco afterwards:

> It took five months of experiments to accomplish the results I sought. I invented special reflectors to produce the ashen hue of death, but something always seemed lacking. I kept David Warfield in New York all summer, standing alone on the stage for hours at a stretch, while I threw various lights upon him. Then it occurred to me that the trouble lay in the kind of clothes he wore. I sent for fifty bolts of cloth and wrapped him in the different fabrics and colors, until I found one which made him look mysterious and far away. Even then his appearance was not quite right. When other characters came on the stage things went wrong. Finally I tried the expedient of casting a cold gray light upon his features from above, while, at the same time, I illuminated the other characters in the play with a faint rosy glow. It was necessary to have many of these lights of differing quality which, one after the other, "picked up" the people as they moved from place to place on the stage. The effect was exactly what I desired, and it proved to be one of the most important factors in the success of the play.

Lucky the lighting expert who worked for Belasco! Nobody has given that much time to lighting a play properly, before or since. Even so, "effect" and "natural" remained the key words rather than "emotional atmosphere."

In general, before the 1930s the designer of a show was overwhelmed by the craft aspects of his calling. Lighting in particular suffered. The designer was expected to design, paint and then deliver a whole production, right down to the illumination, at the stage door.

In Europe, though, at least two mature minds were considering and clarifying the role that lighting might have in enhancing the play. Adolphe Appia and Gordon Craig came to the realization that light could be put to creative dramatic use. They experimented with light on the stage to reveal the form of dimensional objects — trees and castle stones, steps and levels. They evolved a style of stage settings, of stylized dimensional forms representing realistic objects, and they added the use of light as the design element that blended these forms into a unified and composite stage picture.

Later, in the extravagant twenties in America, Robert Edmond Jones, working for Arthur Hopkins, and Lee Simonson, with the Theatre Guild, were visionaries. They believed that a comprehensive visual treatment could support the atmosphere of the play and carry it beyond the simple physical locale or imitations of nature. For a long time they were

---

Another novelty well needed would be the abolition of footlights. The light from below is said to have for its purpose to make the faces of actors look fatter. But I cannot help asking: why must all actors be fat in the face?
— *Strindberg Manifesto,* 1893

... under the domination of the painted set, the lighting is completely dominated by the decor.... Lighting itself is an element the effects of which are limitless; once it is free, it becomes for us what the palette is for the painter.... the actor no longer walks *in front of* painted lights and shadows; he is immersed in an atmosphere that is *destined for him.*
— Adolphe Appia

... the reproduction of nature's lights is *not* what my stage manager ever attempts. Not to reproduce *nature,* but to *suggest* some of her most beautiful and living ways — that is what my stage director shall attempt.
— Gordon Craig

prophets without disciples on Broadway, though art, community and university theatres tried to follow their ideas.

When disaster struck the U.S. economy, and with it the commercial theatre, communication among people caught in a common calamity became a pressing need. In due course the Federal Theatre gathered up the unemployed of the theatre and gave them the means of saying what they had to say — with precious little money to pay for the privilege. The need for a new visual approach was now ineluctable.

The Federal Theatre, the Mercury Theatre, the Group Theatre, Theatre Union and the first Phoenix Theatre could only stay within their pitiful budgets by jettisoning the hefty realistic scenery and the production formulas of the recent past. What they had to say — the new kind of life documentation they essayed — asked for lighting that did much more than calculate the locale and the hour. The idea, the actor and a pool of light to focus interest on the performing area were used to convey the essence of meaning as never before.

These *pools of light* are the true beginning of lighting design as a separate art and craft, for with them begins an understanding of light's separate contribution to the whole. These alone could create theatricality. Varied as directed, downward or angled from back or front, left or right, high or low, each position produced its own plasticity and pattern.

It was at this point in time, with the Federal Theatre, with new forms of dance and music, with experimental groups, pinch-pennied, emerging in an explosion of ideas, that the young Martha Graham, the young Orson Welles, John Houseman and Jean Rosenthal, among others, were thinking, creating, performing and working. Lighting design gradually became accepted as an integral and separate part of the dramatic whole, the collaborative effort. Those of us who followed the profession approached our work individually. I can only speak for myself. What follows is how I myself have thought about my work and carried out what I thought.

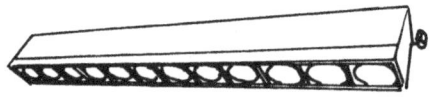

modern fresnel light

Five. Lighting the Play

In the conflicts of the drama, the most important role of light is to expose the nature of the struggle, to set the atmosphere for its development, and to underscore its resolution.

You begin by holding a play in your hand. (In the commercial theatre, when I receive a script I am being asked whether I will do the job of designing for it. In repertory or regional theatre — where the lighting designer is hired by an organization which selects the material — I am already committed to design for the plays they hand me. In either case I begin with a play in my hand.) Even if the play is a classic with which I am thoroughly familiar, it becomes a new play for me. I am older than I was, things have happened, the world has changed, and I shall be working with certain people.

Let us assume, for the purpose of considering the lighting of plays, a single production under a standard set of circumstances.

You know that the dramatic theatre is a system of communication. Its enormous ability to communicate on many levels has three major elements. (One likes to classify.)

— The playwright, who is anxious to communicate what he has to say as *he* sees it
— The director, who has chosen this play and who is theoretically responsible — *in toto* — for the results
— Us others, who will place the communication on the stage: actors and designers, all of whom are helpless without stage crews, carpenters, electricians.

Sometimes one person is involved with two or three of these elements. He should, I think, carry out his responsibilities in exactly the proper order.

The play — the playwright's play — comes first. I believe that everybody involved with a play should concentrate on the dramatist's intentions rather than try to expand or change them. If all facets of a production cannot be disciplined by the script, the play is not worth putting on.

The lighting designer does best, I think, to begin with the play — any play — by forgetting the technical aspects which are his responsibility. Otherwise, his lighting ideas are apt to be, as they once were, purely

> Our playwrights need to learn that plays are wrought, not written.
> — Robert Edmond Jones

for illumination. Read it as a whole; read quickly, all at once, without care for details. If it is a familiar play, try to read it as if for the first time. Look for the "central image" — the "flash" Professor A. Dean talked about years ago at Yale. If and when it comes, hang on to it and never lose it. It will be your constant guidepost all along the way for what lighting can do within its vital function, which is to fulfill the need of all drama for unhurried concentration and full communication.

Light provides important shortcuts to comprehension. It can instantly establish time of day and cover lapses of time. It accents or establishes place and change of place. And light may also uncover and elaborate undercurrents which there is no time to expose in words; or it can express what cannot be expressed in action or revealed by the actors — the unspoken and the taken for granted. In the conflicts of the drama the final and most important role of lighting is to expose the nature of the struggle, to set the atmosphere for its development, and to underscore its resolution.

But first you must have the "flash," the image, the central thread, the idea. Let us say you — using the hypothetical lighting designer "you," really me — have it. You keep this central image clear but fluid. Add in no details at this time. You are obligated first to share this image with the director, your superior authority.

By the time you talk to him, you should have plowed through the script many more times, as many as it requires for understanding it (for *hearing* it). You must have enough background to understand what the director has to say, have a language ready with which to respond to his thoughts and concepts. The theatre is a very autocratic place and can only function autocratically. Within the matrix of collaboration the clear line of authority is based on the degree of responsibility. At the present time the director is responsible and in charge. Even if you have done many more plays than has the director you are working for, which you may well have, you are obliged by the courtesies of relative authority to go to him first without prejudice in your own favor. And to *listen* to him, rather than help him. You do not proffer your ideas at this time. You listen and hear what he has to say.

People are quite curious about listening and often hear only what they want to hear, what suits them, following their own trains of thought from selected fragments of what is said to them. Telephone companies base the required clarity of their equipment on the indication that users hear less than 65 percent of what they listen to. Assumption accounts for the rest.

For collaboration you need a much greater willingness to hear — not in order to agree, but in order that all ideas may go into one pot and be blended into one whole. There is great pleasure in this.

When you have listened to the director, you find to your astonishment that he does not want to do the play as you have seen it. You do not say anything yet — you just listen.

Next, you see your real friend, the set designer. You are again committed to greater authority. This probably came about because scene design was an entity before lighting design was, but there is less of an authoritative gap than there used to be. In recent years lighting is being used more and more as scenery or instead of scenery or to make minimal scenery possible. You may find that the set designer — who has presumably gone through the same process you have — agrees neither with the director nor with you. He may think the show should be very abstract, for instance, while the director visualizes it realistically. Take it easy. It usually proves to be all a matter of degree. Later you can take the director's realism and the designer's abstraction and relate them to your own image.

If all of you think the play *means* the same thing, it will begin to come together. Now you take your ideas back to the director and back to the scene designer and say how you see it. Three people can be honest, honorable and truthful and still be part of a unit, which let us assume for the sake of the play they are. If so, you quickly reach the satisfactory point where you can start really doing your part. You become specific, a specific person.

Before I continue with this happy theory, I must admit that a lighting designer leads a most curious life. For one thing he, unlike a scene designer, rarely can draw very well. Besides, it is hard to draw light — I have tried — as well as difficult to describe something as intangible as air. References to paintings help, not because the lighting is supposed to look like Rembrandt or Constable or Hals, but as clues to atmosphere, color, and the kind of focus the director and you have in mind. The common vocabulary which has grown up for communicating about light — those useful terms such as quality of light, pattern, color washes, downlight and backlight, do help us all.

To the area of agreement you should have reached at this point with your "bosses" you set up the boundaries within which you must work.

Boundary 1 is the degree of reality the director wants to suggest.

Boundary 2 is the placement of important scenes within the set.

Boundary 3 is the restrictions under which the performance will take place: what theatre or theatres it will be in, whether the play will have a long tryout run out of town or will open in New York, and what commercial standards it is expected to meet. Economic restrictions must be respected without slighting the aesthetic respect you pay the script.

You then go back to the play. You study it, examining its surface over and over until it is as familiar as a road you drive daily or the blocks you walk to work. You look for images to print as the frames of a cinema are printed, looking for them within your own habits, relating them to your lifetime store of images.

I was lucky enough to be born with visual recall, retaining images rather than words. When anyone talks to me, I see what they say rather than taking it in on the verbal level. My memory bank is in pictures,

---

Jean was interested always in bringing out the form and individual style of whatever designer she worked with. She did not impose her own aesthetic — she adapted it. She had a great personal sense of style, but she never took over.
— Oliver Smith

Once Jean got what I call "inner design" it was almost impossible to get her to change and I've seen her work with some very tough directors. She was capable of enormous, steely strength — never aggressive — surfaced by enormous charm, graciousness and humor.
— Oliver Smith

Stage lighting is often surrounded by a thick and impenetrable veil of mystery, which is due, undoubtedly, to lack of knowledge of both the limits and the potentialities of the problem.
— Stanley McCandless

Some of my most cherished memories of life in the theatre never actually took place onstage during a performance. Jean Rosenthal is part of those most cherished recollections, such as the first reading of the play, the bringing together for the first time of the creative team of individuals required to mount a play or musical — the marvelous funny protocol of speeches, of hopes expressed, and good wishes and chatter and Equity rigamarole. I first met Jean at such a reading. I remember how she smiled with such fun and joy as we discussed our mutual interest in the play and she nodded her head and I nodded mine.
— Angela Lansbury

but before printing, as it were, the ones that apply to *this* play I remind myself of the distinction Georgine Oeri, the art critic, makes when she looks at painting or sculpture.

"Is it an *image* or an *arrangement?*" she asks herself.

An *image*, unlike an arrangement, however effective, has an organic base. For the stage, an *image* blends into the beauty of the whole, contributing to communication.

By now you are living in the familiar terrain of the play, immersed in its implications and in what lies beneath the surface of stage directions, action and dialogue. You identify with the characters in time, place and situation, with their humor, uproar, conflict or tragedies. The look of the play, the scenes, the places, colored by the emotional intentions of the author, becomes clearly visible. At this point your mind begins to organize the use of light into specific shapes.

Light *has* shape — dimension, edges, entity and quality. When I start to develop a light plot — my parallel shadow-script — I think with the tools of my trade. There are many of them and they will do a marvelous variety of things. I no longer have to ask myself what a lekolite or a fresnel (see "Tools of the Trade" section, page 133) can do. I know as a matter of habit, at forty feet, at sixty, focused from flood to sharp. It is important that a new lighting designer learn to know his tools so that he can think easily, without translating, in terms of equipment. If you play with light, are ignorant about it, you are likely to make arrangements rather than create images. Using harsh colors and moving light so fast that you take the eyes of the audience off the actors distract from the whole and may become the style of the production. If it is unsuitable, as it usually is, the result is disastrous.

I have been called "modest" because I insist on lighting unobtrusively, but it is not from modesty. A play's lighting is most successful when it achieves its purposes without obtruding, without adding its demand for the audience's attention to the other demands for attention, when the audience is unconscious of it, when it is at once seen and not seen.

You, the lighting designer, are ready now to listen to the words you already know by heart read by the actors, probably under stark work light on the stage of that echoing, lonely barn which is any theatre without an audience. You will be lighting, as well as their bodies and faces, the voices of the actors. Proper light is also to hear by.

Since it takes two or three weeks to process and prepare the equipment for installation in the theatre, you are now pressed to plan your layouts and hookups, supply the plots for their exact placement, and specify the kinds of light you need to achieve your patterns and your colors. This work is detailed and demanding, and must be accurately completed before you turn over the mechanics to the electrician. It then becomes the electrician's responsibility to check all your equipment through the shop, to estimate cable lengths, to take over effects — like water, for instance. If rain is called for, he is the one who must make it seem to rain. Should there be a projected effect, he shepherds it through the shop to the balcony or bridge from which it works.

If, while all this is going on, there is mutual understanding between designer and technician, the team makes for the extra magic of performance conjured by the particular respect that keeps each job as cleanly independent as it is interdependent. I remember well when electricians wanted to murder me for using so much slow indiscernible movement of light within scenes, but when they saw what happened they liked it and often were proud of it.

The lighting designer continues to watch rehearsals. You begin to diagram the movements of the actors, continuing all the while to absorb the play. Like music, it yields more and more with each hearing. Light, above all, has the capacity to tie together disjointed moments so that they accumulate into a lasting and significant impression; you are now working out how to manage this sort of unification.

When the lights are hung and the scenery is ready, the time of focusing comes for you. This would seem to be no more than pointing lights where you want them to shine, and the hours it takes are consistently maligned while everyone else clamors for the stage. In fact, focusing is the heart of the mechanical installation of the show. With present-day equipment light can be controlled and shaped into forms and patterns that convey the dramatic intention. Molding light in this way is the hidden part of focusing, with hardly anyone except the designer and the electrician aware of it.

Some shows are easy to focus because they play on an open stage. Musicals I have worked on, like *West Side Story* and *Redhead*, although heavy electrically can be focused much more quickly than dramas like *Winesburg, Ohio* or *Becket*, where as much time is spent in getting to the lights as in focusing them. We use the term "jockeying" to describe what goes on when stagehands maneuver a thirty- to forty-foot "A" ladder with a six- or seven-foot base in and around the units that make up the set.

The first time you focus a show is the thorniest, because this is the moment when theory, ideas, thought and pencil lines become patterns of light — reality on the stage. It is the outcome of all that has gone before, the months of reading, thinking and talking about paintings and degrees of reality and all the rest of it. I have learned to keep a scrupulous record on legal-size paper with columns headed *Circuits, Color* and *Focus,* and in that last one I leave room for minute notations of the lens focus (flood to sharp) and the position of the shutters if the lights are ellipsoidal, and the locations of the hot spot in every case. To increase accuracy, designers have devised a grid scheme to subdivide the stage so the area focused on always remains the same. If the focusing is clean, you have done half your lighting.

During the final days of rehearsal, when at the beginning and end of each working day the play is taken through from start to finish without breaks, the lighting designer works out the cues for the various

---

In working with a lot of rough and ready stagehands, who at one time had contempt for women in the theatre, Jean, really more than any other technical artist, brought them around. Many women have followed — but she was the first one to do it. And the stagehands adored her.

— Oliver Smith

Though Miss Rosenthal clambers about the stage with great energy, she is forbidden to pick up as much as a single light bulb. Members of her union, the United Scenic Artists Local 829, may design light plots, give orders and look, but they must not touch.

— Winthrop Sargeant

I have been in the professional theatre thirty-five years and I can say truthfully that Jean Rosenthal is the only person who ever ordered me out of the theatre. I sat two rows behind her at a light rehearsal. I said, "Gee, that's great, marvelous." She said nothing. I said, "I think that will be all right." Jean drew herself up to her full four foot six and said, "Would you please leave the theatre." I didn't know who she was talking to. She said, "I can't do what I have to do with you here," and she said it would be worse if I sat there and said nothing. So I left. She was right. She had tremendous method in the way that Picasso or Hemingway had a method of work.

— Garson Kanin

63

... an intercom links Miss Rosenthal and the chief electrician, who is buried backstage between ranks of dimmers and switches, and cannot even glimpse what is going on. "Darling," Miss Rosenthal croons softly into the intercom, "please bring 65 to full. Tell George to let me see 7 — Flash 5, please. . . . Yes, honey. You'd better pick up 14 before it burns. . . . Please kill that baby [the reference is to a baby spot]. Now bring 1 to 5 and 3 to 7. Please, darling, bring 3 to 7. You haven't killed the baby, yet, honey."

"Jeannie!" the electrician's voice comes over the intercom, overriding a confused jumble of noise that indicates a crisis of some sort. "I know, darling," replies Miss Rosenthal in the tones of a mother reassuring a child . . . "can't we talk about it a little later? Just bring 3 to 7 and everything will be all right."
— Winthrop Sargeant

operations of the lights. Some cues are mechanical: fadeouts and blackouts that mark the ends of scenes, presets, fixtures turned on and off, shades lifted so sun streams through windows, and so on. Others are spaced through scenes to reflect the ideas and emotions contained in the scene, which is usually best done by moving light so imperceptibly that the viewer is unaware of any change. These are the ones that try the patience of the electricians, who must take the long, slow counts.

With focusing and cue placements finished, lighting rehearsal begins. These sessions are without doubt the most public exhibitions of creative thinking in the world. There you sit in a dark auditorium, usually with the set designer and director as well as those assorted people who are always somehow there. At this time the theoretical design is stated in intensities. It is the time when, if one has absorbed and analyzed the play truly, the ideas and impressions that could not be articulated are suddenly there before you. This session has a rhythm which if uninterrupted crystallizes these concepts rapidly and definitively so that the underlying mood comes clear.

If I may make a plea, it is that this short time (on a dramatic show five or six hours; on a musical, nine to eleven) be unbroken. This is all I plead for. Time is the essential ingredient in the theatre and there is never enough of it. That is why concentration must be brought to such a pitch. Drama is, essentially, a study in concentration.

The playwright, to begin with, must say all he has to say within the allotted span of an evening in the theatre. Plays must progress from essential to essential — even if the essential is only a gag at which to laugh — by the shortest feasible means. Yet at no time may a dramatic sequence seem hurried, its players get out of breath — except on purpose. Ideally, the produced play ends exactly on time with all its intentions fulfilled. The actors relax in prolonged, graceful bows as the audience releases its aroused emotions in rounds of applause — in the one and only welcome delay permitted before the stage goes dark again and the houselights come up.

When a production closes and the company disperses and the scenery goes to the dump, designs and light plots are filed to gather dust along with faulty memories and still photographs. If it is produced again there will be another director, another cast — which is why no light plot can ever be transferred from one production to another.

I would like to talk about some of the plays I have designed for, and I have included my light plot for one of these in the section called "Tools of the Trade," in which the mechanics of lighting are exposed. This is to illustrate, not to impose, how I have carried out what I thought about in lighting the play.

If I begin, again, with Shakespeare, it is partly because he sets the stage so generously that all of his plays may be produced in many ways. He asks you, as in the Prologue to Henry V, to "Think when ye talk of horses, that you see them printing their proud hooves i' the receiving earth."

There is no "best" way to design for Shakespeare. Your choices range from the stringent limitations of his own Elizabethan theatre through the extreme romanticism of the nineteenth century to the most abstract modern manner. Such freedom in conceiving a production would be less heady if it were not a freedom resulting from an overwhelming richness of choice. You never wish to create intentions for Shakespeare or to supplement them, only to dig them out, encompass and understand them, underline them and make them clear.

I owe many of my ideas for other plays to Shakespeare, who understood more than anyone else "the magick of light." Light is implicit in every scene he wrote. If he had been alive in the age of electricity I think he would have taken infinite pleasure — and infinite pains — in carrying out his intentions toward light. Study him carefully and you learn about light, as you learn about so much, including the subconscious mind of man.

Designing the lighting for Shakespeare's plays contains every problem and every solution one faces in dealing with stage lighting. His range of demand is all the way from a blackness of mood so profound that it may only be matched by an almost unimaginable absence of light to an intensity as great as that of the sun on the desert at high noon. Yet such light must be indicated, felt, not overstated, because his words carry their own light and must never be muffled by too much attention drawn to anything else.

I should like to consider, only in terms of lighting, the play in which Shakespeare's intentions are the most complex and least clear. *The Tempest* is not well made as the other major plays are well made. The "story" has complications but little or no continuity. To try to elicit an orderly progression of plot or prim exactitude of meaning is hopeless, and there is no basic, single moral to give this supremely serious fairy tale the shape of fable. It is fantasy, as his fantasy-comedies are, and it is real, dramatizing Shakespeare's attitude toward people, all kinds of people, as realistic as any study of human effort, made with insight, may be real. Try to pull *The Tempest* together and it falls apart. Each separate scene makes its own poetic statement, and the ideas, abstractions and philosophies are most acceptable as statements from the miraculous mind of the poet. This play was neglected in the nineteenth century, when science and the rational mind were engaged in challenging mystery rather than in pondering it. Now, once again, the marvel of the imagination enchants us, with space and its mysteries to explore, and in this climate the man Prospero, the sprite Ariel and the monster Caliban no longer need be "explained."

Of all the elements in the production of *The Tempest*, lighting may serve most loyally to construct bridges from one aspect to another without attempting to impose a rigid, formal logic or rationalization which the play constantly contravenes. Light can indicate the "real" and the "unreal" without harping on the difference, which is thor-

Jean loved Shakespeare. She read him all the time. She was a Shakespearean scholar.
— Oliver Smith

When Jean Rosenthal lit a play (such as *Hamlet*) for me, it was with the most sensitive perceptivity. She adorned the American theatre.
— John Gielgud

oughly muddled in the confrontations between characters from our world, off-island, and the inhabitants of the magical island.

The first scene is "real." A ship is wrecked, in a storm at sea, and the assortment of real people on board are threatened with real drowning. The storm, within the leeway offered by the theatre, may be indicated — retold by advising the audience that one is taking place. Or it may be presented in full seriousness. (Electricians love storms.) Either way works. The dialogue is brisk, human, profane and full of desperation; the variety and character of those humans about to be shipwrecked is introduced with masterly economy; and the scene ends with the human cry ". . . and I would fain die a dry death. . . ."

It is natural to assume that the storm ends before dawn. After the storm, the stage may properly be black. If you produce strong horizontal lines of light which appear from nowhere and fall beyond the eyes' range, whatever is revealed by the rays will be mysterious, the implications not natural, less than lyric, and very "sudden." Reveal the horizontal pattern quickly; it discovers and arrests what the light falls on, printing the objects and holding on to them. Continue to add light and the sea-surrounded island takes shape in the abstract time when "the morning steals upon the night" under an abstract sky.

From here on, the lighting can approach or diminish reality either by reverting to the sense of mystery established during the revelation of the unreal island in unreal light or, alternately, as in the storm, by using nature to familiar advantage. Patterns of light in nature are clear to everyone, earthly. Arbitrarily decreeing that stage left is the east, for instance, makes it possible to govern your stage island by the laws of the compass. Although the play takes place in an instant of time, in the mind, in a "flash," there is no violation of this inner truth in using times of day for the action, dawn through sunset, indicated by the slanting rays of the sun. You can define "another part of the island" by changing the angle of the rays and using cooler light to move action from the sun side to the shadow side of it. Shakespeare's plays are full of cues to nature. Although this place is magical, suspended in place, not real, to the men from outside who walk upon it the leafy dells or seashore dunes are *terra firma,* and the quality of light indicated for an island surrounded by "yellow sands" is of precise and poetical importance to the play.

At times the story is of foremost importance and the philosophy is set down (not laid aside) for a furthering of the plot or for a comedy scene. The stage and the performers are then closely related to each other; the audience is not involved but observes them, objectively, within their setting. At other times, in soliloquies or certain dialogues between man and sprite or monster, the performers and the audience are drawn together to share spoken ideas and thoughts. The surroundings lose all importance and the visual attention justifiably draws in to become a communion of minds.

Once you have balanced nature and magic in the lighting, moving acceptably from an emphasis on one to an emphasis on the other without interrupting the play, only the masque presents a problem. The masque takes place in the imagination of Prospero, not the mind of the poet, and is separated from the rest of the play, neither a "real" sequence nor a "magical" one. The masque cuts across both action and philosophy as pure vision. To justify a sudden and different mood in the lighting, it is possible to presuppose a regathering of the storm just before the masque. Blot out the sun, create dim, cold light in which to present the prologue to the masque. Then the masque can be treated as a dream-within-a-play in light of its own. You can even take advantage of the convention that dreams are blue.

The transition back to "reality" occurs again with Prospero's moving speech "Our revels now are ended . . ." and during the course of this soliloquy the play regains its original shape. Caliban, Stephano and Trinculo return in the plain light of honest day. By the time the epilogue is reached, the suggestion that the sun has set over the island has been made legitimate. Prospero may be left to speak under a starry sky, or better still, out of time and out of space.

If *The Tempest* contains, as has been suggested, Shakespeare's farewell to creative life, it is a most moving one. The symbolic breaking of the staff and the drowning of the book are a leave-taking, whether or not it is the playwright's final one. The lighting may fairly accept the suggestion without insisting on it, by allowing the island to disappear and the sky, with sun, moon and stars, to cease to exist when Prospero ends his epilogue with "Let your indulgence set me free."

Theatre people can seldom resist the dramatic shock of unseemly juxtaposition. To consider *Plaza Suite* immediately following *The Tempest* is not to commit an act of irreverence nor to insert pratfall comedy as a relief from profundity, as Shakespeare so often does, but to yield to that affection for dramatic contrast.

Plaza Suite was a hit. I mean it was a hit before it ever went into rehearsal. That rare and cheerful certitude made us all work like demons. We had an expert playwright (Neil Simon), a marvelous brace of actors (George C. Scott and Maureen Stapleton) and a hit director (Mike Nichols). Oliver Smith designed the set for Saint Subber, one producer who appreciated the importance of plausibility in the look of a realistic set. Saint is also — and I bless him for this — aware of the kind of magic realism that is so appealing in a situation describing an emotional action.

This comedy can be produced and designed in only one way: realistically. The single set, a suite at the Plaza Hotel in New York during the 1960s, is the unifying factor tying together the three one-act playlets. Each play comments satirically on an aspect of middle-class life in that decade. The actors, playing different people of varying ages in different situations, within these walls, have an interesting challenge.

Plaza Suite is also a challenge for the lighting designer if one is

> Simon's plays are paper thin, marvelously contrived entertainment, and that's all they are . . . wafers that grow thinner and thinner in baking. It is much more difficult to light any of Simon's plays than to light a great heroic play.
> — Oliver Smith

> Jean gave anything, the most uninteresting realistic set, a quality. For *Plaza Suite* she worked out a front throw from the balcony rail on a series of cues so that it was almost like a moving spotlight, yet there was never a hard line of light. . . . More than any other lighting designer she was capable of using the balcony rail so that it wasn't just a blast of what I call George Abbott lighting — a great fan of white light — but rather an even, very subtle shaping.
>
> — Oliver Smith

> My sight becomes confused and blurred. I must withdraw it and apply it again spasmodically; just as, to judge the gloss of a scarlet fabric, we are told to cast our eye over it, glancing at it from different views, quickly renewed and repeated.
>
> — Montaigne

> What made Jean unique was that she was an artist in the strict sense of the word, and also a mechanic who knew wattage and circuitry. In one multiple-set show I had had a lighting designer who was the opposite — vain, disorganized, lacking in confidence and concept — so he just had fits and tantrums. Everything took an eternity of time and was so costly. For *Gift of Time* I was in a position particularly to appreciate my need for Jean.
>
> — Garson Kanin

willing to accept it — because one needn't. You may justifiably do *Plaza Suite* in a great deal of bright light, and that can be that. Or you can do *Plaza Suite* by weaving a light fabric that supports the plausibility of the emotional actions on the stage. In that case, the important thing is the view of the suite of rooms as the actors in each play see it. It will look quite different because they are quite different people.

The first character enters at about four o'clock on a winter afternoon. The sun is beginning to set. So much for time-and-place. The woman who enters is in an extremely romantic mood. She is celebrating her twenty-fourth wedding anniversary. She has asked for the rooms at the Plaza to which she came on her honeymoon. The comic complications — this is the wrong suite for one thing — are based on her romantic assumptions. The room should look at first exactly the way she sees it when she comes in.

The second set of characters are using the place for a bit of middle-aged philandering. No memories of a long-ago Plaza suite are involved. This scene, brightly lit at two in the afternoon, is viewed by a slightly tipsy, somewhat moronic couple conducting specious conversational preludes to hitting the hay in the omnipresent bedroom next to the drawing room in the suite.

The third act also takes place in the afternoon. Rain is in the offing. The characters are the exasperated parents of a bride who has locked herself in the bathroom at the moment when she is expected downstairs for a Plaza wedding.

The eyes of the beholders in each act are different. In each act they see these same two rooms differently. I believe that if one studies the inner logic of eyes seeing the same place selectively one can interpret this in the use of the light, giving each episode an additional and subtle variety. Two actors essaying such different roles in the course of an evening can easily turn the drama into a *tour de force*, subtracting from the comic validity of the playlets. The lighting may add immeasurably to the ease with which the different characterizations are accepted.

For that very serious play, *A Gift of Time*, those of us engaged in the production were to a rare extent personally involved. I had promised Lael Wertenbaker, who was and is my friend, that if her book *Death of a Man* should be dramatized that I would design the lighting for it no matter how many other commitments I had. Garson Kanin, who had worked for three years on his adaptation and who would now become its director, accepted my willingness. Boris Aronson, the scene designer, with whom I had so often collaborated, was so moved by its portrayal of a man facing his death that he admitted putting into his designs the profoundest creative effort, the effort he usually reserved for his painting and his sculpture. (Complimented on the beauty of his triple backdrops painted for each act, Boris said indignantly, "Those aren't backdrops — mere scenery — they're *murals!*") Henry Fonda and Olivia de Havilland had played together many times in the past and brought to the leading roles old understandings as well as rare dedication. Hank was to give, I think, the finest performance of his career, and I think he knew this. Marian Seldes, a leading lady in her own right, agreed to understudy Olivia and to play a minor role, for the sake of the play. Down to the children, the cast felt from the first that they were reliving a vital experience rather than playing parts. We did not have a hit — only a hope. The subject of death by cancer was forbidding and the married love story of a middle-aged couple moved toward this inevitable end. No one permitted the uncertainty of success to affect, even subconsciously, his determination to make this play perfect.

The technical challenges were great. It had taken Garson those three years to solve the basic technique for presenting the story on the stage, to solve the time changes and flashbacks, to give the playscript the cinematic fluidity which would carry the multiple scenes. He conferred endlessly with the technical staff. Garson knew exactly what he wanted, and so did we, but not how to achieve it: to create a sense of things remembered, some of which were happening simultaneously in different places.

Boris designed his three sets with three scenic areas apiece. That gave us nine areas in three acts. To have light cover movement between the areas — movement which was peripheral to the action and implied a change of time as well as place — I had to throw out the standard arrangements for lighting. This show was made up entirely of "specials" — one controlled light at a time. Instead of having two to four master boards and one or two auxiliary boards, we had one master board and about fourteen auxiliaries. (See "Tools of the Trade" for explanation of technical terms.) The auxiliary boards were split up into stage right, center, and left. Each design was preset; then, when the master came up to cover a change, an electrician knocked down the preset and set up the next one.

To get the swimming sensation, when people moved between areas, out of time and space, I used key lights, atmospheric, not right for action or for actors, to make a limbo they wandered through. As one area faded down, the next one came up. Cues for light changes were started five or six minutes before the light "arrived" — with long, meticulous counts for the dimmers — so that no area went dead at any time. Those not lit for action kept a faint radiance, a mental aliveness.

The places were specific. Most of the action was laid on the Basque coast in France, and it was important to have a sense of locale, to suggest that this was a certain place in France. The other scenes — on shipboard, in a New York hospital — were also specific. But time was flexible. Within the sets the characters moved in time without specific breaks to indicate the passage of days or hours. The lighting had to convey that the movement in time was through memory, not in the present.

Sometimes all three scenic areas on the stage were occupied by

Jean herself was not quite sure how it was going to work. I think that is why she so enjoyed doing the show: because she was not sure it could be done. I have found it to be a characteristic of really creative people: they only want to do what they think they cannot do.
— Garson Kanin

Jean's touch was tender. In a remarkable way the technique of the light was secondary, the mechanics secondary, to the mood. The use of gels was intensely personal and very feminine. Touches — not obvious — made it touching. This production was not stylized nor abstract: a very thin line between realism and not. She introduced a personal note of delicacy.
— Boris Aronson

In rehearsal I remember how Jean would put her hand up into the light, and it was like a flower.
— Boris Aronson

different characters at the same time — with the action focused on only one area. For instance, at one time, when the man, Wert, was in his tower (left), his wife was talking about him in the living room (center) and there were three people in the kitchen (right). Everyone, onstage and in the audience, was aware of Wert at this moment, "seeing" him as you "see" someone about whom you are thinking and speaking.

During all of these scenes, the audience could never be in a state of confusion, never have to say "Where is he?" "When is this?" The play, instead of proceeding from action to action, had to flow, like a river of memory, continuously. There were no blackouts — in the lighting as in the play the flow of reminiscence must lead from episode to episode naturally and clearly.

The Wertenbakers, about whom *A Gift of Time* told its story, were romantic realists. No aspect of reality was denied or neglected, but that reality was colored by their romanticism. (I never felt that they were basically classical in their attitudes — except in their acceptance of doom.) Tennessee Williams, as a writer and person, on the contrary is a realistic romantic. He treats his "reality" in the grand style. His words distend the size of his characters. They cast immense shadows that are larger than, a distortion of, life.

The Night of the Iguana, after you have read it over and over, gets pretty Victorian, but it plays better than it reads. (Most good theatre does.) In its setting and its lighting, the challenge is to heighten and distort reality without destroying it. (I think that is why the play worked better than the movie. Motion picture "locations" are so inescapably real they resist exaggeration for the sake of mood.) In Oliver Smith's setting of the run-down, out-of-the-way hotel in tropical Mexico, he used a slatted overhead pattern to achieve a heightened sense of light and shade. All the overhead light came through slats, and this made bars and patches of light all over the stage.

The two women stars used the lighting in a way that enhanced their characterizations. Bette Davis, raucous and blowzy, simply took on the colors and tones of the light in the way an experienced motion picture actor does when sensitive to lighting and aware of it. Margaret Leighton, that great English lady of the theatre, playing a New England spinster, had to spend much of her time onstage listening to other people. Half hidden in the shadows, she never intruded on the audience's attention. When it was her time to speak, the audience found itself looking at her before she spoke. Without seeming to move at all, Maggie shifted her weight so that her expressive face appeared right in the center of one little patch of light Not a second too soon, not a second too late.

These women were supremely conscious of light. Less sensitive light-aware actors will head like moths for the hot spot in their stage area, without regard to the balance of the scene or the other actors in it. Those with greater awareness permit the light to "find" them at exactly the proper instant and place. Others may blunder about, especially those who insist they should act as they "feel" on any particular night, whose movements are erratic.

It is a pleasure for me to work with one who takes full advantage of whatever skill I bring to making his or her performance work. I love working with Angela Lansbury, who brings such integrity of characterization to the play-books of musicals. She responds to light like a flower. Margaret Leighton is another who uses the lighting to the full advantage of her characterizations. In *The Chinese Prime Minister* she played a woman who has successfully defied and denied her age until her defiance is crumbled in an instant of shock and she must age two decades in her collapse. She permitted a shift in forestage lighting, unseen by the audience, to age her and make her ugly. The color was drained from her lovely face, harsh lines appeared and she was nakedly old, giving an emotional and dramatic climax to that delicate, oblique play.

Dedication to a script makes for one kind of harmony; the ambience of success another (especially in a business as economically uncertain as the theatre); great acting another still. When it becomes obvious in the course of producing it that a play to which you are less than dedicated is going to flop, morale is a matter of will and of deliberate self-deceit. You have believed in it, for one reason or another, or you would not be there. You must keep hold of *why* you got into the thing and cling to that. Of course you may have taken a job, any job, but when you have reached a certain age and are in reasonable demand, you are in a position to refuse what you have no belief in and must blame yourself, not the others, for your misjudgment.

Experience is a faulty teacher. Memory is stunned by such publicly observed catastrophes as *The Seventh Trumpet* — battered to instant oblivion by critical fury — or bemused by statistical success, such as that of *Hello, Dolly!* — which seems likely to break all records. Only a layman asks a theatre worker why, after so many years, he does not always choose successful vehicles. You may as well ask why sensible adults do not always marry the right people. The theatre is as wayward, capricious and changeable as life is, susceptible to every hazard known, and forever dying in order to live again.

There is a literature of blame, of the violence done by one collaborator to another. Playwrights may curse directors, directors actors, and everybody protests the power of the critics, which in New York is enormous, and in these days it is more important to please the representatives of a single newspaper than anyone else in the world. For a while it was the fashion among theatre critics to praise the cast and lay all blame elsewhere. For a time, the scene designers seemed sacrosanct, with no one mentioning that a set can detract from a show. Quite recently it has become usual to notice the lighting, without due regard for the fact that it is frequently most effective when least observable.

Jean understood my deep desire to play the Madwoman of Chaillot in the musical made of the play (*Dear World*) and I knew she would help me in every way she knew how. I love to feel every character I play can, at some time during a performance, experience a "moment of truth" with an audience — a moment when each person sitting out in the darkened house feels a personal contact with the actor on the stage. Such a moment existed in the second act of *Dear World*. Aurelia, an old, old lady, has fallen asleep on her bed in the presence of Armand, the young man. She dreams, and then half awakens, mistaking Armand for her long-lost lover — and in the halcyon twilight she sings the poignantly haunting "I was beautiful." I remember how I felt each time I moved into the atmosphere of light Jeannie had created for me. At that moment Aurelia was luminous, transparent as a peony tinged with palest pink and fragile as a petal. The old crone was transformed into vulnerable innocence. I knew "they" understood, and we shared the moment to its fullest. The emotion I felt each time it played lasted till the last spot irised out on my face, and I was thankful for the cover of darkness to hide my tears.

— Angela Lansbury

The pressures and hazards of production are many and it is all too easy to claim to know what went wrong after the fact of failure, and all too easy to forget or forgive what is wrong after the fact of success. What must be kept straight are the *intentions* and how well or badly those intentions were fulfilled.

For the lighting designer, as for everyone else involved, adult drama is filled with inconsistencies, some of them glorious. To cover inconsistency, only overstatement in the lighting is basically hazardous. (Except where, as in the *House of Flowers,* the Negro skins, the white houses and the dirt can be blended under blistering white light to rationalize the very inconsistencies, binding them together.)

The lighting designer has his problems even with the simple realism of moonlight and sunlight, and cannot afford to succumb to the temptation to solve them by the use of theatrical clichés. You use moonlight, for instance, which is a cliché conveying lyricism to almost everybody. The audience knows that it is moonlight washing Titania's bank or Juliet's balcony or Roxanne's. But in each case it is a *different* moonlight. Titania lives in a gossamer world of unreality. From Juliet's balcony the clashing of swords can be heard — her moment is ephemeral, real, fragile and, above all, young. Cyrano is tragic in the moonlit shadows below Roxanne's balcony, and also faintly absurd. It is a modern cliché that tragedy unfolds in gloomy darkness, although Greek tragedy used light that intensified as the tragedy heightened. *Othello* is a tragedy played in full daylight in Mediterranean countries where no clouds dapple the brilliance of the sun. I suspect that Shakespeare, in gray England, could hardly have envisaged the saturating sun of Cyprus — so the simplest recourse is a portentous "sick" sunlight.

Every play and every production of every play is a fresh challenge. I really do not find, except for certain basics, that problems or solutions repeat themselves very much. Lighting may be restricted by physical limitations, but it is released emotionally in other ways. I do not believe in too much of a color pot. The scene designer should set the color range. I do believe in total attention to focus, movement, intensities.

Perhaps I like to light comedy simply because I like to laugh and think light-for-laughing-by is so much more than merely bright. I like tragedy because its range is as infinite as light is. Add music to either and the range extends, which is why I like to light musicals and opera. And always the most interesting aspect of lighting is that of the *air* and the *space* — the plastics of the stage, the sculptural values. Perhaps that is why I like best of all to light the dance.

I hope I can find the words to use about music and about dance. It is easier to talk about plays, which live by words.

Technician and dreamer seldom combine. Most people are victimized by experience. Once you know how to do things, that's the end of you. Jean never repeated. She was constantly reborn, found new solutions. To retain her kind of innocence in the commercial theatre is practically impossible — but she did.
— Boris Aronson

At rehearsals of *Luv,* Jean laughed so hard it made her hysterical.
— Oliver Smith

Six. Lighting the Musical

A musical is bigger and brighter and busier than other forms — which does not make it harder to design for.

Modern musical comedy is a twentieth-century-American invention. It's a Topsy — grown every which way from the old-fashioned variety-show-with-boy-meets-girl-plot into an entertainment adapting opera, ballet and dramatic techniques to its exuberant uses.

You treat the script, or book, with the same respect as a dramatic script, whether it deserves it or not. The songs are an integral part of the script; the words are important. You study the movement, the integrated dancing, as you would for ballet. You soak in the score as you do for opera. And you seek the emotional key to the whole. After which you are free to admit that the musical is *not* a drama or an opera or a ballet, but a form of amusement which incorporates the technical demands of all other forms.

The three major design elements of stage lighting are utilized to the utmost: *form,* the shape of the pattern of the light (i.e., the beam of sunlight and the accompanying hard quality around the beam, or the diffuse, formless shape of mist); *color,* the mood of light, achieved by gelatins or by varying degrees of intensity, or by both; *movement,* the changes of form and color, achieved by means of the control of light by dimmers and switchboards.

Your study of light in nature — the earth is lit by a single source so powerful that it has within it all color — has taught you your sense of scale. That is your absolute guide when transposing effects to the stage. In the case of the musical, which is an "unnatural" form — that is, by no stretch of the imagination do things happen that way — your relations to nature become all the closer. That is not a contradiction. It is easy to imagine that a completely realistic dialogue is occurring in natural light, even if the light is a single, very unrealistic spot or pool. For the spoken parts of the musical's "story," realism in the lighting is vital to belief. For the musical and dance sequences, it is unimportant, and mood takes over, along with movement.

For all the designers — scene, costume and lighting — a musical is bigger and brighter and busier than other forms, which does not make it harder to design for. The premium is *on coherence.* If every aspect of the designing does not work exactly with every other aspect, the result is a mess.

The discipline needed to control the lavishness of most musicals and to order their necessary exuberance begins with physical space. A musical is seldom as heavy scenically as an opera — it is larger than life rather than heroic in scale — but it moves faster. There are more changes of scenery, the action occurs in more "places" — and more people move around and on and off at shorter intervals. Speed is essential in each transition. Demands are apt to be fanciful in terms of the actual amount of space you have, offstage or in the flies, and the various elements of the production often try to occupy the same space at the same time. Organization for multiple use of the space has to be carefully planned. It is a giant jigsaw puzzle to fit in all the pieces, including lighting equipment, flying, and moving scenery.

The lighting designer must make double use of almost all the lighting equipment, which is the only way to beat the space-for-hanging problem and retain adequate flexibility. Economy of use is part of the logic of musical production. If your stage is set up scenically rather like an onion, so that each layer peels away to reveal another layer, your focusing problem is to light each exposed layer and not the one before or the one to be exposed later.

Emphasis, in terms of all the elements involved, is likely to be determined by who is in charge of what. If it is a Richard Rodgers or a Leonard Bernstein show, prime consideration will be given to the music. If Jerome Robbins is directing, the ballet sections will become focal points. If a "book" director with any clout has the job, the story will gain in relative importance. When you first regard a musical from *your* point of view, it is just as well to know who will be in charge. Given total design collaboration to create technical unity, complexity need not be complicated. Two of the aspects that may unify a production, which are important enough in all productions, are vital to musical production. These are color and makeup.

Illustrations rather than explanations may be the most instructive. *Hello, Dolly!* was a big, splashy, speedy musical which presented most of the normal problems involved in mounting a musical. Oliver Smith (scenery), Freddie Wittop (costumes) and Jean Rosenthal (lighting) were the three designers for *Hello, Dolly!* Over the years, we three revised our designs to fit five complete changes of principals in New York and sent out several touring companies for the road. The show never disintegrated, and, except for an occasional single disaster — such as the night when the railroad train did not stop but went tootling merrily right on off the stage, chased by a frantic cast — did what musicals are expected to do: beguiled, amused, pleased, surprised and entertained its audiences.

Hello, Dolly! was both simple and complex. We three designers had the advantage of many prior collaborations. So I should like to present it scenically, from the original drawings, here, and include the complete lighting design in the "Tools of the Trade" section of the book (page 133). You can visualize the problems: drops which fly in at various depths, big units which come on and go away again, the

---

I adored Jean, I adored her work, her presence. I never saw enough of her, since she was usually huddled with the "others" — the technical designing people. But the little I did see of her was a constant joy, refreshment, and inspiration.

— Leonard Bernstein

train that moves, the staircase which Dolly descends for the title number of the show, open sets and small areas.

Oliver sent me his marvelous ¼-inch elevation drawings of each set, as well as the ground plans, to work with.

Act I, scene 1. I begin with color. One scribbled note to myself on this elevation: "needs pink and white light." The houses reflect the pink-sand color, New York's "rosy" brownstones. The upholstery in the carriage is pink. The set is outdoors. A pinky-beige sky, over brownstone New York, will prove to be the key to the overall unit.

Act I, scene 2. Grand Central Station has its own light. You never could be anywhere else. Pinky-*gray*. And over the exterior, the beige-pink sky, a New York period sky.

Act I, scenes 4, 5; 6, 7. Logically the lighting colors follow through the golden tones of the country, the country feed store and depot, to the exterior of the hat shop, with a pinky *November* sky, into the gold interior and a return to the pinky sky, married with lavender.

Act I, scene 8. Lavender and blue, with a cool gray-pink sky for the deserted stage, ends the act.

At the same time, I am working with Freddie's designs. He has sent me not only swatches of the material used for the costumes, but beautiful color photographs of his costume plates. (Examples below reproduced in black and white.)

The costume designer also has his palette, his color plot which runs through the show, and his reasons for having a particular color dominate a particular scene. Color reflects mood, both overall mood and particular mood. Color collaboration among all three designers is essential. The lighting can destroy or enhance the effect of color. If the costume designer has ignored the palette of the scene designer, the lighting designer has a very touchy problem. You may have to choose which of the two elements you must harm. Your end choice is in favor of the actor — he must get first attention, so what he wears takes precedence. Everything on the stage must come to vibrant life. Glazing a colored object or costume should be done with all the care a jeweler takes in setting a gem. Freddie's costumes are jewels.

Before I make my final choices for the palette in the lights, I mount swatches of cloth from each costume on cardboard sheets, label the sheets by characters, multiple (as in the chorus) or single, and arrange them by scenes or production numbers. I keep pieces of gel in sample books with me always, and I spend many hours peering at these swatches through the pieces of gel. Most costume designers are aware of lighting basics — what blue light will do to a color, etc. But the more knowledgable the costume designer, the more attention is paid to fabric. In musicals the extent to which a fabric absorbs or reflects light becomes of major importance. In the ensemble numbers, the costumes dominate, overwhelming the faces and the scenery.

Act II, scenes 1, 2, 3, and 4. The second act of *Hello, Dolly!* as you can see, sweeps upwards, fitting the established basic palette.

Act II, scene 5. The show ends with the kind of calligraphy that creates the courtroom, in black, surmounted by that pinky-beige sky which has been there or implied as existing over the whole production.

When the stars change, as they often do in musicals, you check your lighting for minor adjustments, in color and in the lighting of their faces. When Pearl Bailey took over in *Hello, Dolly!* the lighting had to suit dark skin. You do not want warm colors for her. The pinky shades reaching her face are replaced with white.

Makeup is the last element in the lighting picture. It is important for the lighting designer to understand makeup. You may well be blamed if a face is not seen as it should be — although you know that a dozen other people have walked through the same lighting and were perfectly visible. Ten to one the actor who remains poorly visible is using a makeup base that absorbs light. His clothes, the people near him become brighter and more luminous and capture more attention than he does. You, the lighting designer, should *know* what happens to all types of makeup under all types of lights and either adjust the lighting to the makeup or have the makeup adjusted to the lighting!

In fact, so far as I know, the only things you can neglect in the theatre as a designer lighting a musical are the backstage johns. And I am not sure about that, if you have a say in the matter. The lighting fixtures in such places are apt to be of the kind that makes human beings look like poor little white worms. Fluorescent light is cheap

—but it blots out the red in skin color and a glimpse of yourself in such light can depress you, just when you need to feel as attractive as possible.

Seven. Lighting the Opera

Short of music itself, no medium at the artist's command may be as lyrical as light.

I am very often asked whether there are different ways of lighting an opera, or a dance, or a drama, or a building. Essentially the techniques are the same. It is the emphasis that changes.

Before the mid-nineteenth century, the sole purpose of lighting was visibility. Once you had made an opera, or a dance, or a drama, or a building visible, that was it. When lighting gained a "theatricality" it was used for "effects" — and opera as well as drama had many grand effects added in to its illumination. The twentieth century refined the role of lighting so that it could truly aid communication.

As the flexibility of lighting by electricity grows, it is increasingly possible to avoid the hazards of electric lighting — which can be as exhausting as it is dependable. One principle which applies to all stage lighting is still often and disastrously disregarded. That is the fact that a constant middle range of electric light, unaccented and unrelieved, induces tedium. It is hypnotic. The eyes of an audience in a dimmed theatre staring at steady middle light grow tired. People become rebellious, sleepy and disgruntled, unaware of why. This is particularly true at concerts, where the action is also static and the performers are also seated and do not move about and the conductor has his back to you. No one has solved the problem of concert lighting to my satisfaction, and my own design for improving the ability of an audience to listen while enabling the players to see their scores without interruption has never been tested.

On the theatre stage you can use darkness, with its promise and mystery. The dancer, the actor, the singer must see and be seen, the set be explained, clarified in light which does not weary or dazzle the eye, but a judicious amount of darkness lets the voices come through, captivates the eye, holds attention.

Lighting for the drama must be continually logical, but opera is an illogical dramatic form and the emotion of the music allows the lighting its freedom to emphasize the poetic aspects. Short of music itself, no medium at the artist's command may be as lyrical as light. In opera the lighting accompanies the music as it expresses what is going on dramatically, and you always permit the music to dominate, to set the lyric tone. You are lighting what you hear, not what you see. The emphasis is on sound not sight.

Traditional grand opera never permits the music to be subordinated to the drama, plot or action. The music is never absent or set aside, and when the mood is matched in the lighting, the audience senses it instantly — when the moonlight washes Juliet's balcony, for example, or when the shepherd in *Tosca* sings at dawn. The music is the over-riding consideration and it is the music which obliterates opera's inconsistencies.

My extreme pleasure in lighting opera comes, I think, as much as anything else from those inconsistencies. They make opera production a series of practically impossible challenges. Sometimes I suspect that effort appeals to me for its own sake. I do admire effort. Horse races make me cry — all that lovely energy being expended so quickly — and so does a soprano projecting a faint pianissimo into the topmost gallery of an opera house. Trying to unify all the elements of grand opera so that it becomes aesthetically impeccable falls under the head of mighty effort expended on the unattainable. But if your lighting harmonizes with the atmosphere created by the music, you add to it a life, an ease, a suitability, which frees the ear to listen and aids the eye to ignore opera's imperious discrepancies.

All opera requires of its audiences a suspension of disbelief. People do *not* stop and go on about it in song when their actions and emotions are at the peak of momentum. Lighting, of all the mechanical contributions to production, can do most to modify and bridge operatic incongruities. It can enfranchise the singers to move and act convincingly while they prolong each dramatic moment in song. Proper lighting, within any choice of scenic framework, can even establish a logic which will permit the comfortable acceptance of two characters caroling away on the same stage at the same time in full view of the audience and each other while remaining unaware of each other's presence.

Regular opera patrons are by nature tolerant and forgiving. They are also expectant and highly critical, comparing the present with reflections from the past and honoring the traditions of over three centuries which the opera form represents.

Operas tell stories, and all storytelling may be divided into two categories: the listener knows what will happen; the listener does not know what will happen. When a story becomes so familiar that most people know the outcome, we call it a classic. Most librettos, stories for operas, were either classics to begin with — *Don Giovanni, Faust, La Traviata* (Camille), *Salome* — or, if they continue to be performed, become classics — *Madame Butterfly, Tosca, Aïda*. Opera goers know who will die in *Bohème* as surely as we know who will die in *Romeo and Juliet*. For any theatre classic, you have the choice of presenting it in its historical idiom — or differently.

There is a general tendency among directors to take a classic story which everyone knows, set in some period everybody knows, and reinterpret it. This is valid when you get a unified *mis en scène* — as you do in that perfection of nineteenth-century opera repertory at La Scala in Milan. It works badly when everyone involved is permitted to go out for himself. I must admit that lack of central artistic authority has made a mishmash of some well-intentioned innovations at the Metropolitan Opera in New York.

Innovations in staging opera can only be secure and helpful when based on full knowledge and respect for the origins and evolution of opera. Nevertheless I can think of no traditional opera which cannot profit from modern invention, from inventive staging. Too much respect for the past may well preserve, along with honorable and time-tested traditions, the past's outmoded etiquettes. To regard with alarm any change whatever, as some opera impresarios do, does not derive from opera's total inheritance, but from *la belle époque,* when opera was very grand indeed.

Pre-nineteenth-century operas were mannered, designed to entertain and not to involve the audience emotionally. In the seventeenth century, when scenic perspective depended on a series of wings painted continuously to suggest a single picture, the sun was a golden disc hauled upward on a string. Opera houses were as flimsy as other theatres; light flickered from candelabras and tallow candles. Librettos based on retold myths or those written for comic opera, in the later part of the century, had all the delightful air of perishability which characterized the theatres.

In the eighteenth century, opera production was dominated by the French. The mechanics were still innocent and never intended to deceive. Although the content of librettos was fuller, characters, with such stunning exceptions as Don Giovanni and Figaro, were as two-dimensional as the settings.

With the nineteenth century, opera turned tragic. Librettos were more often than not bloody and broad, and ended in monumental dying. The complications of human emotions were added to the music, and human figures raised outsized voices in towering states of rapture or pain. Stages were huge, to hold large choruses, and everything was out of scale — doors bigger than they needed to be, windows bigger than they needed to be, with nothing on a human scale. The images were immense, keyed to nature, and meant to be believed. With Wagner, heroic myth, intended to be believed, was added to super-realism. (I have always tried to avoid lighting Wagner.)

The form of opera may defeat naturalism, but the nineteenth century insisted upon it. Castle walls were painted meticulously to look as if they were built of solid stone. (On such sets preserved too long, a sharp light is fatal — tattered canvas does *not* resemble crumbling stone.) The chorus in *Aïda* paraded on a solid series of ramps. All that lumber! Opera goers were complacent and the audiences, in the loges and opera pit, were as opulent as the productions.

Atmosphere on the stage was kept low-key. Murk from which sound emerged was the convention. When gaslights were replaced by electricity, the equipment in opera houses was firmly restricted to the same old positions: there were two master positions, front bridge and fly floor perches. Permanent sidelights, except for tormentors at the proscenium, would be in the way of offstage choruses, and so were not used. Naturalistic effects were heightened — lightning strikers worked overtime during storms — and accented touches of realism, such as slashes of light through windows or prison bars, were used. (These are effective at first but tend to grow irritating.) The use of color developed conventions which haunt the opera house still: red for danger, blue for romance, green for ghosts, white for revelation.

It is interesting to note that most opera houses, the great ones of Europe and the old Metropolitan in New York — before it was replaced in 1966 — continued to use low electric loads. Contrast the amount of light for the average opera and the average musical; you will find the ratio about one to three. At the old Met, for instance, the distance of the light throw was 145 feet with one-third of the wattage of a musical comedy house, where the average throw is 40 feet. Opera audiences have no expectation of true brilliance.

As twentieth-century eyes grew more selective, the dramatic theatre began to discard its exaggerated and elaborated realism. Movie-educated audiences were no longer convinced by the painted cornice. In America, through the 1930s and into the 1940s, opera played to half-empty houses. Then long-playing records brought in new audiences, in love with and familiar with the music. Our opera houses filled again. Faithful buffs, like lion tamers or cruise directors, demonstrated the proper and special etiquette of opera going, and novice buffs picked up their cues. The new audiences wanted spectacle too, but required it to be less overwhelming than *right*. Even the sopranos slimmed down for them, sometimes at the expense of high notes or chest tones, and small tenors took to elevator shoes.

Outside New York, and in New York outside the Metropolitan, the lavishness necessary to grand opera began to be simulated with more use of the imagination and less scenic realism. This was partly for economic reasons: all opera these days runs to deficit. At the Metropolitan, under the dictatorship of Rudolf Bing, the nineteenth century was upheld *in toto*, in spite of directors and other experts hired from the dramatic theatre from time to time.

I have concluded, after lighting opera under many conditions, that it does not really matter much what visual framework is selected. Traditional opera can be presented in museum replicas of the scenes in which the opera is set, or with photographic montage, as Sarah Caldwell has done it, or with minimal scenery and maximum use of lighting, as it has been done in Dallas. In Bayreuth, Selsenstein and the two Wagner grandsons have done everything to explore twentieth-century techniques. The entire visual scheme is placed within the design of the lights; the decor is formalized, a framework for grouping the performers in terms of lighting design. (It is immense.) You can adapt any variation within that scale of realism to abstraction, provided it is *unified*.

I began to light opera as a natural result of my experience and interest in the lyric theatre. Opera combines all aspects of lyric production. It can be scaled down, as Gian Carlo Menotti does it, by scaling down the melodrama, without losing the quality of opera. But for nineteenth-century opera, a lofty, outsized *style* is necessary even when it has to be scaled down because of physical restrictions or economic counter-lavishness under a tight budget.

My education in lighting opera repertory mounted in the traditional manner took place at City Center in 1951, where I lighted fourteen operas, under ten directors, in fourteen days.

The directors were refugees from Europe, old-timers who had staged hundreds of operas thousands of times. I was called in, on an emergency basis, because I had lit the ballet season at City Center and they would be using my layout.

Fortunately I had with me a master electrician as experienced as any of my directors. He was one of those incredible craftsmen of the operatic theatre, unsung and non-singing heroes, with an absolutely accurate eye for focusing, thorough familiarity with opera, and an uncanny ability to comprehend and turn lighting ideas into practice.

Our layout was perfectly good for conventional opera repertory. It consisted of three pipes at different heights, each six feet apart going upstage. On the first were twenty-four outlets, the second thirteen, and the third twelve. I isolated each lighting unit so that they could be used individually to separate out forms and create the strongest possible contrasts with minimal light.

The simplicity of the layout really helped. The lights remained in the same positions; you could use only variations. You could use a few special lights, focused for a particular opera at the time they were setting up the scenery for it. You had a basic set of colors and control of the movement of the light, in cues, to dramatize whatever you wanted to at a particular time. It had to be very orderly and exactly planned — especially as all rehearsal time for opera is strictly limited. Leading singers rarely give more than eight hours to stage rehearsal — and the show that opens on a given night is not the one which was rehearsed that day.

To prepare myself I listened to recordings of the music from each opera over and over, read and reread the librettos. With each director I talked his opera through, to find out his images and his ideas. Then I worked out the cues.

Opera scores are fantastic, full of cues written in the music rather than the action. There are practically musical *instructions* for the lighting. Listen to nineteenth-century operas and you hear the naturalistic effects, from seasons to times of days, birds and running brooks.

The music told me so much and the directors were so well prepared and taught me so much, and we planned everything so well before coming into the theatre, that those were fourteen marvelous days, totally committed, wholly unhysterical.

Opera repertory works technically like this. The night crew takes down the production just ended. Then they go home. The day crew comes in about eight A.M. to set up the opera that will be rehearsed that day. About eleven the orchestra arrives, unless it is a piano run-through. The rehearsal continues until around four P.M. Then the day crew sets up the show for that night. And they go on like that all the time! Every moment is charged with the threat of disaster, which all theatre people seem to love and on which all theatre so curiously thrives.

Working with total concentration on those fourteen operas, I relied more on skill than analysis. The eyes and the images somehow controlled the situation. With unlimited time and facilities, given the premise of conventional production, I do not think I should have done them very differently. Every opera has a capsule, a central problem, and the clue to the solution lies in the music.

Rigoletto, for instance, rests on nature. It builds through a night, a day, and a night toward its last-act storm and the lightning.

One clue to lighting grand opera naturalistically is that you are inclined to use one great beam of light rather than a lot of little beams. You use light in terms of design, which makes it seem to be traveling great distances. If it is moonlight, you really want the effect that light is coming from the sky — not the reduced sky of the theatre, but the real sky, beyond the roof, far away. That sunrise you hear in *Tosca*, for the dawn execution of Mario Cavaradossi, comes up over the hills of Rome beyond the Castel Sant'Angelo, beyond the invisible field in which the shepherd has piped his sheep. So the storm toward which *Rigoletto* has been building encompasses the stage and exists far beyond it.

The storm is full of lightning and you can hear the lightning in the music. When it came, we did not use the regular "lightning flasher" which flashes all over the stage. I preferred to use the design aspect of flashes of lightning to reveal each piece of dramatic action. On the doorway, which was an entrance from the courtyard, we focused a special and simply lit it to look like lightning and flashed it so that it had the quality of lightning. While Rigoletto waits for his victory, we used a follow spot to reveal over and over the sack holding Gilda's mortally wounded body, flashing the iris again and again. The whole stage became nothing but lightning, cued and organized within the stormy darkness, so that you saw what you should be seeing. The music tells you what you are supposed to see — and the crew got so caught up that they began to hear the music. You really could not cue fast enough, but they heard the music and got it for themselves. The stage shimmered with lightning and the action kept being revealed. I must say it was very exciting.

Traviata, on the other hand, demands a constant romantic, lyric atmosphere. There is only one basic decision to make. Is the story, as Verdi once suggested in a letter, told as a flashback, memories from Violetta's deathbed, or as a Dumas melodrama? Franco Zefferelli directed it once as Verdi had suggested: focused on Violetta as a person. She was costumed as a gossamer moth, circling the flame of her life. At City Center we told the story in a perfectly straightforward manner, ballroom to deathbed, in soft, diffused lighting which equalized the characters.

In opera you do not need to see facial expressions, which do not dominate the means of communication. You need to see entrances, exits, crossovers, but you already know the detail; either you have built it up in your mind or somehow you just know it.

For *La Bohème*, another romantic story opera, motivation cues the lights. Candle in studio; cracks of light through boards; streetlights outside the Café Momus; a snowy daybreak; a wintry day in an attic. You can use — as the Met did when Rolf Gerard built for *Bohème* a practically habitable Paris studio circa the 1840s — wholly realistic scenery. Or you can suggest it. We had a studio window against black velour curtains. Either way works and the lighting is much the same for both.

The cliché that tragedy should be played in gloomy light is no truer than the cliché that comedy must be bright. (In many eighteenth- and nineteenth-century comedies mistaken identity is the cream of the jest, made plausible only by dim lighting.) Perhaps these preconceptions of dark tragedy and bright comedy linger from the far past when a man was terrified at night and his fears were dispelled with the rising sun.

Brightness in any case is curious and based more on contrast than on candle power. The stage becomes as bright as it has been dark. If you light one candle for nighttime, five seem as bright as day. For contemporary comedy, where you have an enormous amount of brightness, you can have a lesser dark. The principle is that the *less* light you have, the *more* you may seem to take away. What you preserve is the ratio, the contrast between light and dark.

Even for *Carmen*, which calls for contrasts of sun and shade cut across as with a flashing knife — the *sol y sombra* of the Spanish bullring at five in the afternoon — you can establish these extremes with very little light.

The Marriage of Figaro is a comedy with a constant surface sparkle, witty and enchanting. But real emotion lies close beneath its bantering surface. Even the buffoonery is never inelegant, just as Mozart never wrote a bar of inelegant music. The light must move and sparkle, with constant shifts for the byplay, and yet never be chilly as it is for farce. The last act — where everyone is fooled into accepting a comic masquerade of mistaken identities — can become preposterous if the audience is not permitted to connive in the masquerade. We used a shaft of light falling through the palace door in which the characters revealed their true selves to the audience, sharing the joke, before they moved back into the light-and-shadow play in the garden at dusk.

Der Rosenkavalier, a serious romantic opera with moments of true buffoonery, resolves itself into a series of portraits of the heroine, the aging Marschallin. The entire show is hung with these portraits, lingers on them. Her light is the important one, and when she moves her light goes with her. However exquisite or humorous the interludes may be, when she is not on the stage you are waiting for her to return.

There is a special problem in lighting *Salome* — besides whether or not the soprano can dance as well as sing. *Salome* must be played, for the most part, in what seems to be constant light. The music is written in spirals, coming back and back to the same places in ascending circles. Even the seduction scene is endlessly repetitious. Vary the lighting too much and the changes become monotonous through the necessity for repeating the changes. Treat the story realistically, and it becomes unbearably explicit, including that bloody severed head. At City Center, I divided the stage into four quarters: Herod's throne, with the court; Salome's area; the cistern; and the far side of the cistern. Nature got only a nod: moonlight, but no moon. Without visible movement the light could shift, as if filmy clouds crossed the moon, from Herod to Salome. Jokanaan's cistern was a black hole and his voice rose from total darkness. There were only three basic changes of light: for the dance, for the delivery of the head from the well, and for the final catastrophe.

That most perfect of operas, *Don Giovanni*, is as strenuous to light as to stage and to sing, and sets the standard for all the rest. For the production at City Center we had a unit set, for economic reasons, and Thomashevsky, the director, who had staged a thousand *Dons*, simply put aside all that nonsense about different places and let the lighting become very important.

The basic statement that the *Don* makes and that creates the central lighting image is the contention of good and evil within one person. The struggle is never between good and evil but between two concepts man has of himself. So you cannot use the lighting clichés indicated by a lover in the love scenes, a man fleeing his discarded mistress, a man struggling with a ghost (or fate) unless you contradict those clichés at the same time. The lighting should, as the music does, constantly restate the essential struggle within the Don.

The complexities within the marvelous flow of the music and the novelistic plot are infinite. Take one seven-minute scene in Act II. You deal with seven variations in the emotional atmosphere on the stage:

1. End of a serio-comic chase

2. Flippant colloquy between the Don and his comic servant, Leporello

3. The Don's confrontation with the statue of the Commendatore, whom he has murdered

4. The coming to ghostly life of the statue

5. The Don's bravura invitation to the "statue" to come to supper

6. The statue's acceptance for what may be the Don's death feast
7. A flourishing exit by the Don; a craven one by Leporello

Such variety can be coped with by swift but not nervous movement in the lighting and by the use of sharply contrasting colors. I chose green and white for contrast, although other choices would have been equally valid. The connotation of green-for-ghost was useful in this particular context, so that when the Don retreats from his involvement, within this scene, into his role as man and lover, he becomes "white" — connotes the hero. Yet "white" — which is "good" — must not seem dominant for the Don, since the Don is both good and bad. You avoid too close an association between "ghost" (green) and "good" (white) by constant movement in the light. Besides, you cannot hold static light of any color for long on the Commendatore-statue without having the audience speculate helplessly on how long he can stand perfectly still. Nor may his ghost-green be too insistent, or the effect will be spooky rather than mysterious.

By barely perceptible and constant movement in the light, which keeps the electricians busy, *pizzicato*, you bring each stage of the scene to a pitch, its climax, and then erase the image to make room for the next. It should happen in the way light vibrates on water — freeing the audience after a moment of high tension, returning each individual to himself.

Don Giovanni tells a highly complex story, of course, but an opera audience is never distracted by the need to follow the plot. It knows the answers in the back of the book.

For City Center in New York I had done considerable research on lighting effects which had worked in Europe for opera. There had not been time to invent very much in the way of design, only to take everything I knew and everything I could find out and to get the season on. Using my "keys" to each opera as the unifying factors one after the other, the operas had worked well enough. Now Lawrence Kelly, who knew of me only through my work with the dance, invited me to come and see what could be done with the Chicago opera season in 1955.

He warned me that I would be lighting what he called playfully the "Mary Garden sets" bought for Chicago from Manhattan opera companies circa 1908 and on, with maybe one new set built on the traditional scale. I liked the spirit of the young people who were trying to make something of the production end and I wanted to work with Maria Callas, the greatest singing actress of them all, so I made time and went.

The Chicago management had been using illumination — which meant that it was either daylight or dark — and some "effects." I looked at their layout and made a most difficult demand. I asked for a lighting rehearsal after the first dress rehearsal, beginning at midnight and continuing until four or five in the morning. Rescigno, the

> The difference Jean made was a revelation to me. Rescigno and I listened to all that counting down . . . 10, 9, 8, 7 . . . without much comprehension while we watched an absolute transformation. Yes, she made it *believable*.
> — Lawrence Kelly

> I compare Jean to Maria Callas not because they were both stars possessing the intangible thing of the great artist, but in their ability to cope, as craftsmen, with any and all circumstances.
> — Lawrence Kelly

Lyric musical director, was reluctant, but Lawrence Kelly persuaded him and the two of them sat there and watched while I worked.

The hardest thing to do with huge, traditional opera sets, especially if they have seen better days, is to make them *credible*, somehow convincing. That was what they — Kelly especially — later referred to as my "magic." Actually it was *reality*, an increased sense of reality, in the relighted sets that they appreciated.

Perhaps more than anyone else, Maria Callas brings reality to the most exaggerated operatic roles. She is a consummate *dame du théâtre*. Lighting her as the bride in *I Puritani*, I found that one need make none of the concessions one usually accords a singer — who must act, if at all, with his or her mouth wide open, or stand, ostensibly listening, for unbelievable intervals. You could afford to light her face, disastrous with most opera performers. She brings to opera such musicality and to acting such burning intensity that she creates the necessary sense of being bigger than life while remaining true to life.

Gian Carlo Menotti, one modern composer of operas which have, on a small scale, the vocal opulence of grand opera, has a theory that opera can be written realistically and accepted very realistically. His *Medium* is a perfectly straight story of a mock séance, and his *Consul* is essentially a perfectly straightforward documentary drama.

In New York, *The Consul* played on Broadway on a straight-run basis. It was realistically produced. The production was designed to concentrate on the documentary aspects of the drama. This worked very well. Since then, I do not know of anywhere that it has been part of any opera repertory except in Germany, where the subject is too close to the people to be ignored. There it has been sung over and over again.

At the Staedtische Oper in West Berlin, an old theatre with a superb modern working plant for repertory, *The Consul* was produced as if it were full-scale grand opera, which has a dominant visual opulence. Ebert, the director, achieved the effect of opulence by placing all three sets for the three scenes on a turntable. Over this he hung a grid, in effect a ceiling, made up of little crosses. When the table turned during scene shifts you saw it turn through this lattice, tipped down the way a garage door tips down, as a curtain. At the end, when Magda commits suicide, the ceiling tipped down in the opposite direction and you saw what looked like a graveyard in the background, full of crosses.

The New York production was acknowledged for the brilliance of its realism, its realistic attitude, and it succeeded. The other was praised for its extraordinary and romantic visualism. Either way worked and neither violated the feeling of the music.

In *The Medium* there is only one digression into arbitrary opera. This is the aria "I am afraid . . . ," in which the medium faces herself in a florid soliloquy. For the séance scene, which this aria interrupts, the designer, Armistead, painted black-and-white wallpaper on scrim. Lit so that the scrim seemed solid, it seemed to be a very realistic little room. Behind the scrim he created a plastic abstraction in reds, mauves and greens, with nerve-like tendrils. When the "I am afraid" aria interrupted the action, I simply took all the light from the front of the stage, kept a little votive light focused on the singer's hands, and lighted the abstractions at the back with movement in the light which created a faint spiraling among the tendrils, suggesting the interior of a brain. After this dramatic and musical separation, an imperceptible change back to the earlier lighting returned the medium to her little room. It was particularly effective because you never really knew what was happening.

The other capsule problem in *The Medium* for the lighting designer is how to inform the audience that the ghost summoned by the medium in the séance is a fake, a trick ghost. Here you can take advantage of color preconceptions. Since one expects green ghosts or blue ghosts, such a ghost would trick the audience. But the medium should trick only her clients. So I made the ghost a pinky color, which a ghost is never expected to be, and this suggested that the ghost is a phony.

Both these bits of lighting come under the head of "living dangerously" — they can so easily be tricks themselves and thus fail of their purpose. I must say living dangerously is something you can seldom afford in opera.

Few of opera's people have ever turned down an offer from the Metropolitan. Like the mountain to mountain climbers, it's *there*. (And a kind of Everest.) The Metropolitan, in eighty-four years of existence, had never had a lighting designer as such when impresario Rudolf Bing asked me to work there for a season. I said yes.

Scene designers and directors who had bruised their creative egos trying to move the monolith under Bing warned me. Others urged me to accept. For years some of the directors and designers had asked for lighting designers at the Met, and the resident director and designer had led the fight to get me asked. They hoped, I think, that the prestige I had gained in the field would change the Met's attitude in a season. I knew better than that — having been with Maria Callas when she was fired from her contract. I only hoped to pave the way for a future change in policy. Anyway, one takes on impossible assignments for one's own curious reasons: I agreed to take on a mammoth misconception for the World's Fair at one time just because I would have a chance to use seven follow spots all at once. My reasons for going to the Met were partly critical. I considered it outrageous of them to have built a brand-new building incorporating a monstrous and archaic lighting system. The cumbersome control room, with its 228 channels, 248 dimmer buttons and 2,480 handles, was based, I think, on the principle that the old Met's system worked for their old repertory cue sheets. These cue sheets would have needed revision if a

"I tell you one thing," said one of the stagehands, talking to me about Jean Rosenthal, "it's a good setup for Jeannie. She likes her lights going up and down and sideways all at the same time."
— Joy Manson

more flexible and sophisticated system had been installed. As a theatre building consultant, if I was going to be critical I had best back my criticisms with practical working experience in the building.

From the beginning, I was only permitted to give my instructions through one person, chosen by the management. That was costly. Ninety people stood around while orders were laboriously transmitted — and we were monitored by closed-circuit television to see that we obeyed the rules. (It was pretty uncomfortable.) Really, one thing I cannot abide in the theatre is waste of time! It is so uneconomical. The slow part, the creative thinking and planning, the preparing of what you have to say to your workmen, should be done in advance and thoroughly. Once you have the stage, you should be able to work at top speed, the speed you have gained through experience. It is easily possible for me to set up from six to twenty-five cues in an hour with a system like the Met's. The average maximum number of cues here seemed to be fixed by the department head at one per hour, and he made it impossible for me to work any faster. With millions in deficits plaguing the opera, it drove me crazy to operate as if backstage we had money and time to burn.

Working at the Met was like working with an army which had no chain of command. There was the commanding general and there were his captains, with no effective authority in between. Whatever I managed to achieve there in the way of atmospheric lighting was by stealth and insubordination. My one attempt to live a little bit dangerously taught me not to try.

Deiber, the director (and hence a captain, not, as elsewhere, a major general) for *Romeo and Juliet,* was essentially an actors' director. Oriented toward theatre, he expected opera's singing stars to go to any place in a scene where he told them to go. For the balcony scene, Deiber wanted a certain effect. I created the effect.

We had a balcony bathed in moonlight. The stage was shadowy, with trees silhouetted against moonlight. On the ground there was one small, particular puddle of moonlight for Romeo to step into and sing.

Now, singing stars are seldom interested in the *mis en scène,* how the chorus sounds as it backs up a voice, the balance with other voices, or how anyone else moves within the action to create a dramatic and visual whole. Such discipline is imposed by the director, whose authority, to be effective, must be backed by that of the impresario.

Romeo in this performance was Franco Corelli, a fine tenor. Corelli was interested in only one thing — the sound of his own voice. He had discovered one spot on the stage from which his voice, he thought, sounded its best, a little secret of acoustics. He was staged and rehearsed, to which he was amenable, and when the night of the performance came, there was that puddle of moonlight waiting for Romeo to step into and sing. Corelli never went near it, but headed straight for his private acoustical spot. Now that was living dangerously and losing. When the director of *The Medium* told

---

When they did the electrical layout for the stage at the new Metropolitan, three very important lighting designers would gladly have contributed their services at modest fees — Jean Rosenthal, Joe Mielziner and Abe Feder. All superb in their own ways. And the Met, which operates on a fourteen-million-dollar deficit, said it could only afford five hundred dollars for a consulting fee. So they had no lighting consultant. It's unbelievable — when they were spending three or four million on equipment!

— Oliver Smith

The arrogance of the Metropolitan is unbelievable. It was the only time I've ever seen Jean defeated, literally defeated by a system, which was an artistic gestapo. She didn't have a chance, and she could have saved the Metropolitan two to three million dollars a year on their budget, let alone lighting the singers so you could see them for the first time. It was a major disappointment in her life, one of the few battles she lost. She lost that battle. To Mr. Bing.

— Oliver Smith

It is the balcony scene, bathed in blue moonlight. The audience bursts into applause. "That's for you, darling," Deiber says, putting his hand on Jean's shoulder, but she is concentrating on Romeo, who starts to sing, standing to the left of the stage. "Come out, Franco, come out into the light.... Please!" Jean Rosenthal begs under her breath.

— Joy Manson

Marie Powers to sit in a certain place in a certain relation to the light, she did it. When the director told Corelli where to stand, he did not do it.

Perhaps it is as well that the Metropolitan under Mr. Bing has retained as the unifying factor in its productions the nineteenth-century style — although at Bayreuth, where the very stones breathe of tradition, everything is done to explore new techniques.

Over the years I have designed the lighting for perhaps two-thirds of the operas used in standard opera repertory. I have also probably done more new operas and more historical rarities, such as Handel's *Julius Caesar* and Purcell's *Dido and Aeneas,* which were treated as if they were new, than anyone in the country. Some of this lighting, especially in Dallas and in Kansas City, has been done under circumstances where I had considerable freedom and control.

When Lawrence Kelly left Chicago and went to Dallas, he was committed to a tripartite attitude toward opera production, with authority at the top in all three areas: general management, artistic management, and production management. He was general manager, Nicola Rescigno was artistic director and I was production manager.

Time, authority and freedom — these I was given. I was not supposed to be their lighting designer, except for certain productions, but was to set up the production system. So far, many designers have worked with the setup, in their own way, and have found it, I believe, satisfactorily adaptable to their needs and styles. I was able to hire and train a staff and I was permitted to take a chance on unknowns. Larry occasionally complained that I took too many chances — it did not always work out; but often it did, and that was important. One comparatively unknown young man, paid eight hundred dollars to design costumes and scenery for a production, was Franco Zeffirelli! And after attending the "free university" — as Larry once called it — at Dallas, Nananne Porcher and H. R. Poindexter have become topflight lighting designers in their own right. One of the things lacking in this country is proper training grounds where young people can work with established professionals and be given their opportunities.

Dallas was a truly collaborative undertaking, organized for collaboration. This, I think, was the important basis of its success. And it was there that I had the opportunity to design the lighting for opera at its most challenging, at its best. And in it, Maria Callas gave in *Medea* one of her most unforgettable and glorious performances.

The production of *Medea* presented all of us who worked on it with breathtaking freedoms of choice. Madame Callas is so informed a musician and so brilliant a singing actress that she has no need for the security of traditional opera etiquette. We were in a theatre accustomed to modern staging, which rests on a minimum of scenery, a premise which fills any lighting designer with excitement.

Medea the opera is a hybrid. Its libretto (French) is solidly con-

After the performance, the Met's ballet mistress, Markova, congratulated Jean and said to me, "Jean is just so unusually musically aware the timing of her lights works in with the score."
— Joy Manson

Jean's major contribution was philosophical ... not the lighting jobs she did. One remembers her lighting of the *Italian in Algiers,* the Callas concert she made into a visual event, the *Medea* in Dallas or her *Dido and Aeneas* in Kansas City ... these were shows she literally physically pulled off. But her most important contribution to the whole was to create in the minds of everybody in the theatre that stage management is something you consider and nurture and develop. So many people in the theatre today were her protégés. And contemporary lighting in the theatre today, as far as I can see, is the invention of Jean Rosenthal.
— Lawrence Kelly

Jean was a genius in her work, the only real magician of lighting. And I wish to remind you that her lighting of *Lucia* was as difficult and important as *Medea.*
— Maria Callas

structed on the tragedy (Greek) which Euripides wrote four and a half centuries B.C. Composer Cherubini (a Florentine) wrote his *Médée* for the Théâtre de la Foire de Saint Germain in Paris in the late eighteenth century. This baroque period, addicted to classicism, presaged the Victorian Gothic of the nineteenth century. Cherubini, an unforceful composer working with powerful Greek drama, created for *Medea* a forceful score.

Thus we were offered a wide choice of styles: classical Greek, eighteenth- or nineteenth-century Italian or French, or the most modern manner. In Dallas we mixed them all, and the bastard hybridization of styles worked like a dream under the inspired direction of Alexis Menotis of the Greek National Theatre.

Our visual skeleton was naturalistic and also classic. Yanni Tsarouchis, designer for the sets and costumes, used a separate and individual style for each act. The first was formal: could have been eighteenth century, could have been ancient Greek — because the columns were dimensional instead of painted. The second act was played on platforms, on which there were quite realistic little temples. The third-act set was nineteenth-century, duplicating a version performed at the Vienna State Opera some years before. These disparate backgrounds so suited each act that you forgot one when you came to the next. Consistency was maintained visually by the costumes, which were supremely elegant. Woven by ancient Greek techniques in Greek materials, they had the kind of craft beauty which pulled the whole thing together.

In the lighting we exaggerated naturalistic effects so as to create a kind of hysteria in the atmosphere. The clouds were not like clouds, nor the fire like fire, but were eruptions of violence. We *forced* nature — so that it became the primitive view of nature rather than the naturalistic. This suited the added dimension in the music. When Medea decides, in a long aria, to kill her children, the scene is maniacal and unnatural. The lighting may bespeak its fanaticism. Massive lowering-cloud effects were projected on the sky — running left to right because the projector unreels them that way. A second set of clouds unfurled downward in spirals, crossing the horizontal to distort the pattern. We kept the mechanics unnoticeable, and the effect was wild. When the temple was set on fire, the blues washed out and the reds blazed unmixed. Motivated by the "real" phenomenon of fire, this did not break the line of reality, but stabbed like a knife into the heart of tragedy. The crowd, witnessing the fire onstage, were silhouetted against the dark background, bathed in the color of blood. For the final explosion at the end, the lighting was treated as if it came from hell, not heaven. There was a brilliant flash, a puff of smoke, and then what is known in the trade as a blackout. The fire reds took over again, with dying intensity, and curled over the whole stage.

Maria Callas knew exactly what we were getting at and made it part of her performance, which dominates any opera she is in, and she moved like a dancer in the rhythm of the lights. When she took her curtain calls the audience rose, yelling its collective head off. This memorable performance of hers was given, as it happened, on the night of the day Rudolf Bing turned down her conditions for singing at the Met.

It is for such a night that opera lovers live.

Eight. Lighting the House

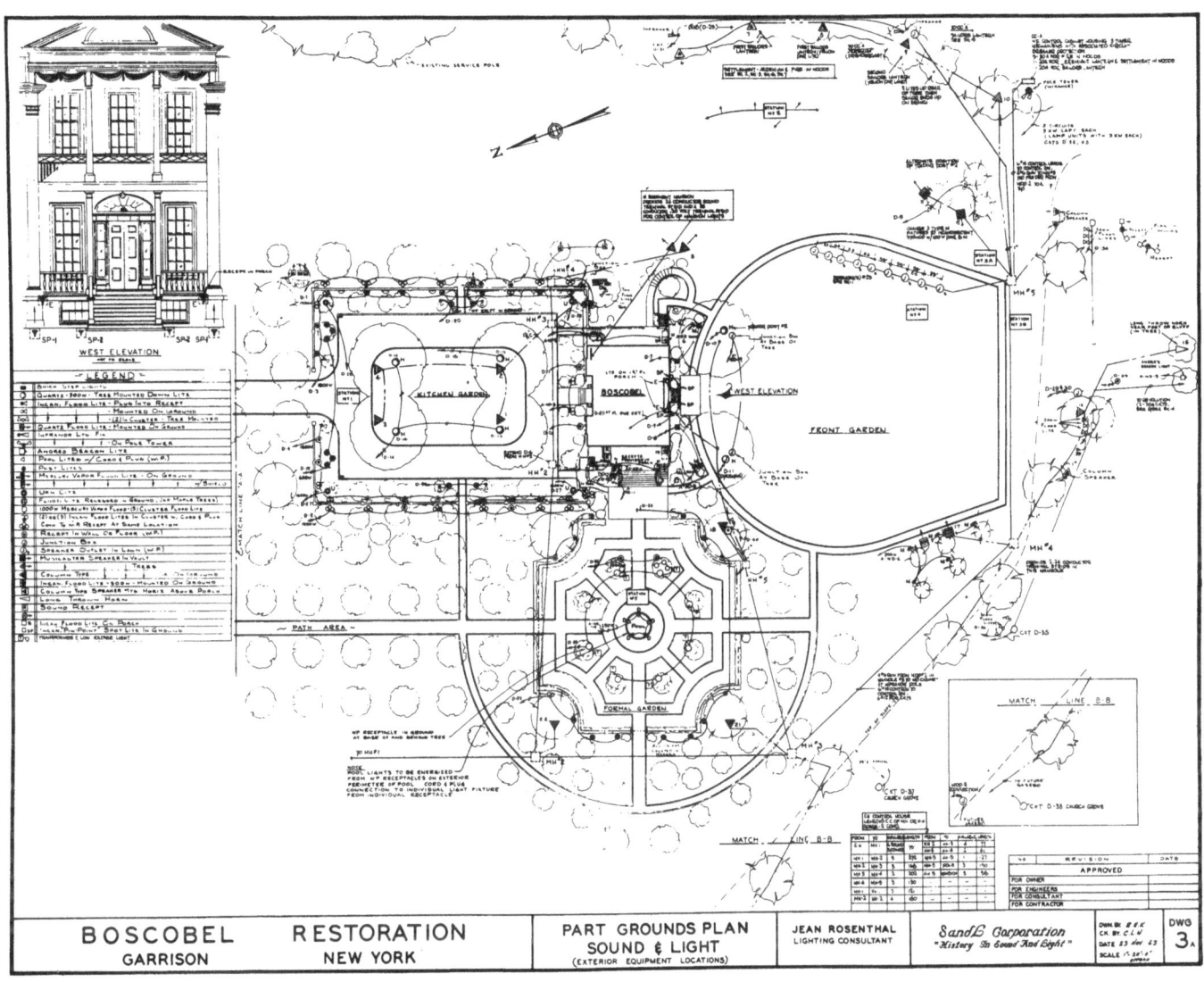

At Boscobel we worked outdoors at night and were eaten alive by Hudson River valley mosquitoes — which would be expensively banished by extensive spraying when the audiences came.

This chapter is not about domestic lighting. I am no expert on that. I have been a consultant on the lighting of public buildings, but that is outside the scope of this book. What I should like to do is to talk speculatively about the future of lighting design in two fields — for theatre houses and for historic houses or buildings, the former in terms of the whole design, the latter in terms of a theatrical form which is widely used in Europe and only beginning to be used in the United States — sound and light shows.

Greek amphitheatres were constructed to hold audiences drawn en masse from a given travel area. Patrons, populace and patricians sat in tiered seats bearing down semicircularly on the stage, indifferent to social distinctions in the seating and egalitarian in the relation of audience to performers. We are returning to the amphitheatre style of seating, recognizing that the direct relationship of observer to performer is enhanced by an unobstructed view afforded by steeply raked seating. Symmetrically designed, the amphitheatre approach is serene and enduring.

The simple stage for the commedia dell'arte was raised and curtained. The attraction was mystery. Attendance was accidental; people without interest in each other gathered; box-office returns were based on how much the performance pleased the curious. In Elizabethan times, stages were thrust into the audience areas. Scenery was left to the imagination. Lighting was for the purpose of seeing the actors, who communicated directly with the spectators in monologues and asides, and so that the audience members could see each other. Seating began to have social significance.

In the nineteenth century theatre going became social, formal and spectacular. Promenades, the entrances and exits of the audience, were of equal importance with the stage performances. The worst places from which to see, the boxes, were the status seats because their occupants displayed themselves best. To compete with their audiences, productions were massively scaled and brilliantly lit, and stage machinery was elaborated to the point where it was necessary to mask it from view by creating a frame, the proscenium, which itself became progressively elaborated.

As realism replaced romantic realism, the great advantage of the proscenium theatre was the ability to create illusion out of make-believe. Exact-scale scenery and the magic of moving a common object out of the ordinary house and placing it within a theatrical production made the stage almost habitable. Lighting may have been pretty static, but it was as realistic as the running water from stage taps. Camera reality excluded this type of stage realism, and we began to create our naturalism with light, dimensional reality, and sculptured abstractions. We used to say in the theatre, "Give us a bare box and points of support, and we will fill it with whatever we need for any production." The proscenium theatre was that bare box and it is still adaptable to the most modern playwrights, however ornate the frame, if that frame is modified by an intermediary masking step known as the tormentor (torm) or portal.

The theatre of the future will not be as limited as a box. Audience demands for comfort are greater; technical developments are becoming more and more sophisticated and lighting equipment more and more flexible and capable of subtlety. What is needed is for the creative and decorative minds in the theatre to work in collaboration with the practical and technical minds to achieve an all-purpose theatre that fulfills all our modern expectations.

In show business we always speak of a theatre as a house. It is the "dwelling place" where our lives are lived at their greatest intensity as well as the place where we earn our livings. Management and performers usually speak of a "good" house as a single theatre at a particular time drawing the largest number of paying guests. Technicians talk about good or bad houses in terms of backstage installations. For example, our Broadway houses vary in size and charm, but they are all period houses with old-fashioned equipment and space arrangements. Actually they are considerably less exalted versions of the ornate nineteenth-century European theatres, reduced in style, cramped in seating and stage space, and for economic and social reasons they are likely to remain so.

Since the 1930s there has been a search for a twentieth-century style in theatre design, which has resulted in many different kinds of theatre buildings, constructed for the most part away from New York in other cities and on university campuses. At present, no dominant style has emerged. We have not yet written and produced a solid body of new plays to guide our aesthetic judgments in building new theatres. We still produce pre-nineteenth-century classics with an unjustified reverence for their original stagings, thereby hampering fresh and innovative theatre design. In rejecting proscenium stages out of hand, we fail to find ways to take advantage of their considerable technical assets. Experimental building has included multi-purpose theatres combining thrust and proscenium stages and using a multiple mess of technical devices in order to adjust the audience to the stage. Arena theatres discarded the stage walls altogether, achieving remarkable intimacy between audience and performers but limiting many valuable aspects of visual reality. For example, all properties must remain part of the stage action for an entire act or be of such a nature that they can be carried on and off by an actor.

Lighting systems — sometimes masked (the source of light, the instrument, hidden from the audience), sometimes exposed — have coped imperfectly with two new problems created by thrust and arena stages: how to light from all sides exposed space where there is no scenery without disturbing the audience; how to create for romantic or realistic plays the illusion that what happens on the stage happens only there, with the audience privy to private events.

Houses are built, and lighted, in response to economic, social and aesthetic needs, with available materials and techniques; and then, mistaken or inspired, they last awhile. I think our major error in building new theatre houses has been to try to correct rather than take advantage of the past, to overcome with complex technology rather than to accept the limitations that any form of theatre building establishes. We have learned enough since the 1930s to know pretty much what we want and where we are going. Our new theatres can become houses in which our playwrights can operate freely, our revivals can be presented without losing their specific aesthetic bases, and our audiences can have the comfort we demand in our nontheatrical houses.

Sitting in the auditorium, the "front of the house," should be as comfortable as sitting at home in front of TV. That means perfect sight lines; adequate foyer space, sanitary arrangements and parking space; and adequate sales arrangements for buying tickets.

Stages must be flexible, to meet the expectations of productions which reproduce the past and also to permit our playwrights future freedom. We need to make full use of the space below the stage; trapped areas in the stage floor have many uses. We need maximum overhead support, using the space over the stage and even over the audience area for rigging systems to support our contemporary realistic dimensional forms, such as formalized scenic walls to replace prosceniums and back the acting areas and to support lighting systems which can, when necessary, surround objects with light and light the actors from at least three sides.

To create the illusion of whatever degree of reality a production demands, we need to have an adequate masking system. I do *not* believe in exposed mechanics, except when they are specifically part of the production. Lighting positions should disturb neither audience nor performers. Ideally, the lighting draws no attention to itself whatever. The magic of revealing a picture by raising a curtain may be replaced by the magic of actors appearing out of the dark, but to bring an actor into light which has a visible source is to diminish that magic. Our lighting expectations have been increased, and now lighting must function in the most sophisticated manner. Complex lighting for the proscenium stage is still a designer's luxury; for the thrust stage it is a necessity.

Since we have as yet no unified aesthetic concept for theatre houses, we are obliged to honor and be guided by a technical approach to theatre space, which, overlooking specific tastes and styles, does provide mechanical flexibility to allow the creation of many different styles.

Sound and light is a dramatic form that is the direct result of a technical development. *Sound and light* is not just a phrase. It is a new dramatic way of recreating history, in terms of places, of buildings, of houses where that history took place.

If you have never seen a *son et lumière* production in Europe, where the form was invented, the idea is confusing. It is and is not a pageant staged on historic ground. It is and is not a play, using episodes from history. It is a production, but it cannot tour, cannot be moved from where it is performed. It is history retold in sound and light, without live actors, and it was made possible by the technical solution of cuing lights from a central source so that the lights and the taped sound would combine to work as one.

The lighting in sound and light productions is a major dramatic element. It is used to people the darkness through the imagination, not to create effects for their own sake. The script — the play and narrative — is taped. As in radio drama, the actors act with their voices. The narrator or narrators bridge the acted episodes. The dramatization of events that actually happened is accomplished through actors impersonating the people who took part in them. Sound effects, as in radio drama, make the guns fire, doors open and close, blows fall, weather happen, crowds murmur and shout and move. Taped music accompanies the drama when bands play or someone sings, or as background or for mood or to create an interlude.

The script on the tape is designed for the place. The stage *is* the place, in Europe a famous château or the palace at Versailles or the Tower of London or the Forum in Rome. The place is where what is on the tape happened. History in terms of place goes back in time. Light provides the *action,* the *movement* and sets the *scene* on the "stage." It provides the atmosphere and the setting for the sound. The audience supplies the imagination which peoples the scene set by the light and inhabited by the voices.

Son et lumière was conceived by a French architect, Paul Robert-Houdin. Watching a thunderstorm one night at the castle in Chambord, of which he was curator, he saw the walls come alive in the colors, sounds and lightning flashes of the storm. France had always taken the lead in lighting its public buildings, but that was fixed light. Robert-Houdin thought of moving light, within which the history of the château could be told in sound. The first *son et lumière* production opened at Chambord castle in 1952.

Sound and light shows became a feature of European summers, a major tourist attraction. With government financing and participation by actors from stage and screen, the rich history of *places* — within massive ancient walls or on bloody ground — was brought to life. Production and especially installation were expensive. *Sound and light* was projected for American monuments, but government patronage was not forthcoming and there can be no profit in it, except in terms of tourism. Where productions were financed and put on in the United States, in my opinion the adaptation of the European conception was too literal.

I felt that sense of challenge on which a creative craftsman lives when I was approached to design and produce a sound and light drama at Boscobel, an enchanting Hudson River house restored by Mr. and Mrs. DeWitt Wallace of the *Reader's Digest*. My experience with buildings, with outdoor lighting, with drama in all other forms would all add in. Since no one had succeeded in creating an American sound and light production I admired, I put together my own team. I have faith that something good will result when good professionals work together.

Clyde Nordheimer, the electrical engineer who had often designed special systems for me, evolved one for Boscobel. It was a fully automated digital computer system with 11,310 positions. The sound tape had four tracks, three for stereo music, sound and voices, the fourth for memory control. Electronic impulses could handle about 700 cues, switch 325 lights off and on, handle the dimmers and switch 86 speakers on and off, with control of the volume of sound from each speaker.

David Butz, the sound engineer, decided to use high-fidelity equipment rather than a public-address system, with its lower sound quality. The speakers would be planted in trees and shrubs outside the house. Some would slide out of underground vaults and then slip back after each performance. Nothing would deface the lovely grounds and nothing would need to be taken down between performances. Once the system was in, the taped drama created and cued into the system, anyone could "run the show" by pressing a button for it to start and rewinding the tape afterwards.

I insisted that Lael Wertenbaker accept the challenge of writing the script, on which everything depended, as it does in all drama. Her partner in free-lance projects, Suzanne Gleaves, would handle the research. John Houseman agreed to direct it.

Lael's "flash" occurred, as may often be so, out of desperation. Nothing much had happened in that beautiful house. The man who built it died before it was completed. His widow lived there. A child was born. And the last inheritors died within its crumbling walls. For restoration the house was moved, piece by piece, many miles up the river from where it had originally stood. As history, Lael said, it was furniture. She decided that Boscobel must be used as a prototype of the grand Hudson River houses and the land around it as a crossroads through which history passed. Actually, the problem and the solution apply to much of America's heritage in places. Within European historical monuments, centuries of events have taken place. Blood and ghosts abound. Americans have been too peripatetic, too quick to destroy and rebuild what they have. Most of our historic places *are* crossroads which history arrived at, entered and exited.

Lael's script was a joy to me. It was conceived in terms of the lighting of it. Incidents from the history of Hudson River life in that area were chosen so that they could "happen" convincingly in the woods that lay beside the gardens, in the gardens, along the riverbank and on the river, as well as in the house. She began with the house as it is today. The hostess — marvelously voiced by Helen Hayes — welcomed the audience at the gates. Music by David Walker danced the audience from there across the lush green lawn, as the lighting led them to a vantage point beside the woods. Then the house went dark and history took over, with a narrative in the voice of Gary Merrill. There was only the wilderness that Henry Hudson's men had explored three centuries before. Incidents from history seemed to "happen" on that riverbank, in woods and garden. Then the house was built, as it had been after the American Revolution, growing upward in light, and people lived in it and the incidents of their time "happened. . . ."

It would work. Lael and I flew out to California to cut the script with John Houseman to a playing time of fifty-three minutes. Then Clyde, Dave and I went out to Garrison, N.Y., and up the road to Boscobel to supervise the burying of hundreds of feet of cable, to install light outlets and speakers. The cast was made up largely of those marvelous actors from radio days who knew how to portray character by voice alone. The tape was made in a New York studio. A thirty-five-piece orchestra recorded the score. The mix was made. Now we carried the tape out to Boscobel and began to cue the memory bank. The seven hundred cues directed the sound into the right directional speakers, the music into its channels. The lighting was designed to isolate the scenes, to create the space in which the sound would combine and appeal to the imagination so that the action would be "seen" as well as heard.

We worked at night and were eaten alive by Hudson River valley mosquitoes — which would be expensively banished by extensive spraying when the audiences came. First each light was focused. Then the sound sequences were tested. Some of these were noisy — a Revolutionary War battle of ships on the Hudson, a cracking of winter ice along the river, the thunderclaps of spring. The neighbors, although quite a distance away, complained. After that we conducted these "rehearsals" at low volume, conferring by two-way radio. The night we tried out the "fire in the woods" — a fine fire, using equipment I had bought from a defunct musical, *Jenny,* I had designed — the effect was so realistic that fire departments from all over the county showed up to put it out.

Except that no one of us succumbed to personal temperament, I suspect this was as hectic as any show I have ever done. Everything depended now on the exact cuing. We ran short of cues at one point where the stereo sound needed the same speakers as the dialogue. Those giant infranors — which swept the lawn where pre-Revolutionary gentlemen were bowling as they argued the merits of revolt — had to be cued twenty minutes ahead of time in order to warm up and arrive on the instant. For a while it was an insane jumble, voices tangling in speakers, lights going wrong. But one by one the colored pins were fixed in the computer board. The horse galloped as it was supposed to, downriver and then up. The land was explored, settled, peopled, warred over — and one man built his house. On opening night, as is mandatory in show business, it all worked.

As a distinguished audience gathered at the gates, the house was brightly lighted. Helen Hayes, as visible as if she were standing in that lighted doorway, bade it welcome. "Boscobel is the fulfillment of one man's dream — a fine house beside a broad river, a house to honor a man's ancestors and harbor his progeny. You will find in its private drama our heritage from Europe and the story of America, her rivers and her people." One review spoke of the magic moment when, that night under an appropriate half moon, "we heard the sailors from Hudson's *Half Moon* scramble up the river banks. Across the misty river, the ancient cannon of West Point boomed retreat and only the hissing of automobile tires in the distance reminded us that the time was the present." When history came up to the house itself, we built it in light, gave a party in it, lived in it, and then watched it decay, as it had, and rebuilt it again. This was truly American history.

I am now hoping that two other sound and light shows which have been proposed will come through: the St. Louis waterfront and the Smithsonian Institution in Washington. To me, it is wasteful of our heritage if we fail in thus dramatizing it. Fluid as it has been, less obviously glamorous perhaps than the royal procession of history in Europe, our history is very exciting. So far Boscobel, although out of the way, has attracted audiences each summer for two performances a week. All it needs is spring cleaning each year, a careful refocusing of the lights and a check on the sound channels, which tend to leak and blur if not corrected each year. The drama of history then repeats itself.

I watched recently when a gang of teen-agers showed up there. Casually dressed, noisy and withdrawn as a group, they were hostile to the world they did not make and saw their world in their own images. I do not know why they came. They loudly disavowed the values of restoring Boscobel. To my surprise, from Helen Hayes's first greeting on they were totally attentive. I believe they left enriched by a sense that a great deal had gone before them.

At times the production takes on breathtaking proportions. For example when the lighting and sound track reenact a naval battle in the river. Startling, too, is the crying of a newborn baby.
— *Variety*

We heard the *Half Moon*, sails flapping and cordage creaking . . . there were arrogant redcoats and hot-headed patriots, an orchardful of angry farmers and an indignation of Tories. A lonely woman read bedtime stories to her children in an upstairs room in Boscobel — and the house dreamed in moonlight as one by one the candles were extinguished downstairs. . . . Nothing . . . surpasses the incredible beauty of this great house . . . in the floodlights that are magnificently handled, changing the mood of the house as the story is grave or gay.
— Tarrytown *Explorer*

Nine. To Dance in Light

If I leave anything to posterity, it will be, I think, most importantly in the field of dance lighting.

Dancers live in light as fish live in water. The stage space in which they move is their aquarium, their portion of the sea. Within translucent walls and above the stage floor, the lighting supports their flashing buoyance or their arrested sculptural bodies. The dance is fluid and never static, as natural light is fluid and never static. Designing for the dance has been my most constant love. I have designed the decor as well as the lighting for a good many ballets and I have designed and installed the basic systems with which I have worked in dance repertory. If I leave anything to posterity, it will be, I think, most importantly in the field of dance lighting. My extraordinary good fortune was that I came along at a point in time when Martha Graham was creating and when Lincoln Kirstein was backing George Balanchine to create new and fresh uses of the ballet form.

Until after World War I ballets were the "girlie" shows of Europe. In the opulent nineteenth and early twentieth centuries, Russian aristocrats attended the ballet to choose their mistresses. In Paris the ballerinas were ordered to be in the green room before and after performances to meet gentlemen guests. From the touring corps de ballet of Ballets Russes, one of the stars married Maynard Keynes and another girl married Pablo Picasso. (It is not possible to imagine the young Martha Graham or Maria Tallchief waiting backstage so that a grand duke might take them on or a Paris blade take them home or even to meet a man who might marry them.) Ballet was expected to be pink and pretty. The systems for lighting it were inflexible. Equipment, standard in European opera houses, consisted of first-pipe positions, a boom or tormentor, one left and one right. Supplemental lights were borderlights and strips of light above or on the sides, simply hauled in, one to twenty of them, at four feet to six or seven feet. There were a couple of what we privately called "belly-button crosslights." (Actually, they hit the crotch.) So the first ten feet of the stage was lit for visibility and available for change of color — blue for *Swan Lake*, pink for *Les Biches*. After that there was just scenery light, flat and without depth or mood.

My system required fixed booms along the side at every entrance as a basis for flexibility and for lighting the whole stage. That made

Perhaps one day Jean Rosenthal will be able to write some of *her* theories about stage lighting because this American woman has made the greatest contribution to lighting stages since Adolphe Appia's death. She has turned lighting into an art that has become an integral part of ballet's composite construction rather than just something which makes it possible to see dancers, choreographers' patterns and designers' settings. She can create atmosphere, violent theatrical effects and complete visibility.
— *Dance and Dancers* (London)

traditional ballet positions

the ballets look different, which roused the ire of the European choreographers and designers for Ballet International in 1944. At the time it upset dance critic John Martin, too, because his eyes were accustomed to traditional ballet lighting; but he changed his mind with later viewing and became a staunch proponent of mood and depth in the lighting for classic repertory as well as for the most modern and innovative ballets.

To plan your system for a dance company you need to study thoroughly at least eight of their ballets. You cannot just take the first one and then add in, one by one, the rest. You will find that each company has, besides a style of its own, an aesthetic, a way of using the stage, that is particularly theirs. You cannot change the hookup or the focusing once the lights are set. It is vital to have one basic light plot, one set of controls — plus a handful of specials which can be focused for a single ballet. You can only change the color for lights that can be reached with a short ladder during a fifteen-minute intermission. You use a basic — and distinctive — palette for each company.

The blue and the pink which suited Ballet Society were a different blue and a different pink from those which suited Ballet Theatre. Ballet Theatre, although eclectic and never wedded to one choreographer or one style, told stories. Even when they performd Balanchine ballets, they chose ones which broke conveniently into movements, so that in their way these ballets built simple dance stories. Ballet Society and later New York City Ballet, on the other hand, did not tie their ballets to plot or story. They were Balanchine-*styled,* and what you lit for Balanchine was form in movement.

Every ballet company requires a distinctive look in its lighting. The only common denominators for all ballet are the requirements of *beauty* and *ease*. Ballet is beautiful. Even portraying evil and ugliness it is beautiful. The dancers' arms, their necks, their faces must be lovely. Heavy color is invariably inelegant and totally unsuited. Most of the different palettes are pale ones. For ease, the cues should be worked out so that the light is securely *there* when the dancers arrive. Before the musical transitions indicate them, the lighting transitions should begin to happen. It got so the dance stage managers never asked me, "Where do you want me to take the cue?" but, "Where do you want it to have happened?" The audience and the dancers should not be aware of transitions, so the lighting anticipates the music and the movement by the minutest fraction. If it is that same fraction behind, all that marvelous energy that goes into making the dance appear effortless is destroyed. Even if it is simultaneous — except occasionally for the deliberate purpose of shock — there is the faintest clash, a hint of strain.

There is a key to lighting each company. For Ballet Theatre it was total decor and story form; for Balanchine, patterns in space; for Martha Graham, interior impulse. When you have studied say thirty-three out of a company's total repertory, you find that the need for certain specific lights appears in at least nineteen of them. That becomes part of your setup. Then, within the setup, including the basic needs, you consider the individual ballets. Do you want a shaft of downlight, or high sidelights, or low sidelights? Does it need crosslights from the pipes? Is there a star turn?

You have established the key for the company and the look of the company, the hookup and the focusing, the palette. You have your repertory setup and you work within it for variety. You work within its *limitations*, the ones you have established. If you do not, you will be in trouble. Your lighting system will be used for as many as twenty-one separate artistic entities within a single week. These are subject to last-minute changes of program and last-minute substitution among the leading dancers.

To dance in light is never a single challenge, but a constant series of challenges.

The monumental egos and towering talents of Lincoln Kirstein and George Balanchine devoured other talents, somewhat in the way Orson Welles had. Lincoln ate up designers and George fed on dancers. Perhaps George was the more comprehensible carnivore since he had a vital hand in cultivating what he devoured. Pygmalion to his Galateas, if he created a *ballerina suprema* he — five times over anyway — married her.

Nan Porcher once braved the pride of Maria Tallchief and asked her why she had married Balanchine. "I guess the thing is," *ballerina suprema* Tallchief did explain, "that you are a ballerina. George is the most important choreographer in the world. You are young and ambitious. And he turns all that incredible charm and dynamic force on you. It is like a searchlight. You realize your own potential. All of a sudden one day, after he has created works for you, and you are becoming an important person in your profession, he turns to you and he says, 'I need you.' And the idea that George Balanchine needs you is so overwhelming, of course you marry him. And you find out immediately that he does not need you at all, he just wants full control. And that is the way he gets it."

Lincoln is also an elemental force, like a forest fire or a waterfall. He had no real outlet for his talents. Instead he used artists to carry out his very definite ideas of the visual look ballet should have. He could have taught them a lot, because he was immensely knowledgeable but he was not tolerant of their separate genius. I suppose I survived for eighteen years as production director and lighting designer for Lincoln because mostly I wanted to do what Lincoln wanted done. Lincoln never really told you to do anything — that is, he never said "I insist" — but his ideas were so clear that he was able to impose them and he kept total visual control in his hands.

I met Kirstein through John Houseman. Lincoln knew my work for Martha Graham and invited me to work for him. His Ballet Caravan was on its foundering way to South America but he had unlimited plans for the future. The war interrupted. Lincoln knew what scholars knew about paintings and went off as an expert to help uncover and restore to their original owners works of art confiscated by the Germans. On his return he reassembled a company. Ballet Society really represented the performing members and graduates of the School of the American Ballet, and its opening performances were in the highly unsuitable auditorium of the Needle Trades High School on Twenty-fourth Street.

Nevertheless, Lincoln was creating productions at the height of perfection. The works were created by or heavily influenced by George Balanchine and based on marvelous pieces of music: Ravel's *L'Enfant et les sortilèges*, concertos by Hindemith and Stravinsky. Lincoln was exploring ways of translating the visual promises of ballet — which had attracted painters like Picasso and Bérard and Miró to design for Diaghilev — in such a way as to apply them to contemporary painters. When he inherited his money from his father, he founded a whole lyric enterprise with George Balanchine, all under the aegis of Ballet Society. I headed the technical staff, partly because Lincoln trusted me to translate the designs of easel painters into workable stage designs.

He used painters he himself was drawn to, and he kept casting painters for different works. His relationship with these artists as scene designers was paternal, or in one of the oldest traditions of paternity. There would be a meeting with the artist, and with me, usually at Lincoln's extraordinary, stimulating and book-filled house. For the meeting Lincoln would have made tremendous preparation,

It was a stroke of genius on the part of Kirstein to acquire her [J.R.'s] collaboration with the organization. All through the existence of Ballet Society and now, in the New York City Ballet, this shy, unobtrusive magician of the incandescent lamp has brought saving illumination to many a drab setting and colorless costume or to an entirely bare stage. . . . [Her] lighting brought to life the designs of such varied artists as Chagall and Noguchi, Beaton and Smith. More than that, working with lights alone, she managed to give form, direction, and space to many ballets in the repertoire that had no decor at all.

— Anatole Chujoy

La Valse, Balanchine,
New York City Ballet

Serenade, Balanchine,
New York City Ballet

Four Temperaments, Balanchine, New York City Ballet

would have done enormous research and would know exactly how he wanted the ballet to look. He would impose on the artist all those books and illustrations. Not one of the artists failed to accept the work offered with interest, but they still hoped they might be able to bring something of themselves to the design. Being a sponge by nature, I learned a good deal from that sophisticated education in the literature of design. The Spaniard, Estebán Francés was almost the only one Lincoln permitted to do his own designing. Among the rest, some artists were tougher than others. Rouben Ter-Arutunian was the toughest. He managed, no matter how much research was poured on him, to retain the idea he originally had, using his excessive rudeness as a weapon of defense. Rouben missed a lot, because much of what Lincoln offered was good and useful material, but he did retain his own identity. The other designers suffered considerably because they did not like having Lincoln's total point of view imposed on them, and this created many frictions and emotional upheavals.

As Lincoln's money diminished, so did the use of expensive decor. We began to develop a look which followed George Balanchine's famous dictum "less as possible!" George was exploring the use of ballet stripped of all the decorative details that were so identified with the great ballet companies of Europe. He cheerfully accepted the cyclorama and velour drops that became our standard space arrangement — the area was simply filled with light and the emphasis of the visual look was the lighting. It was not particularly that George liked or did not like my lighting. What he wanted was an adequate area which left him free to do exactly what he wanted to do and for the audience to see the bodies of the dancers, which Balanchine manipulated so heartlessly and so gloriously.

When Lincoln's fortune ran out the whole thing would have foundered, except that Morton Baum came along and City Center became the home of the New York City Ballet. Our production look was very dry and very clean, in decoration, lighting and costumes, and this is the look we would take to Europe in the 1950s.

Painted sets can be beautiful — Estebán did some perfect ones for Balanchine, and so have others. They can also be both beautiful and impossible to dance in front of.

When Balanchine did the *Firebird* at City Center we bought the sets Chagall had designed for it earlier. The ground cloth was a mélange of colors. Wings, borders and legs were painted in orange, yellow, pink and green. There were the forest drop, the princess drop and the wedding drop. We threw out the ground cloth. The forest drop — rich, dark green forest and a magic tree with a man embedded in the tree and a cockerel painted upside down — was the one Balanchine used, doing the whole ballet in front of it, with black legs and borders. It was typical Chagall but dark, and against it you could see the dancers and the design of the dance. When the story was told and the firebird's last solo danced in low light, and the firebird had waked

122

the prince and princess to go off and be married, there were eight minutes of music left.

"Now," said Balanchine, "we can look at Chagall," and for eight minutes he staged a series of tableaus. Down came legs and borders in a great cadence of color. Down came the princess drop, bright yellow and white, with a huge green upside-down monster with a trap door in its stomach for the company to walk into. The trumpets sounded for the wedding. The princess drop went up and the wedding drop came down, in gorgeous reds, oranges, pinks and purples, the painted bride and groom floating off at an angle. Lined up on the stage was the full company. They wore Chagall's costumes, hand-painted on canvas, which no one had seen before. (You could not dance in them.) The dancers bowed to each other, walked down, bowed to the audience — and on the opening night, to Chagall.

Chagall was furious. Balanchine had the right to use the sets and costumes his way because he had bought them, but Chagall demanded that his credit be removed from the program. I think he was wrong.

Balanchine was right to demand "less as possible" for his ballets. Take the brilliantly choreographed *Four Temperaments*. Against a complicated drop it had been a flop. At City Center we used only the blue cyclorama and lights. The light cues were kept extremely simple — the dancers, in black and white practice clothes, were simply etched in light, each body defined in light. Mood, music and movement were married in light and the unchanged choreography, previously dismissed by the critics as uninteresting, amazed both John Martin and Walter Terry, the most important of them. *Four Temperaments* became a hit.

Perhaps no book that treats of the New York theatre may be written without reference to the critics. They have, for economic reasons, more power over the New York theatre than they have over any art anywhere else. If I speak of them thus casually at this point it is partly because a lighting designer's work is so often best when it goes wholly unnoticed. This is true of no other of the creative elements in the collaboration that is theatre. Critics are human and fallible, and in the theatre, most particularly in New York, when they praise you it helps and when they hit you it hurts.

George Balanchine was very touchy about the critics. He was supremely certain of his undeniable genius and he resented what he considered misunderstanding more than he did outright dislike. One ballet of his, choreographed to Mendelssohn's Scotch Symphony, got rave notices. The choreography, said two critics, was *exactly* what the music indicated. George was furious. He felt dismissed.

We were in charity with one another at the time, he and I. George rarely interfered with me — unless I had been singled out for critical praise for the lighting of a ballet; then sometimes there was trouble. But for the most part, for many years, he accepted my collaboration pretty peacefully. This time we collaborated on a way to turn the tables on the critics. Balanchine picked out Schönberg's Opus 34, background music used for a 1930s movie. It was eighteen dismal minutes long. He created an abstract, esoteric ballet for which I designed a black background. We used a white ground cloth and the dancers wore black tights. The choreography was pure 1929 *ballet moderno*.

At the end of the fadeout, the music began again, repeated for another eighteen minutes. This time Balanchine's ballet told a wild series of interconnected stories, using soap-opera episodes. For the first one, a black "thing" — a black scrim tube — crept downstage lit with pale green and lavender downlights over a stage covered with paper cambric. It looked as if coal had come alive. Downstage ballerina Tanaquil LeClercq was in a costume designed as a nerve chart and Herbert Bliss in one designed as a muscle chart. In a pas de deux the dancers were overcome with pain. Doctors rushed in with an operating table. And so it went, with dancers appearing and disappearing, and ended with a battery of lights upstage focused meticulously so that everyone in the audience was blinded.

We had a wonderful time, rather like naughty children thumbing their noses at the critics. The critics were pretty flabbergasted — but it turned out to be a very popular number in the repertory.

The "look" evolved by the New York City Ballet had moved far in the direction of sculptural objects for decor within the light-box stage rather than of painted scenery. Lighting on objects, like lighting on bodies, must make full use of a hookup employing the full stage. Marvelous designs like Noguchi's stand out, and costumes become as important as sculpture. When funds were really low, I was often asked to do the scenic designing in addition to the lighting and the technical realization of scene designs. I enjoyed scrap-heap designing as some artists now enjoy combing the dumps for sculptural material.

My set for *The Cage* was about $35 worth of cotton rope. For *Faun* the white-walled dance-rehearsal studio was constructed of yards of china silk hung on a wooden frame and suspended by cables. Black bars and a fan behind the back wall to make the silk ripple on cue completed the decor. For *The Comedians* there was no budget at all. Brilliant-colored felt panels against a black backdrop made a statement that had to do with clowns and circuses.

When it came to *Metamorphosis*, I tried a design of curved bamboo and hung from the bamboo bedsprings sprayed with gilt. They looked like bells, the soul and sound of bells, and the light glinted from them. Karinska, the costume designer, had dressed the dancers to look like oriental bugs, but she could not decide on headdresses. The day of the dress rehearsal Karinska rushed in announcing, "You will not believe! I have the headdresses to go with your bells! I have found the most breeze-taking but-sles!" They *were* bustles, tapered at the sides and bulging at the middle to go over the buttocks. And they made perfect headdresses. All off the scrap heap.

The Cage could not be more perfectly set than it has been by these means (bits of rope, a few leftover floor cloths and a yard or two of old curtain) if the best designers in the field had sat up nights working at it and the construction had cost fabulous sums. And pity any designer, however gifted, and with whatever budget to work with whose work has to be adapted to that particular stage without her [J.R.'s] direction of the process. Between the drawing board and the performance, Miss Rosenthal is a crucial figure. A producing budget of $82 with Miss Rosenthal is more potent than $82,000 without her.
— John Martin

I remember Buddy the electrician at City Center, a "turn-on-the-lights, fix-the-switches, put-tape-on-the-connections" sort of electrician, a "dese dem and dose" tough guy. By the time he had worked with Jean a few seasons, he was a ballet expert. Buddy came up once and said, "Jeannie, in that *Muffmorfuss*, I don't think they've got it quite right to do what you want it." He cared so deeply, and *Muffmorfuss* was not right. Jeannie thought we should design a toy bear called Muffmorfuss. She had that capacity to expand the vision of the people she worked with.
— Lucia Victor

The Cage, Jerome Robbins, New York City Ballet

We took our light-box staging and our clean, dry look to Europe on tour. The Europeans had never seen anything like it and it was very successful. Balanchine was hailed as the genius he was and the company from America was praised in the countries of the great ballet traditions.

I went ahead of the tour to see about the theatres. The very first one I went to, the Gran Teatro del Liceo in Barcelona, was fair warning of how hard it would be to change the traditional methods of staging and lighting physically, let alone changing any attitudes toward it. It was a glorious house, with a 115-foot stage. The dancers would require extra rehearsal time to get used to the rake — an 18-degree rake like the side of a roof, not quite as steep as Caracalla in Rome but very steep. For lighting there were only two small spotlights in the bays left and right downstage, dipped lamp footlights and borderlights, and one little arc spotlight. I told the management that we must have more equipment for our lighting, but they were pretty skeptical. After all, they performed Götterdämmerung in this setup. Finally the management and the impresario agreed to order and bring from Paris minimal equipment, of which I left them a list.

Nan Porcher, as the lighting stage manager, went with the company to set up my designs. When she arrived in Barcelona, a week ahead

July 1950

Dear Miss Rosenthal:
I was in front last evening [at the Royal Opera House, Covent Garden, London] for the opening of the New York City Ballet, and want to congratulate you, most especially, for your beautiful lighting of the ballets. I know the "local difficulties" of this House only too well and I am all the more filled with admiration at what you achieved.
 — Christopher West

of time so that the dancers could rehearse with the rake, she found only that little light left and that little light right, the borders and foots and the little follow spot up there. When she asked about the supplemental equipment, Nan later wrote me, the manager rushed to his safe.

> He considered your little piece of paper so valuable, Jean, that he had locked it away among, I presume, his will and his stocks and bonds. It was intact. Too late to order from Paris. I bullied and cajoled and had hysterics. Finally a friend of the manager's opened up a moving picture studio warehouse and let me borrow some of their equipment. So I had DC water dimmers, 100-volt AC resistance dimmers and 220-volt movie equipment. If anyone got careless and patched the wrong plug, the whole thing would blow up. Fortunately I had a perfectly marvelous Catalan electrician and we did open with a fair approximation of your lighting. Yes we did. You know, they had never seen anything like it. We got raves.

There were even lighting notices for the New York City ballet sent out on UP and AP from Barcelona. It was very gratifying. And when Nan returned to the Liceo in 1959 the manager embraced her. After the New York City Ballet played there, they had redesigned the whole lighting system.

I think it was just as well Nan was with the company instead of me. I am more inclined to compromise in such situations as she ran into. When it comes to doing my lighting my way, Nan is fierce and implacably determined to carry out my original intentions.

The Rome Opera House presented her with another crisis. The opening-night program included *Waltz* and *Cage*, for which I had designed the decor as well as the lighting. Nan demanded a follow spot, which, said the theatre manager, was out of the question. Impossible. The premises were sacred. The Rome Opera House was a national monument. Nothing could be changed, altered or defaced. There was no follow spot and there would *be* no follow spot.

I have another cherished letter from Nan, which I have kept.

> So how the hell do you light *Waltz* or *Cage* without a follow spot? Well, I began lighting with the assistant engineer out front. The chief engineer was a very old man, named Santini, and he sat up in his little box. When I was into *Waltz*, I turned around and said, "Well, here's where everything goes out except the follow spot. It's an integral part of the concept. It's vital to the dramatic unity, not just to follow a star around. I don't know what to do."

The Viking Nan must have sounded pretty poignant. She says she felt that way and even cried.

> Mr. Santini told me to go on to the next cue. So I did. Then I heard a violent altercation in Italian and fifteen minutes later a crashing sound. I walked back — just in time to see a gilt cherub's plump arse disappear from the curved cornice at the top in the rear of the theatre. I think the penalty is probably death for defacing that decor, but Mr. Santini had done

Swan Lake, American Ballet Theatre

it. He had remembered a storage room up there and through the hole made by the cherub's loss of his posterior we had the damnedest follow spot you ever saw. There was no room to stand up, but the electrician was hung in a bosn's chair.... "I looked at the stage," said Mr. Santini. "Anything so beautiful as that deserves everything."

At the end of the week in Rome the entire company were presented with medallions, and they brought one home to me.

Lucia Chase is to American Ballet Theatre what Lincoln Kirstein was to Ballet Society. She devoted her fortune and literally beggared herself in the service of the dance. When she was joined by Oliver Smith he threw his resources into the company, not only designing for it but raising money. His impeccable eye was on the stage, so that for all the company's diversity of production, you could say, "This is beautiful and this is Ballet Theatre."

Ballet Theatre has never had a home theatre, only a home school, in New York. Its dancers are trained in both classical ballet and modern dance and the repertory is eclectic. It has become the repository for ballets ranging from *Swan Lake* and *Giselle* through the works of José Limón and Jerome Robbins and Alvin Ailey, who is creating new works for their repertory. Ballet Theatre has given new choreographers their chance — win, lose or draw — knowing that the successful ones, such as Michael Kidd and Elliott Feld, would pull out to form their own companies. The very first ballet Jerome Robbins choreographed was for Ballet Theatre. Before 1960 Ballet Theatre really did

Rodeo, Agnes de Mille, American Ballet Theatre

not have a lighting system. Many of the designers lit their own productions. For their seasons at the Metropolitan, a good stage manager could make the company look very good, but on the road, I believe, the lighting was fairly disastrous.

Oliver and the technicial advisor, Randy Brooks, asked me to come in for their three-week New York season in 1960. I got Nan Porcher to join me. We put together a layout, imposed strict limitations on it, and sat down to light thirty-three separate and disparate ballets from scratch. (Or rather, when I got up, Nan would sit down and keep the lighting going. When she got up, she would hand me the next batch of scenery sketches.) One opening followed another. Some of the ballets I knew well, others I did not.

Most of the ballets were cued to stories. Even the Balanchine works they performed, such as *Ballet Imperial* and *Theme and Variations*, broke conveniently into movements, fast, slow, etc. At the end of a movement, as at the end of an episode in the story ballets, there was a light change and a mood change. Here came the pink set or the blue set; it was fast, slow or full company. That kind of formality is easier to light than interior drama, such as Martha Graham's, or pure form. The use of scenery made it impossible to be as spare and disciplined as in setting up for the New York City Ballet. If a light for one ballet hit a piece of scenery for the next, you simply had to pull the plug and eliminate it.

In 1965 Ballet Theatre moved into the New York State Theatre. Oliver redesigned or had others redesign all the ballets. The important thing about the lighting was the same principle as for the whole: to impose an organization, to create a setup, that could do all the diverse things the company did, tidily, and anywhere. That meant flexibility, presentability and a color scheme which worked in many moods.

To compare the color range of Ballet Theatre with that of the New York City Ballet illustrates the kind of thinking the lighting designer uses for repertory. For the New York City Ballet I used a grayer blue; for the Ballet Theatre a greener blue. The warm color for the New York City Ballet was a real pink, a pink-pink, flesh or Degas pink; for Ballet Theatre, the pink was bastard amber, which can be either warm or cold. The basic downlights for the New York City Ballet, keyed to a repertory which included *Orpheus* and *Cage*, were lavender; for Ballet Theatre they had to be blue. I did at times very much miss that lavender, but if you must have blue downlights for some ballets, you cannot also have lavender, except for those few you can reach with a short ladder during a short intermission.

Now this company is where so much is represented — the body of Antony Tudor's work, the best of Agnes DeMille's — and for the record, I have left with them, in addition to the light plots for the New York State Theatre, an analysis sheet for touring. When you have to cut for the road, it is important to see every circuit in the repertory laid out and know how it is used for every single ballet.

The ferocious dedication that its artists bring to the dance calls for matching technical dedication. You never make money on the dance. It demands everything of you without paying very well, except in the satisfaction of doing your utmost. "Utmost" has a richness of its own and I am grateful to all devotees of the dance, to those impossible perfectionists George Balanchine and Jerome Robbins, to the passionate patrons Lincoln Kirstein and Lucia Chase, to all the others who have given me this richness.

And most of all — and this takes me back to my beginnings — to Martha Graham.

Martha is a peculiarly American genius. Her heritage is Black Irish Catholic and Puritan (tracing back on her mother's side to Miles Standish) and Presbyterian. She was raised in California with Japanese and Chinese servants. Her nurse was Irish Catholic. To this complex cultural heritage and conditioning she added an intense association with ancient Greece and its timeless mythology.

When I was sent to her at the Neighborhood Playhouse as a reluctant student dancer, the first thing she said to me was, "Well, you have *one* qualification — you have peasant feet!" I did not want to dance, and I suspect she knew it. We had one particular bond in common, which was a passion for Greek myths. Martha had a spirituality, a God-consciousness, which I lacked, but I was raised on Bullfinch. Martha used the myths brilliantly, retelling them in her own marvelous language of the dance.

Dance is to theatre, I think, what poetry is to literature. Martha always began with a very literal idea, with a literal story, with direct thoughts and simple emotions. In their finished form, her dances are powerful abstractions, poems in motion.

From the beginning of my work with her backstage, I was comfortably aware of Martha's silent collaboration. She works silently to bring out the best in you, her silence a recognition of the dignity of another person's talent. She so strictly minds her own business and does her own part with such a sense of direction and perfection that you have hardly any choice except to do your best yourself. You are forced to get onto her wave length, since she recognizes no other. It is not an aggressive wave length, a dominance, but a sort of short-cut called a wave length. It is simply her world and if you wish to enter that world and perform properly for her, you of necessity become part of that environment. She never tells you what to do, but her silence is full of communication and challenge. And you simply respond, within her world.

The lighting came from Martha, from the interior of Martha. The changes were keyed to the physical impulse, the human body, not to the music or the form. There had to be a kinetic connection, an interior reaction. Nowhere in dance, except in an occasional Jerome Robbins ballet or once in a while in Tudor, does the light lead and

> I am partly Puritan, so I understood Jean's occasional compulsive Hebraism. She was so gentle, and so implacable.
> — Martha Graham

> Jean was a very pure person. I have never known her to compromise. If she could do it, she would, if not she said no. Hers was the religion of the individual — dedication to as near perfection as possible. She never deviated from that . . . and had discovered the wonder of life. That is not easy.
> — Martha Graham

> Jean knows — I cannot help using the present tense — that the theatre is a place to project the interior landscape, which is man's soul.
> — Martha Graham

Martha Graham Dance Company

move with the dancer as much, cued not to the music but to impulsive action.

Martha commissioned more original music than anyone else, but like everything else about her work the music seemed to come from Martha. The music was there because she needed it to move on, like a platform. You might take the curtain up and down to the music, but the lighting was organic, not illumination or illustration or even mood, but cerebral, from Martha's mind. This totality, this instinctual realization of a mind and a spirit, could be hair-raisingly beautiful.

For Martha, there was always a single key light, coming from very high up. I do not know of any other dance repertory where there was a key light of this kind. This light, for Martha, has to do two things: create a high angular pool of downlight and a high diagonal that will run all the way upstage. You never lost the diagonal for her. I think of it as Martha's Finger of God.

The palette for Martha was mysterious, often cold, cerebral light — and that high diagonal coming down from the narrowest point. She rarely used painted drops. The stage was set with organic, not decorative, sculpture, so that these were also alive, organic, and the costumes also were sculptural and organic, alive. (One happy accident made a perfect blackout for Martha. During a rehearsal for *Cave of the Heart* I had a wall of hot red light against the backdrop. The light was intensified until the curtain fell. I told the electrician to "'wash it out" — to cut all the lights. He threw the switch and because the red lights were so violent, the eye was left with the impression of gray-green light bathing the stage. This lasted for only seconds — but it had the effect of turning the dancer's world suddenly to ashes.)

You never knew when Martha would say, "I am going to have a season in two weeks." You never knew when she would call you to tell you the story of a new ballet for the first time — and when she did this it was very clear and factual and literal. I went to her when she wanted me. To do one or two new works for Martha a year was a part of my life and a renewal of my own interior spirit.

Hers was the first work I did, and I hope it will be the last.

Martha Graham would be doing one of her introspective works in which the woman Martha was playing withdrew into herself to work out a personal thing. To Jeannie that was Martha going into her little house, her own private world. And Jean lit it as though it were Martha's little house. You could see the walls through the lighting, into which Martha was withdrawing. Or she went down the path to somewhere else, and that path suddenly bloomed with lights. It was as clear as a movie scenario. The audience was not expected to say, yes, that is a house, that is a path, but the audience had the emotional response you have to a house or a path.

— Lucia Victor

With Jean at last on the premises, seated against the wall between the mirrors in the same position Martha herself has occupied all these weeks and months, Martha gives way to the inevitability of performance. Jean's presence seems to banish uncertainty. Jean has brought the stage and all its intricacies and technicalities with her, and that is deeply reassuring.

— Leroy Leatherman

Another performance without her? I don't know how I'll do it!

— Martha Graham

Tools of the Trade

Edited and Illustrated by Marion Kinsella

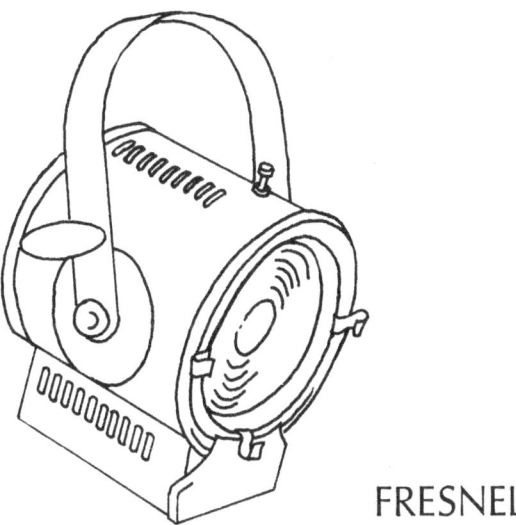

FRESNEL

This light is small (normally 750W capacity) and quick to focus, and has a special light quality: it has a soft edge, a sense of brilliance, and an enormous range. It is suitable, with its low wattage, for interior settings, where not only does it furnish a beam of light, but its fuzziness bounces all around and makes a kind of haze in air. (It is very important to keep in mind the use of light for air.) The fresnel is also useful as a kind of abbreviated borderlight for interiors. You can do a good deal of toning when you use it on flood focus rather than sharp focus. On flood focus, the light does not register as a beam but as general haze, with the beam scarcely visible. On sharp focus, there is a definite beam pattern.

The beam spread (the distribution of light) is important in making a decision which size fresnel to use. For a blast of light, as in certain musicals, you use an 8-inch 1000W fresnel.

If you use fresnels for general toning light but only have room on the pipe for one or two, the fresnel on sharp focus with a frost gel will give a hot center with a very soft edge so that the audience cannot see where the light falls.

Used as a sidelight, the fresnel gives quite a lot of accent and contrast without being hot.

One of the hardest things to achieve in lighting is an even, allover, general soft light that isn't mushy. By use of focus, or sometimes by using frost gels with the fresnel, you can get a very soft light that still has quite a lot of sparkle in it. Because of its unique combination of softness and sparkle the fresnel is a very good light to use for ballet or for general washes of light.

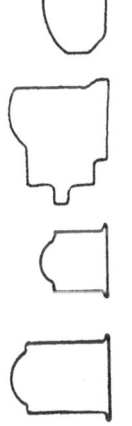

SYMBOLS

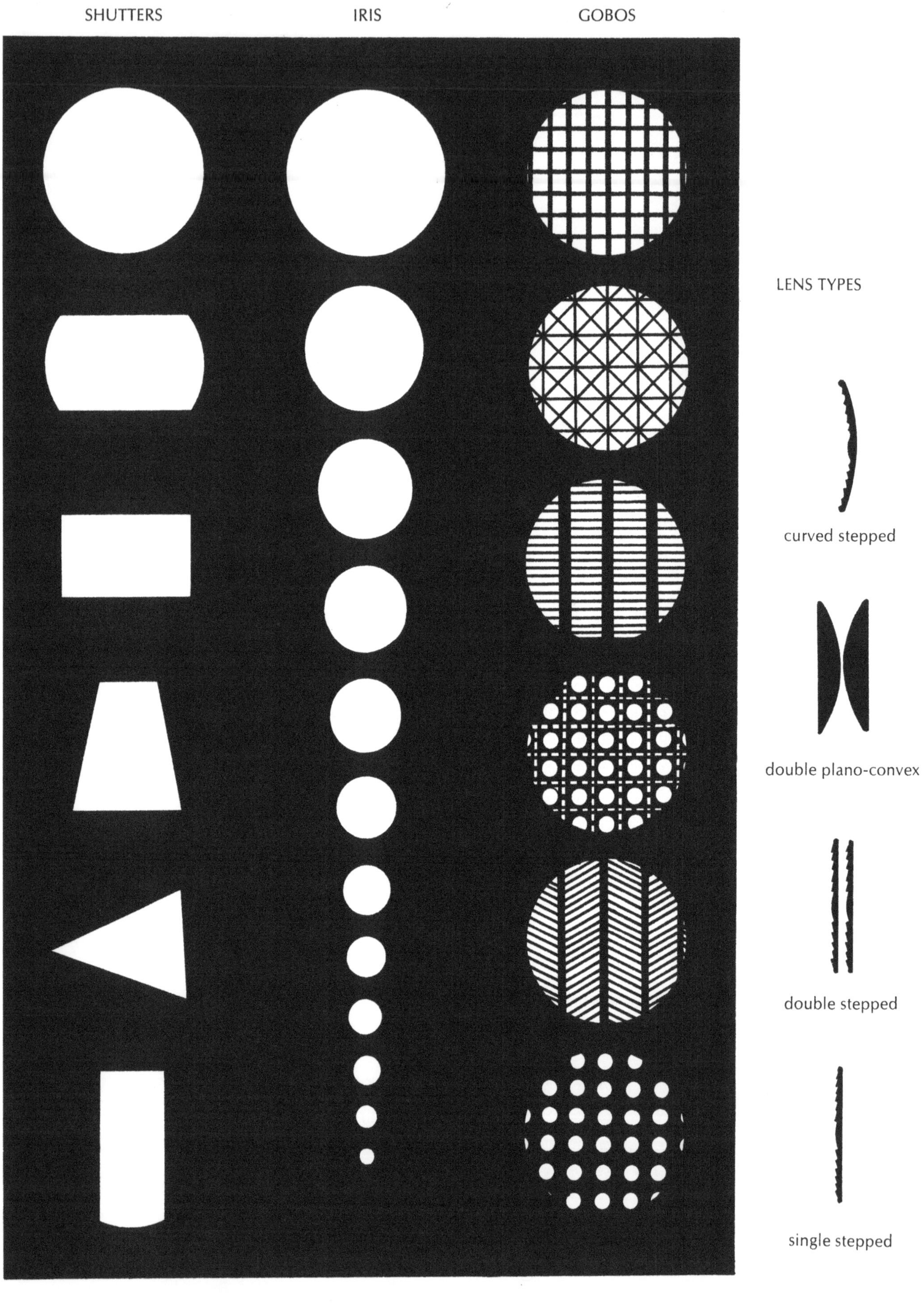

| SHUTTERS | IRIS | GOBOS |

LENS TYPES

curved stepped

double plano-convex

double stepped

single stepped

ELLIPSOIDAL or LEKOLITE

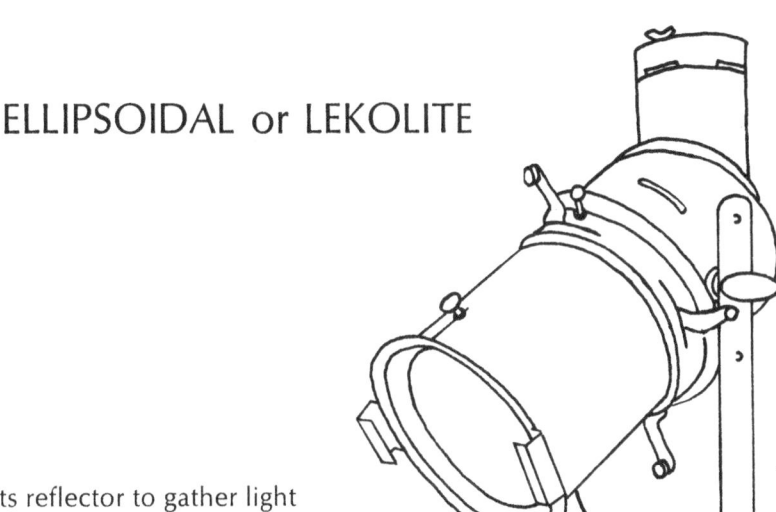

This light is based entirely on the ability of its reflector to gather light and project it in the manner in which one projects an image; that is, the beam is reversed: the top is the bottom and the bottom is the top, left is right and right is left. It has a very hard edge, a very spectacular light quality, and in terms of its shape a very smooth field of light. You may get an absolutely even wash of light using a group of well-focused ellipsoidal reflector lights. They are most often referred to by the more familiar trade names, such as Lekolites (Century-Strand) or Klieglites (Kliegl). Some have better reflectors than others, some have better lenses. It is the built-in shutters which are the important factor, allowing the light to be shaped.

The choice of lens sizes — 6" x 9" and 6" x 12", double plano-convex being the most commonly used — depends upon the distance the light must travel and the amount of area to be covered where it lands, since the width of the beam spread will vary according to the lens size. For instance, the Century-Strand 6" x 9" plano-convex lens claims a 24-degree angle, and the 6" x 12" lens an 18-degree angle.

An ellipsoidal light on soft focus will have a hot center with a fuzzy edge, and on sharp focus will have a hard, clean edge. Some ellipsoidal lights have step lenses, which give a softer edge when the light is in sharp focus.

The light patterns shown on the opposite page will give an idea of what can be achieved in terms of control by the use of built-in shutters (first column). When a circle of light desired is smaller than that obtainable in the normal beam spread of an ellipsoidal light, then an iris unit is called for. An iris unit will give you any size circle of light you may wish, from the normal width expected from that lens size down to the smallest of pin spots (second column).

The gobo patterns, or templates, shown in the third column are of the standard type carried by the manufacturers of stage lighting equipment, but for special purposes they may be either custom made or made by the designer himself out of aluminum, using, for example, oven liners or pie plates.

Gobo and iris units must be specified, as they are not usually standard equipment on an ellipsoidal light.

SYMBOLS

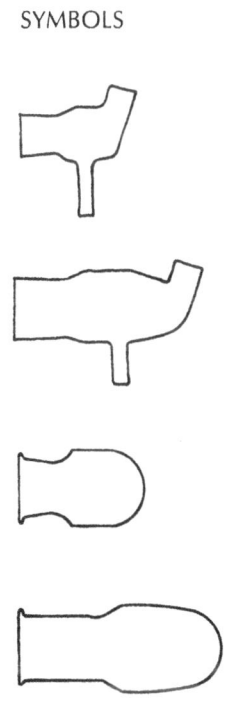

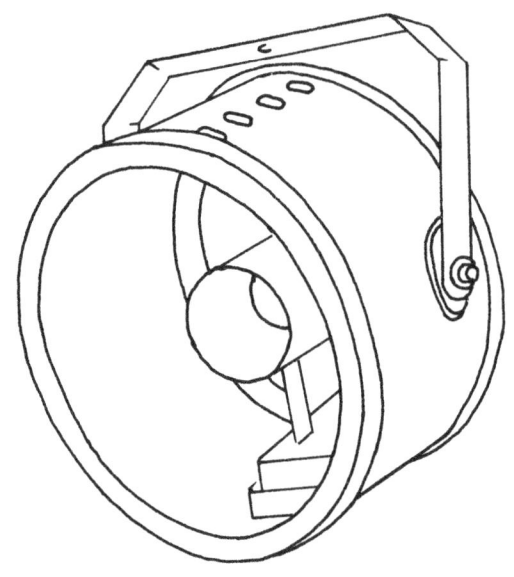

BEAMLIGHT PROJECTOR

SYMBOLS

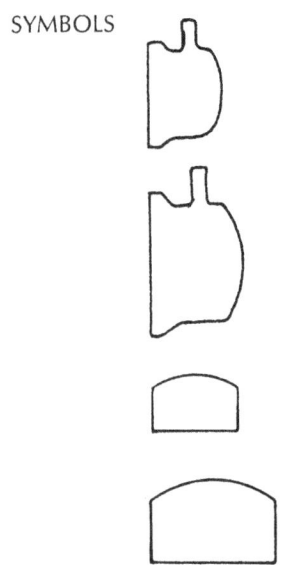

The beam projector is a light that people have a tendency to ignore. I find it very valuable because of its shape, and I like to use it where I want to define patterns without sharp edges. The beamlight has quite marked striations of light and dark. (Recent "improvements" by some manufacturers tend to lessen the striations. I do not consider this an improvement, as it diminishes the shaftlike quality of this light.)

When you use the beam projector you can build a wall of light with a quality of brilliance and no hard edge. It is excellent for backlighting, marvelous to use in opera or such places where you have enough room to spread the light. In tighter places it does have an exterior edge that can be a little annoying. The beam light has two really defined shapes in its soft focus position and its sharp focus position. In its sharp position it has a lot of fuzz around it, but it makes a beautiful column. This light is very easy to focus and very easy to maintain, and has a marvelous capacity for shape.

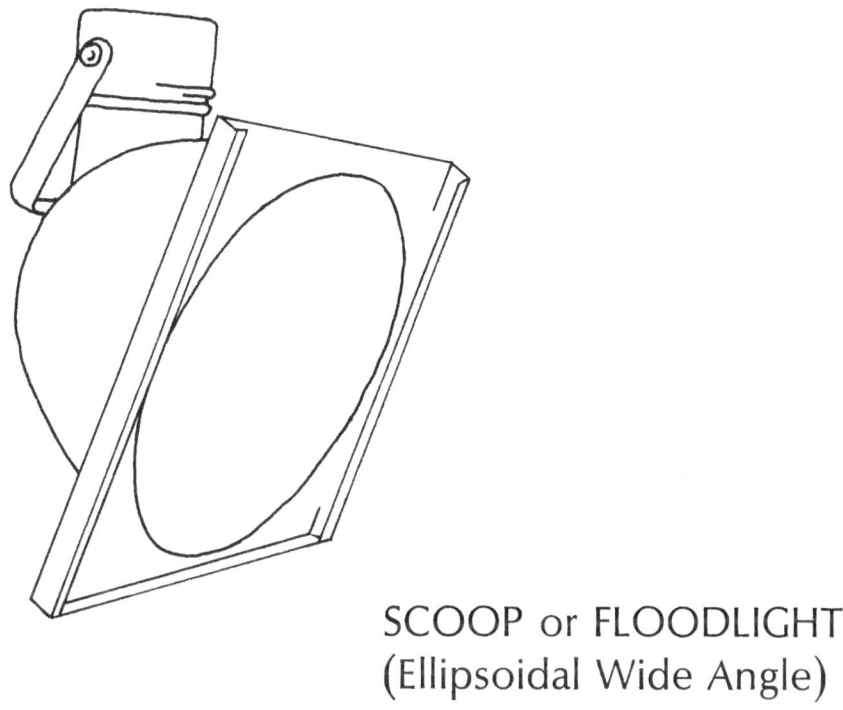

SCOOP or FLOODLIGHT
(Ellipsoidal Wide Angle)

While the scoop is not a "people" light, and can produce no pattern, it is particularly good for curved cycloramas, where the straight lines of a borderlight make even coverage at the curves difficult. It is also useful for giving certain sections of a drop extra intensity of light without edges. Some painted translucent drops respond very well to lighting of this kind.

This light may be used in conjunction with or separate from the conventional borderlight or quartz borderlight.

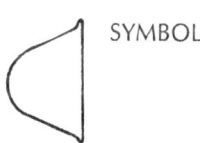 SYMBOL

A Photo Essay on Light

The following photo essay was shot on a miniature stage (scale: two inches to one foot) using small versions of the fresnel and the ellipsoidal spotlights. The figures are sculptor's scale-model manikins.

The essay is preceded by a mini light plot. The symbols on the plot represent the types of instrument used, as shown on pages 135 through 139.

The essay was designed to show in simple terms how light coming from the standard theatre lighting positions will look when focused to light an actor in a given area on the stage. The mini light plot is a ground plan showing where the light pipes and instruments are hanging in relation to the stage. The plot also has on it an elevation of one of the tormentor pipes (or "booms," as they are sometimes called) for side lighting, and the ground plan of the tormentor positions used in the photo essay.

Each of the photo essays will refer back to the mini light plot for position of the instrument used. Through the use of this reference, the logic of why instruments are positioned as they are to achieve the desired angle and effect will become evident.

The light plots for three different situations in theatre lighting are shown at the end of this section, and they of course are much more complex than the mini light plot. However, a better understanding of how to read these larger plots can be gained by using the mini light plot as suggested. The mini light plot will also serve as a guide to understanding how to translate the examples shown of a board hookup and a focus chart.

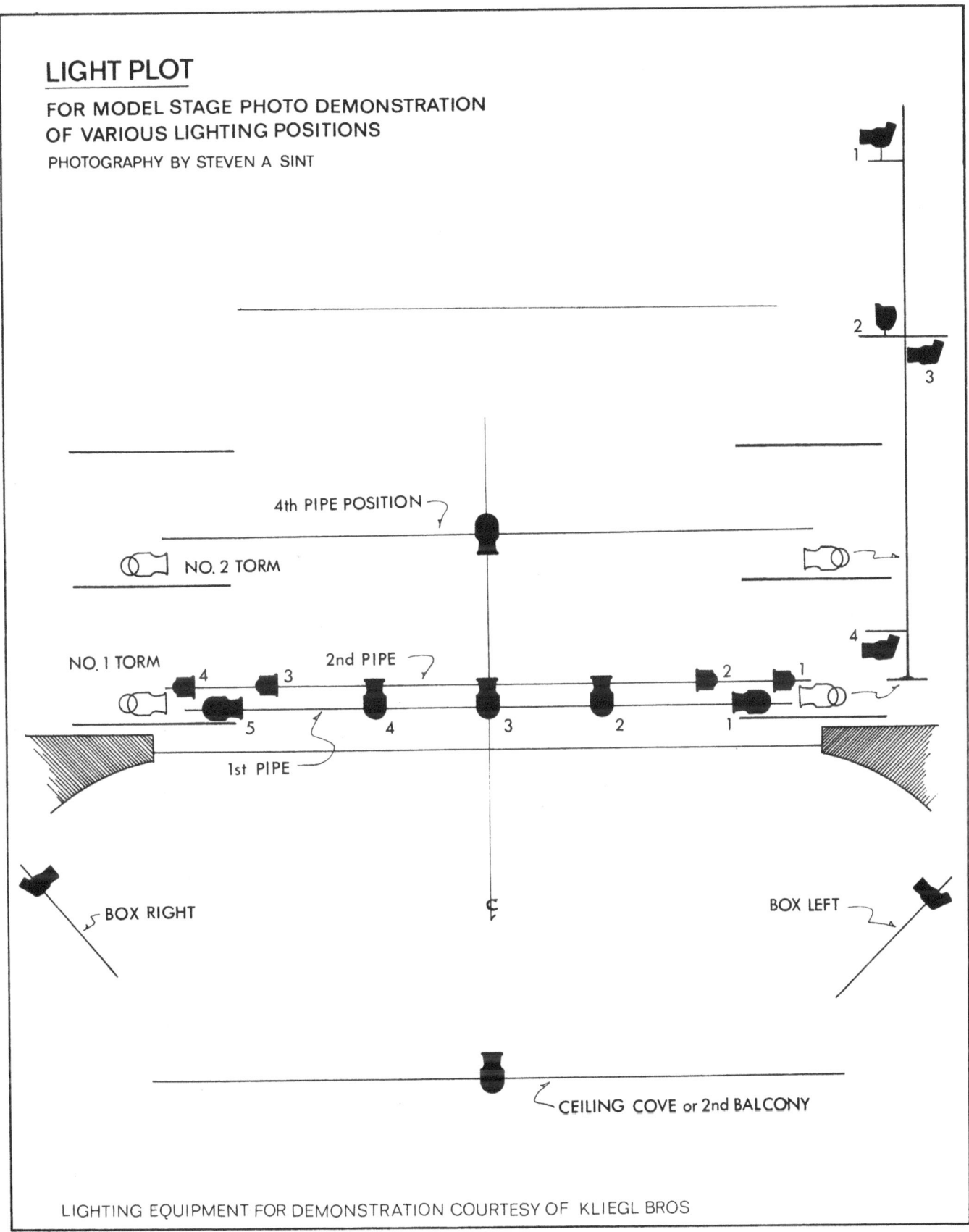

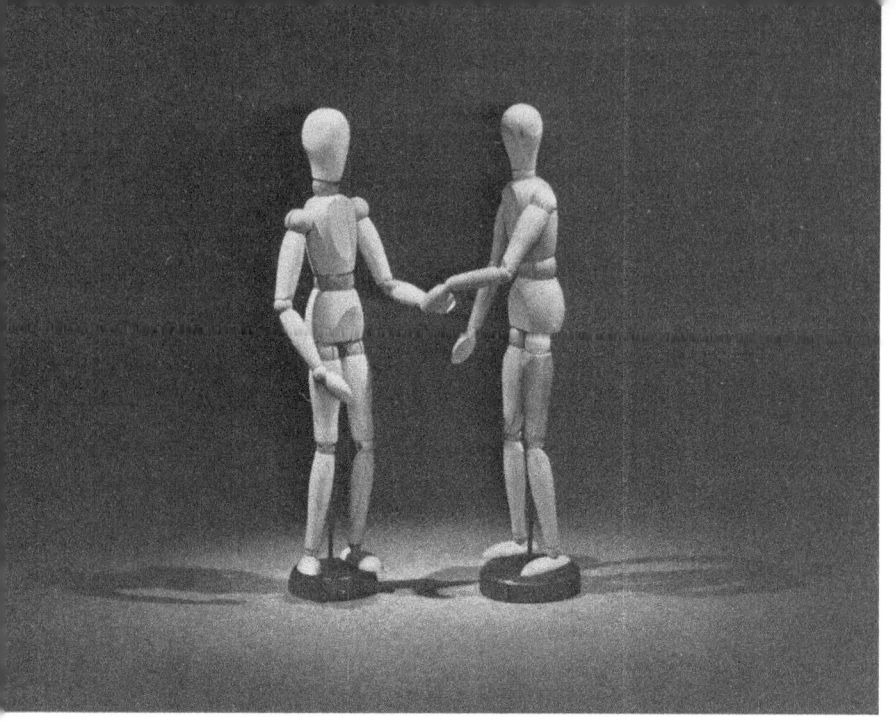

No. 2 pipe diagonal x-lights. Fresnel lamps no. 1 and no. 4 on a 45-degree angle cross-focus to center stage. Both lamps are on half focus.

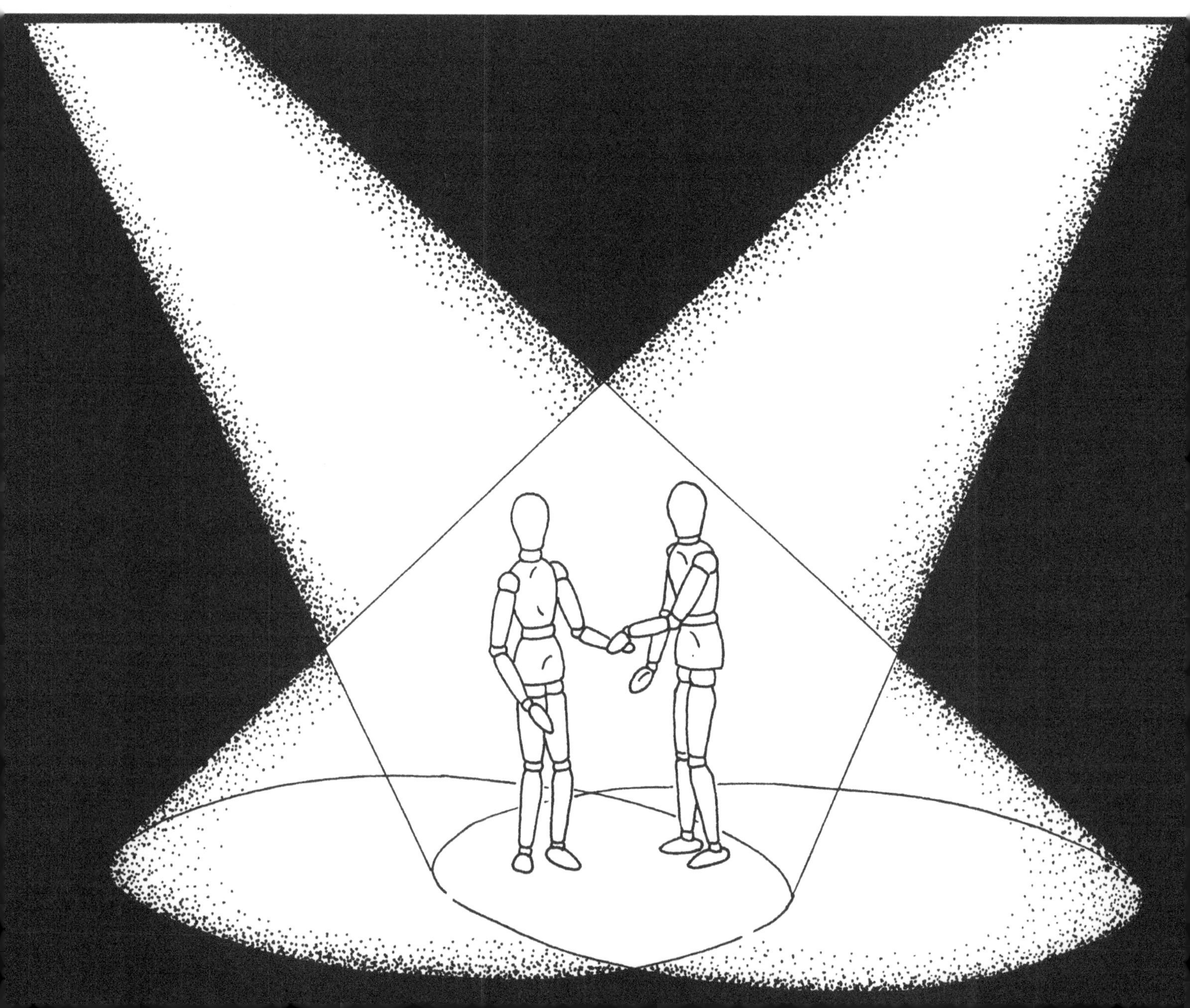

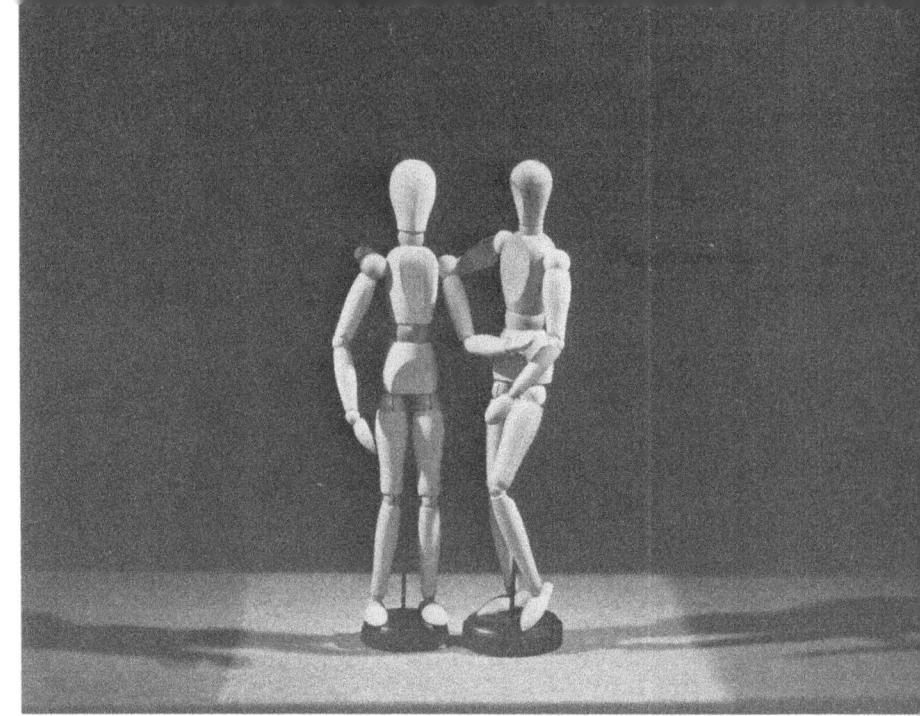

No. 1 pipe ends. Ellipsoidal lamps no. 1 and no. 5. Both are focused diagonally to center stage, and both are shuttered upstage and downstage to stay inside the first bay. The onstage, or bottom, edge of each light has been squared off on the shutters to keep the floor pattern tidy.

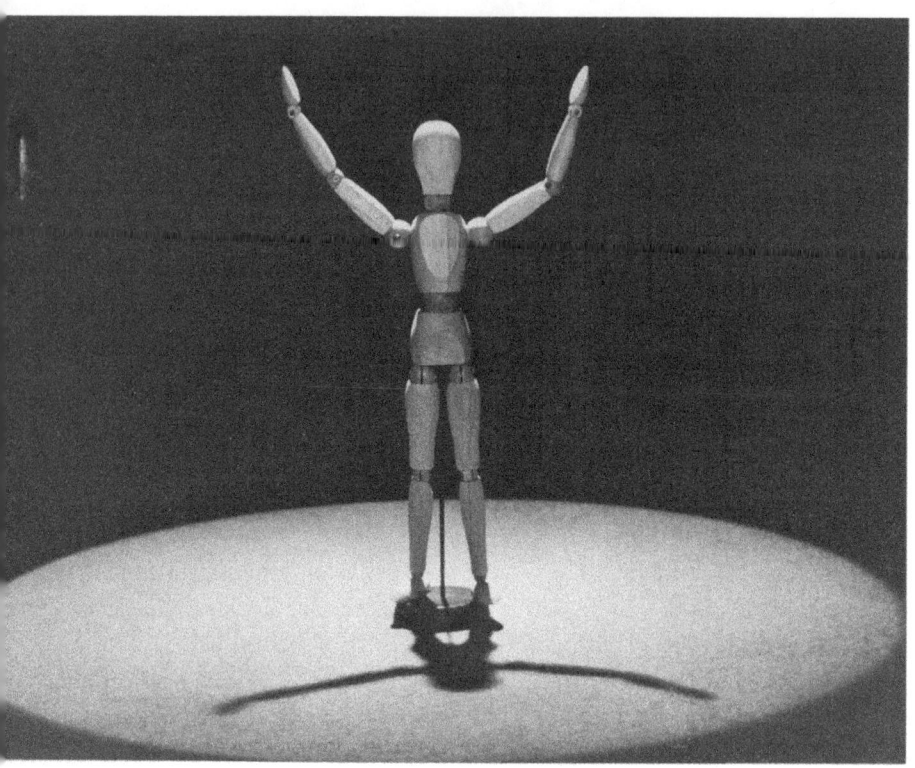

Backlight. ABOVE: ellipsoidal backlight from the no. 4 pipe center position, on sharp focus. BELOW: fresnel backlight, from the same no. 4 pipe center position, on half focus. RIGHT: a section showing the beam pattern of a fresnel from the no. 4 pipe center position, backlighting down center stage.

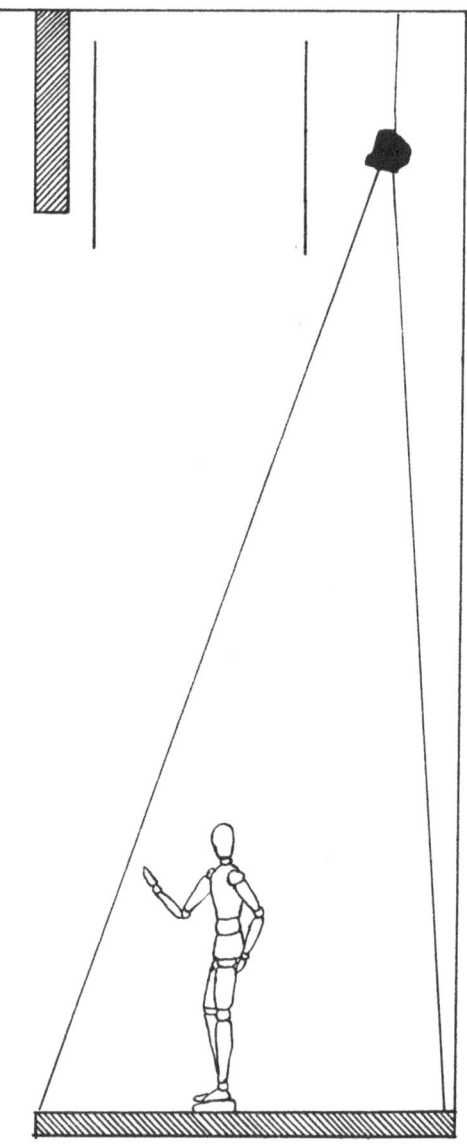

Combination showing no. 2 pipe fresnel x-lights and a no. 4 pipe fresnel backlight, all focused to downstage center, all on half focus (no. 2 pipe lamps no. 2 and no. 3, no. 4 pipe center position).

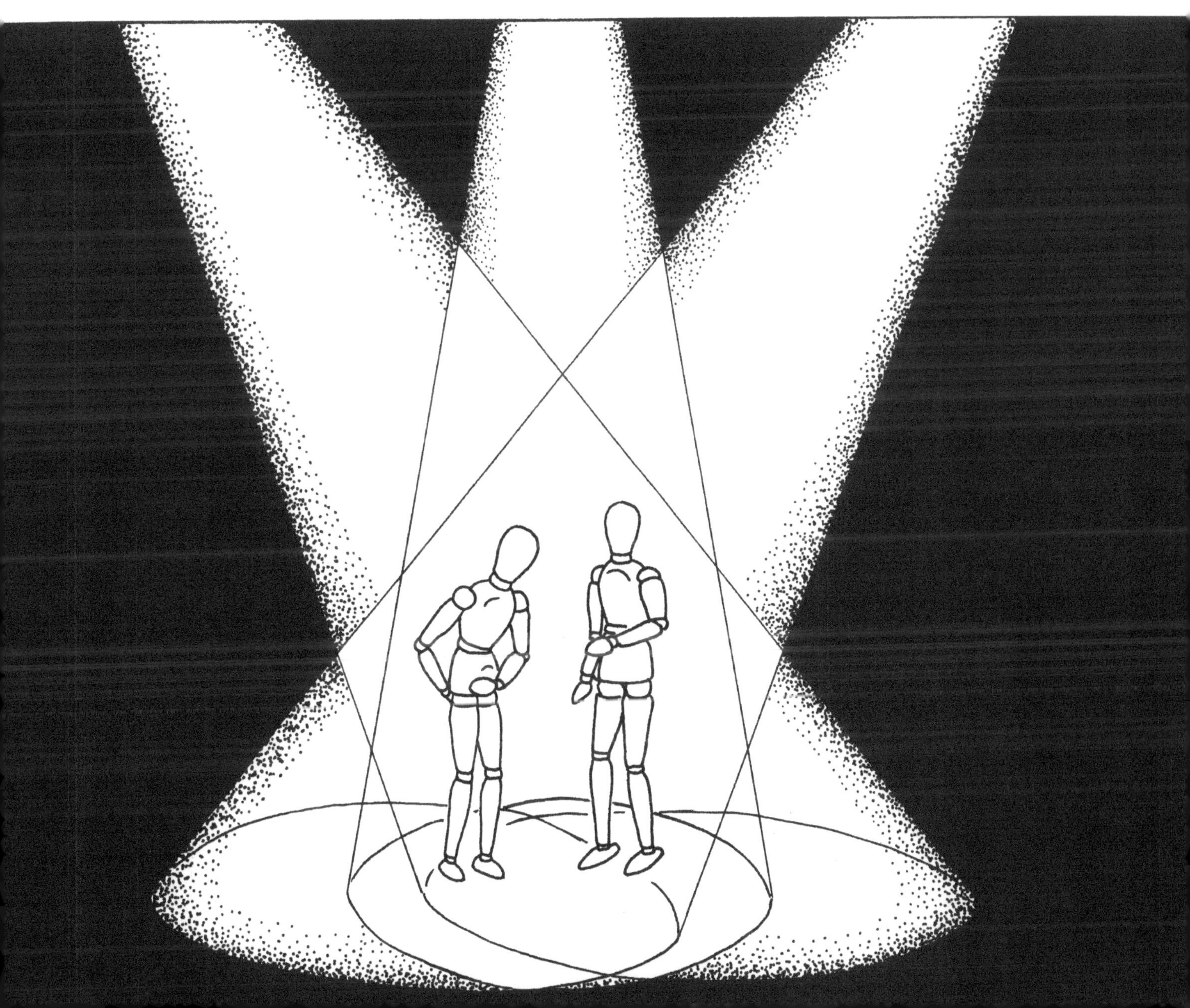

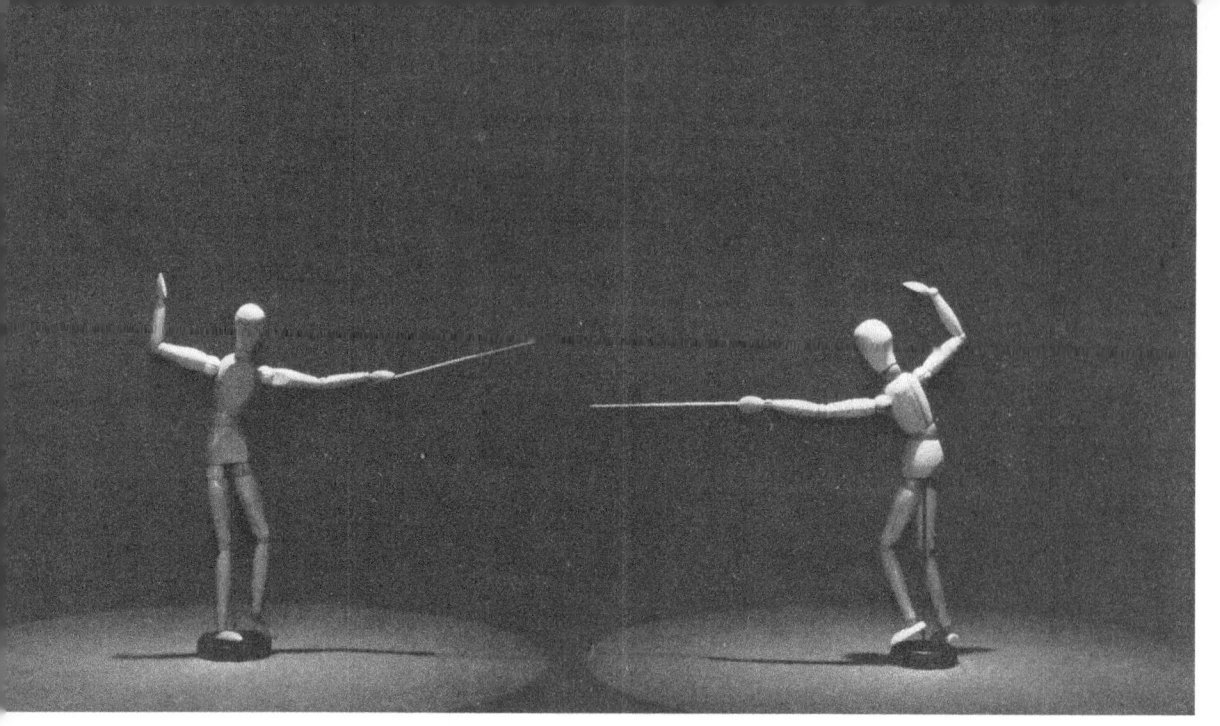

Downlights. No. 1 pipe ellipsoidal lamps no. 2 and no. 4. The focus is straight down and sharp. The downlight can be very dramatic but is not very good for faces.

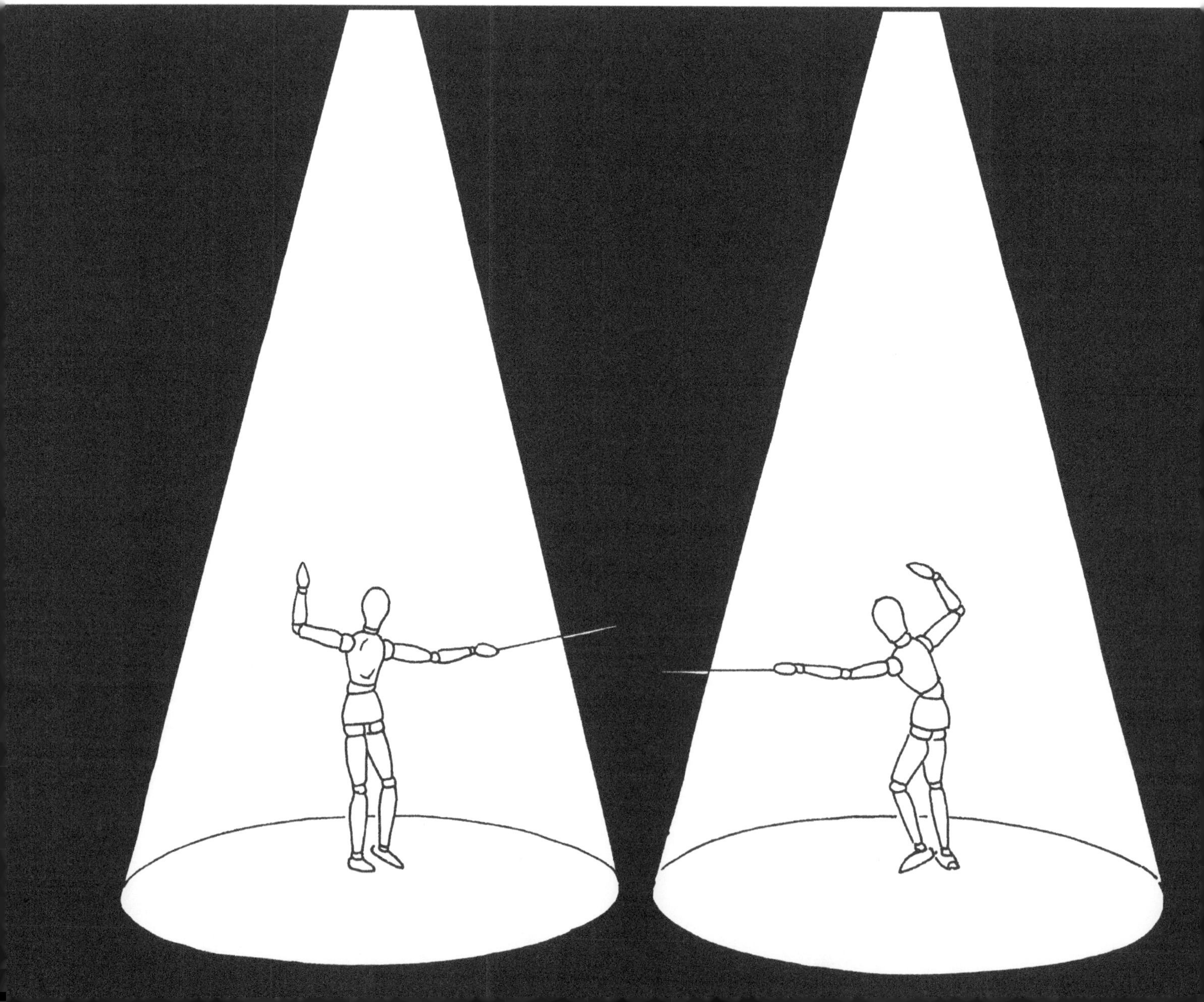

In order to show the comparison of control of the light beam in an ellipsoidal with the ambiant haze light of a fresnel, we have placed two figures on the stage. One figure is in the center of the light and the other is just outside the ring of light. Although the photograph exaggerates the situation a little, it tells the story clearly. In the top picture we have an ellipsoidal downlight on sharp focus, and we cannot see the second figure at all. In the bottom picture we have replaced the ellipsoidal with a fresnel, and the second figure has become visible in the ambiant haze of light, even though the fresnel is also on sharp focus. Both lamps are from the no. 1 pipe no. 3 position.

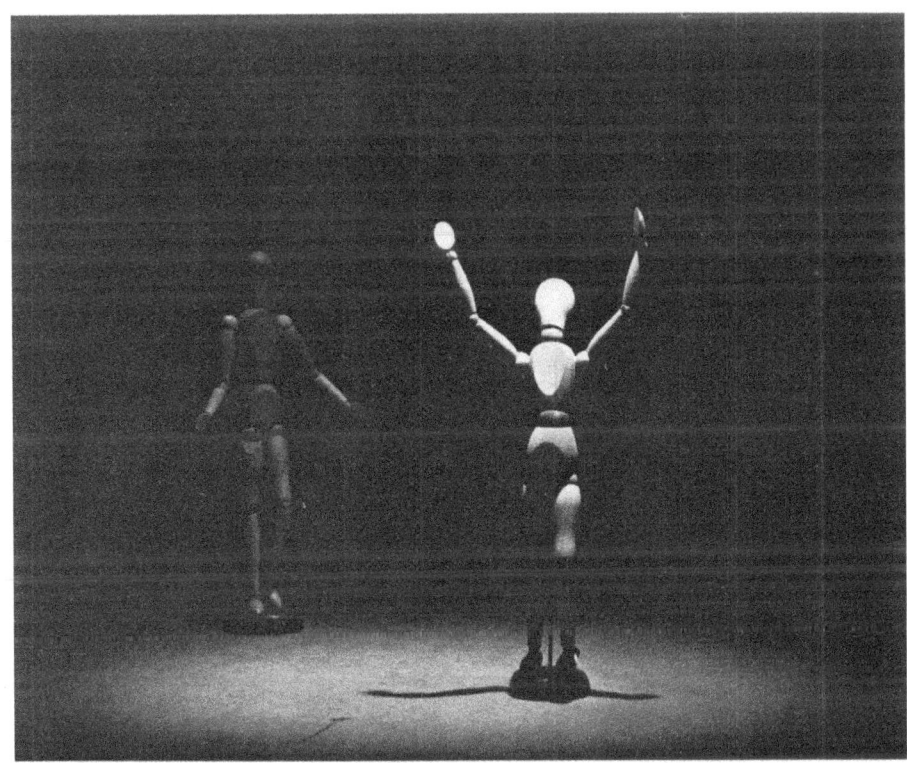

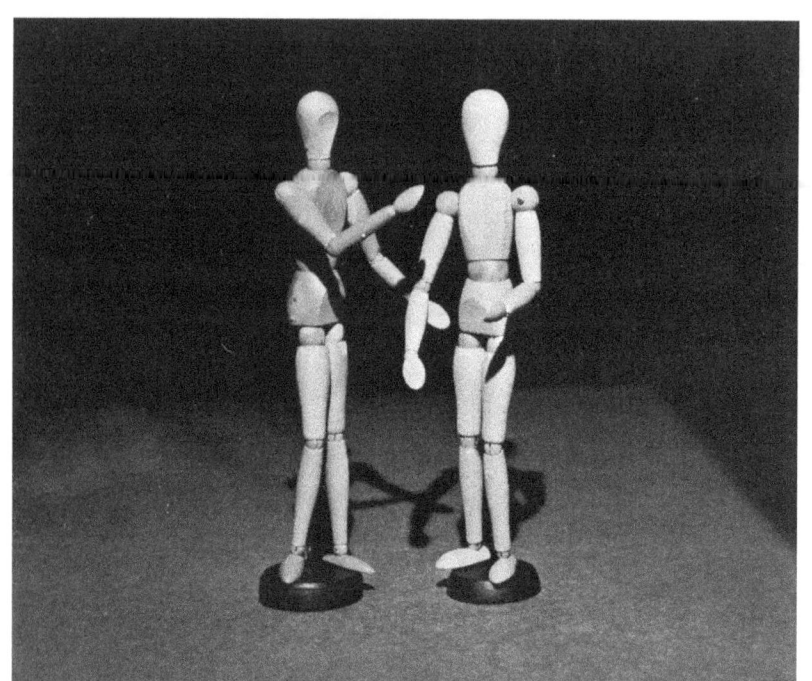

Frontlight. LEFT: An ellipsoidal from the ceiling cove, or second balcony, position, focused to downstage center. Upstage the shuttering is off the backdrop; downstage it is to the edge of the stage, and the sides are squared off for a cleaner floor pattern. By itself, this frontlight gives a very flat quality to the figure, even when x-focused, but it is good for seeing eyes in faces. BELOW: Section showing the beam pattern of the frontlight.

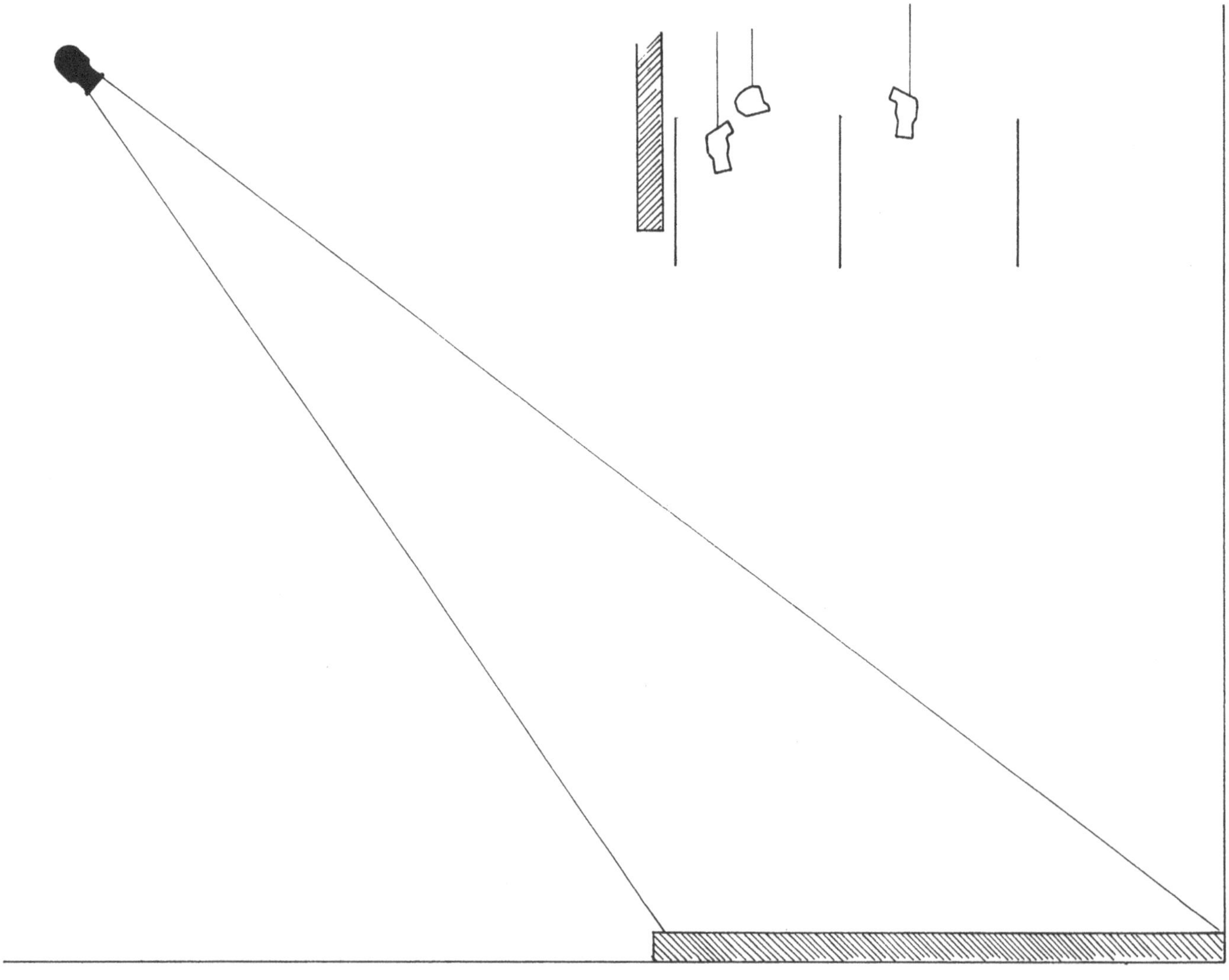

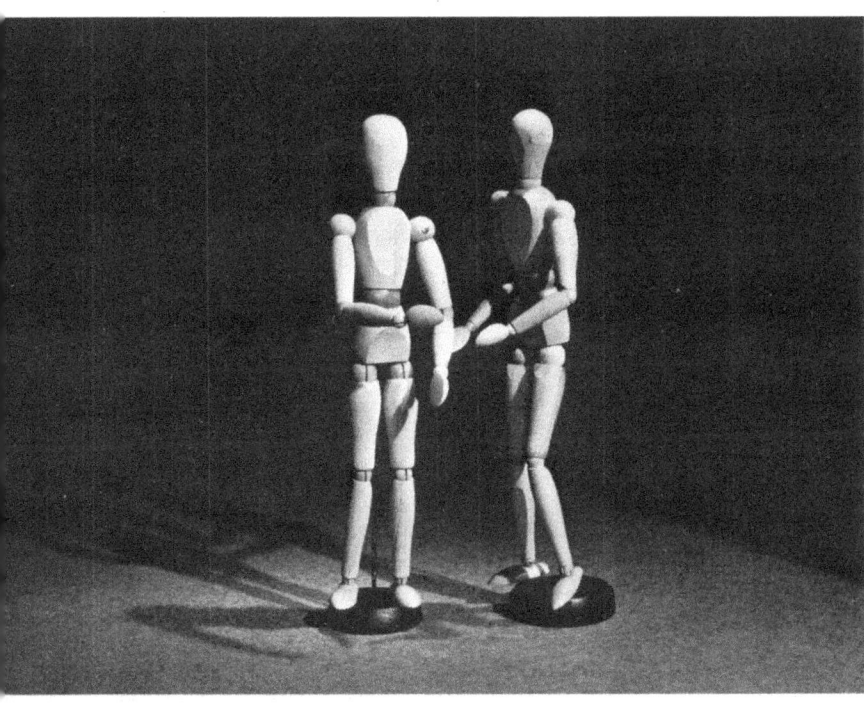

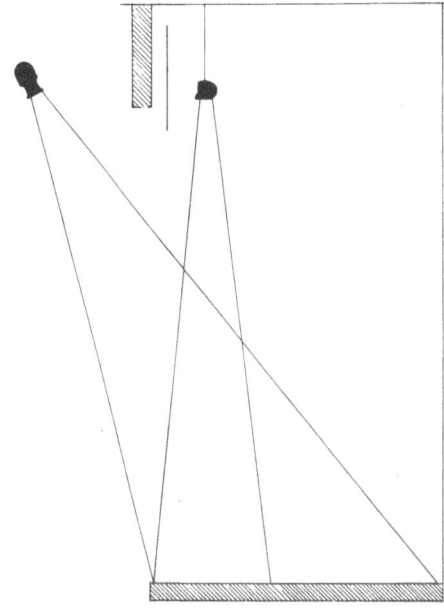

Box lights. ABOVE: an ellipsoidal from the box-left position combined with a no. 2 pipe fresnel (lamp no. 2) focused to downstage center. BELOW: an ellipsoidal from the box-right position. In the shuttering it has been cut off the right proscenium, the upstage drop, and the edge of the stage downstage, which would include staying off the proscenium on stage left. RIGHT: a section showing the beam patterns from the box-right ellipsoidal and the no. 2 pipe fresnel.

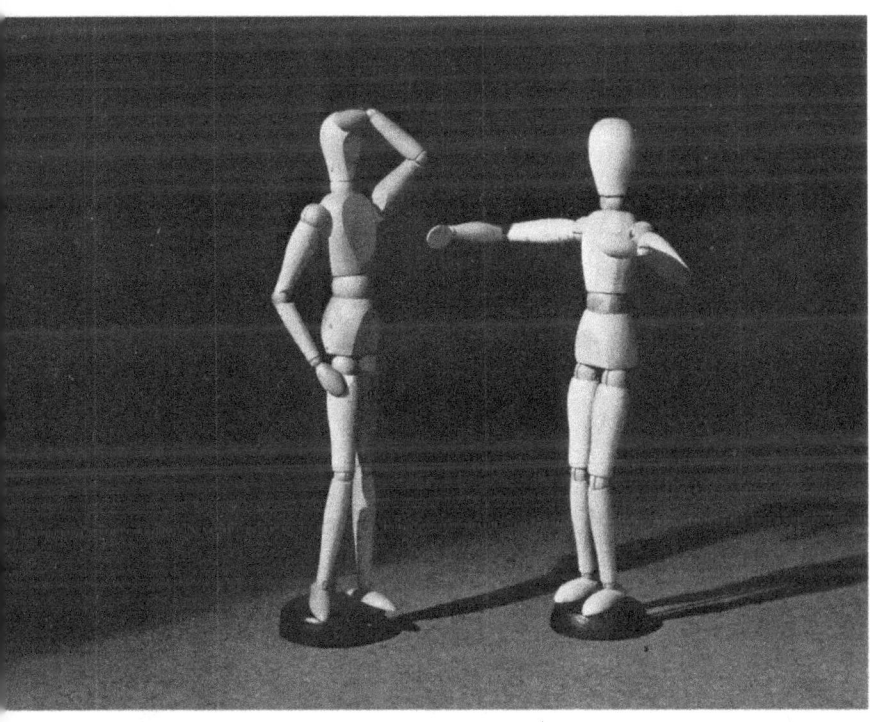

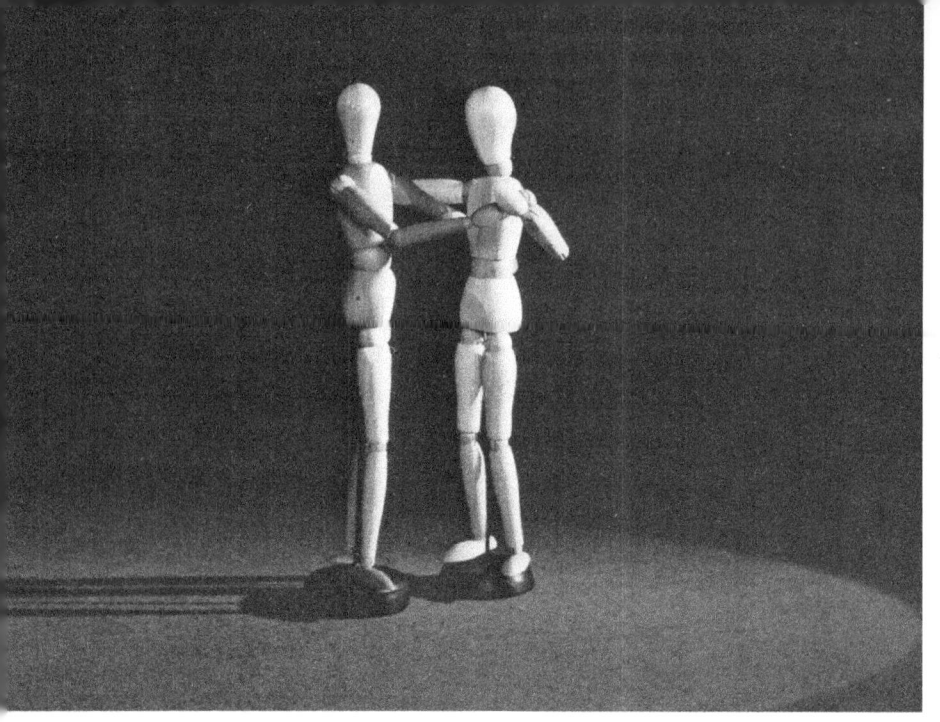

Torm x-light. No. 1 torm left, lamp no. 3. An ellipsoidal focused straight across, covering the stage for the figure from stage right to stage left, or full x-stage coverage.

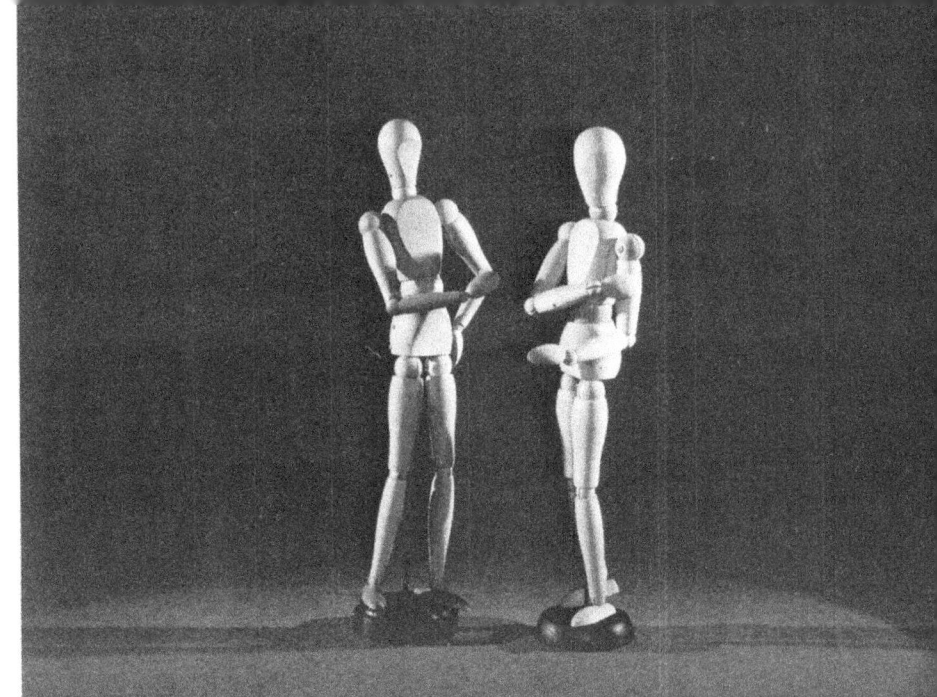

Torm x-light. From both no. 1 torm left, lamp no. 3, and no. 1 torm right, lamp no. 3. Both are focused for head high at center and give full x-stage coverage.

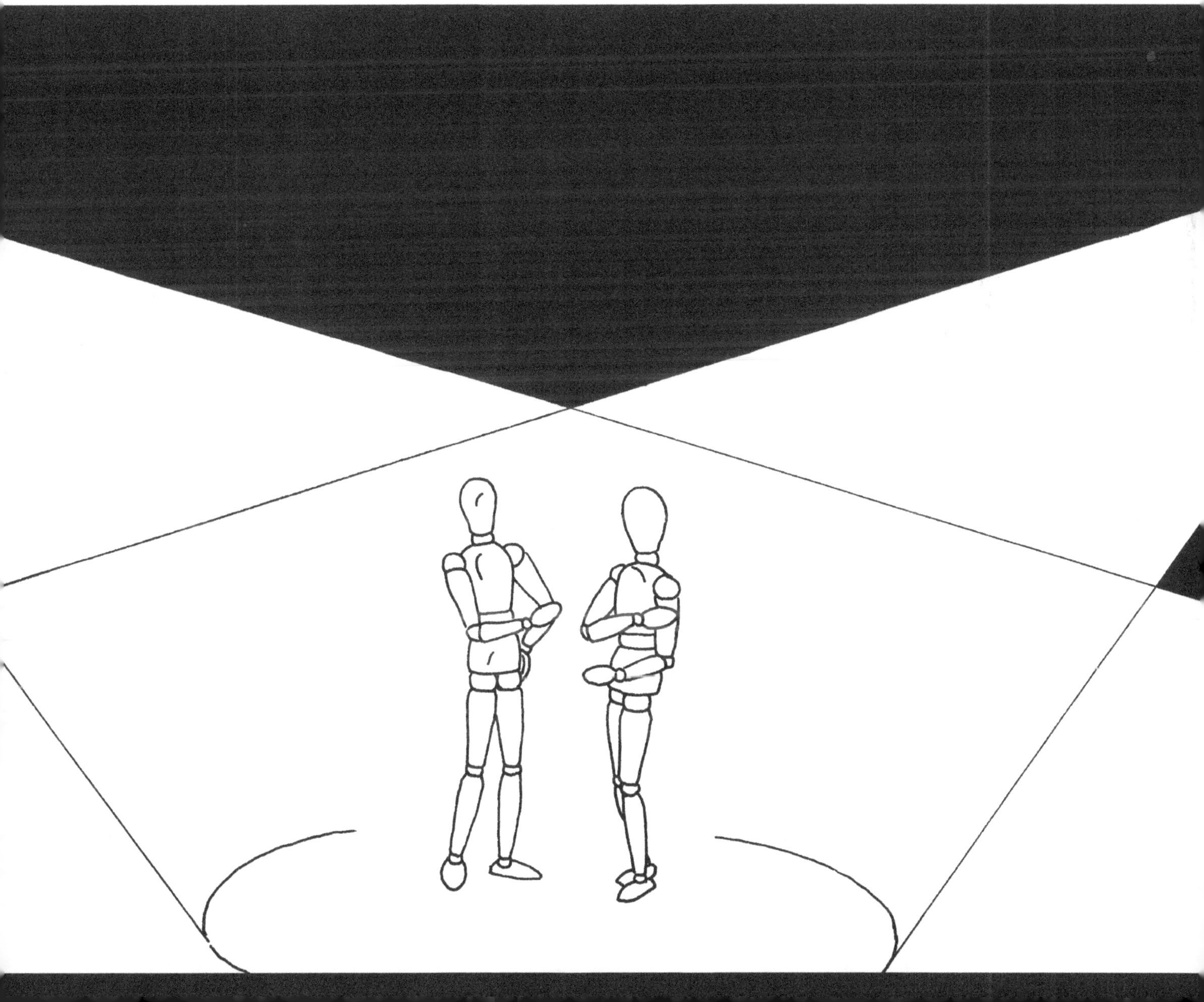

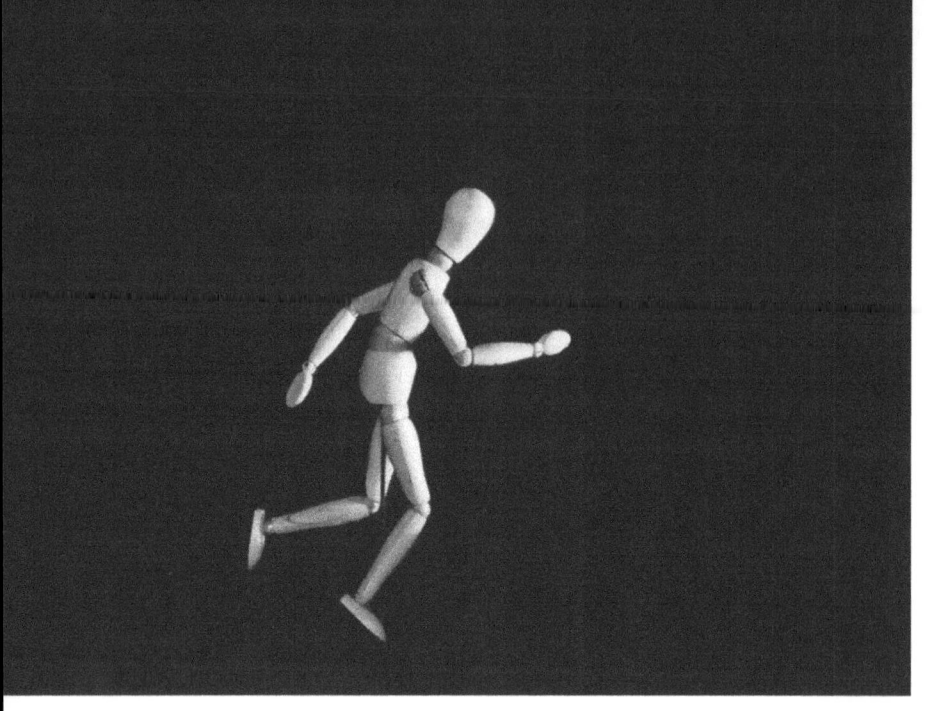

Low x-light, or the "shinbuster." No. 1 torm left, ellipsoidal lamp no. 4, focused straight across the stage and shuttered both upstage and downstage off the opposite, masking legs. It is also shuttered off the floor with the bottom of the light, making the beam invisible until someone moves into it.

Uplight. Ellipsoidals from the no. 1 torms left and right, lamps no. 4. They are focused to head high at center stage. There is no shuttering upstage, and the light has not been shuttered off the floor. The only cuts are off the downstage masking legs (wings) opposite each lamp.

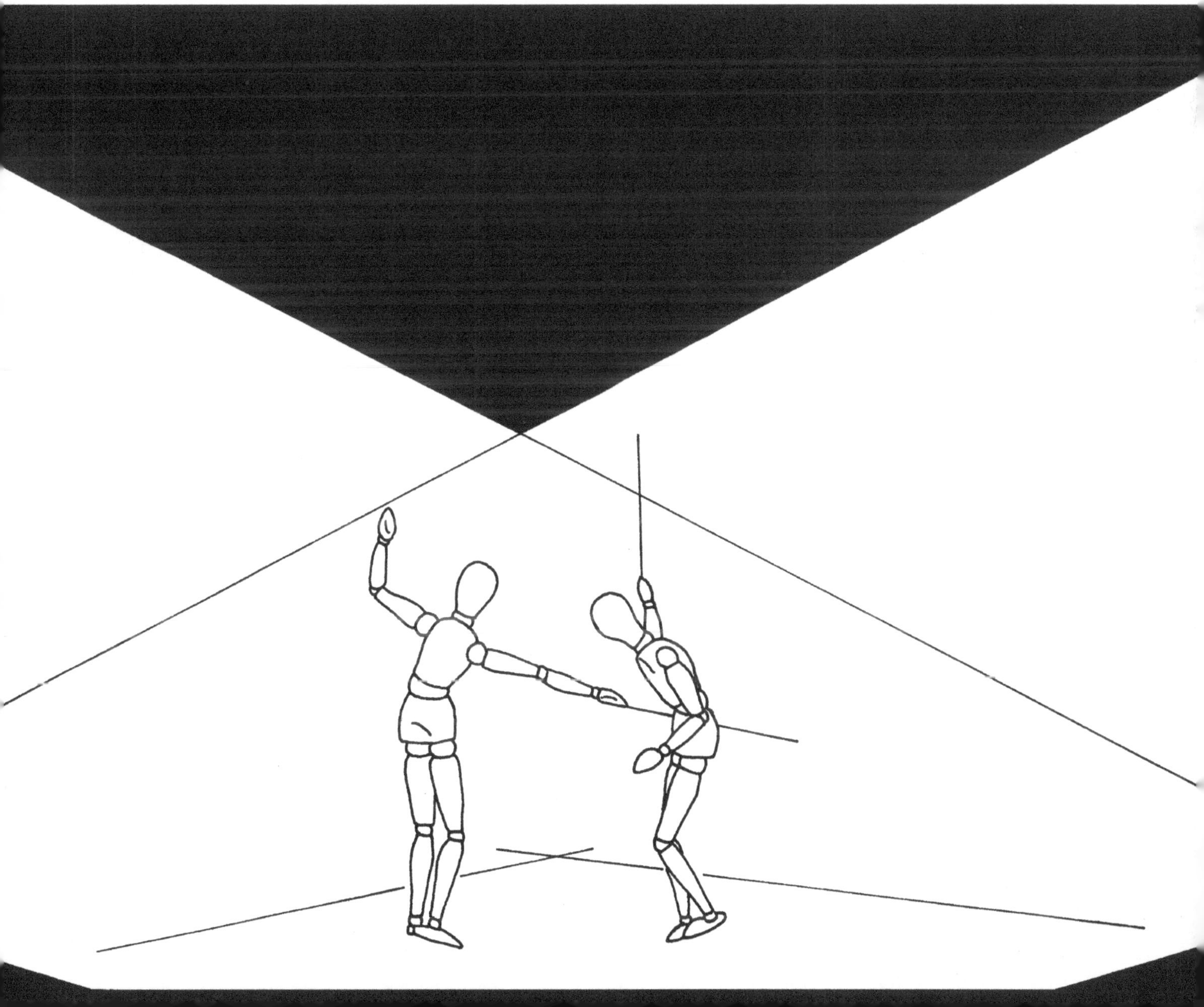

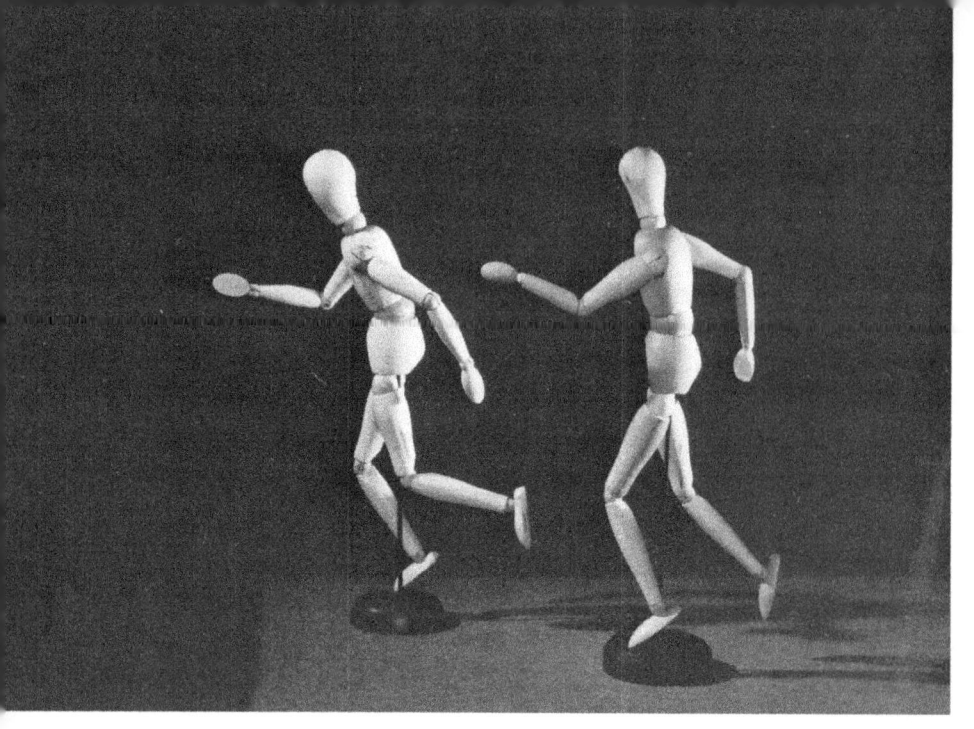

A combination of uplight from no. 1 torm left no. 4 ellipsoidal and a high torm x-light from no. 1 torm right no. 1 ellipsoidal. The high torm lamp is shuttered off both the upstage and downstage masking legs. The stage right, or onstage, edge of the light has been shuttered to square off the pattern as we see it on the floor.

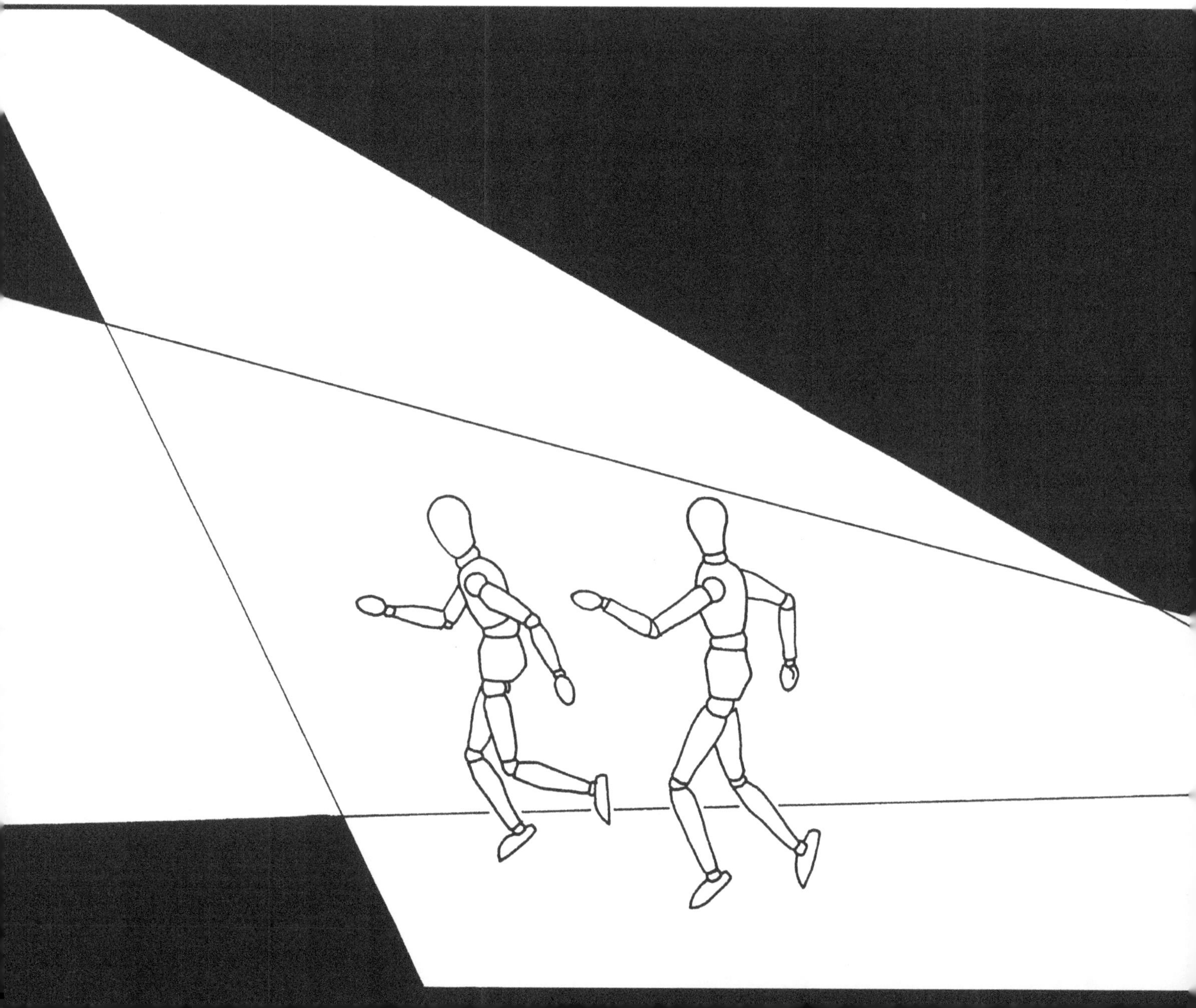

High torm diagonals. Ellipsoidals in the first and second bays stage left, no. 1 torm left no. 1 ellipsoidal and no. 2 torm left no. 1 ellipsoidal. Focus is to center and covers the figure from left to center stage. BELOW: light beams of ellipsoidals as shown in ground plan.

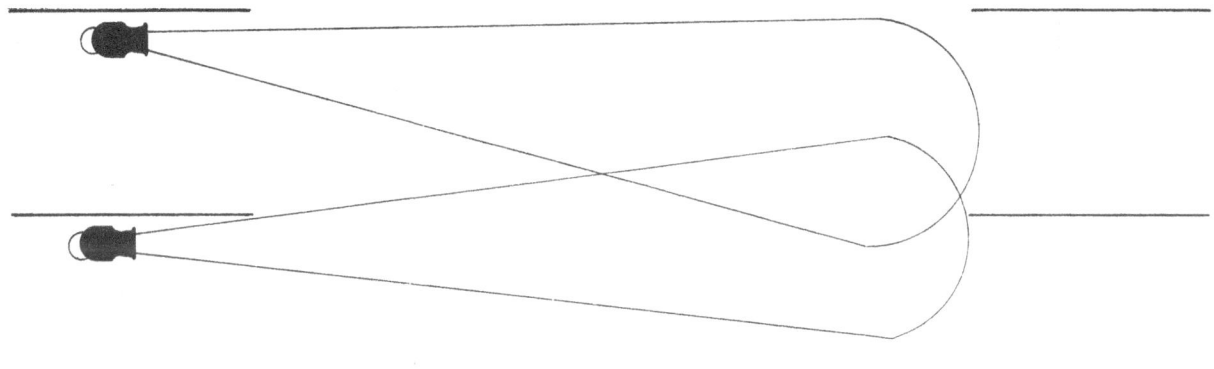

RIGHT: To the high torm diagonal ellipsoidals we add a midtorm fresnel x-light in the first bay, no. 1 torm left no. 2 fresnel. The addition of the fresnel in the first bay gives more distance and separation to the two figures. The fresnel is focused straight across for full x-stage coverage in the first bay.

Combination: no. 1 torm left no. 3 ellipsoidal, no. 1 torm right no. 3 ellipsoidal. Ellipsoidal x-light. No. 2 pipe no. 1 and no. 4 fresnels. All are focused to center stage. (See pages 142 and 151.)

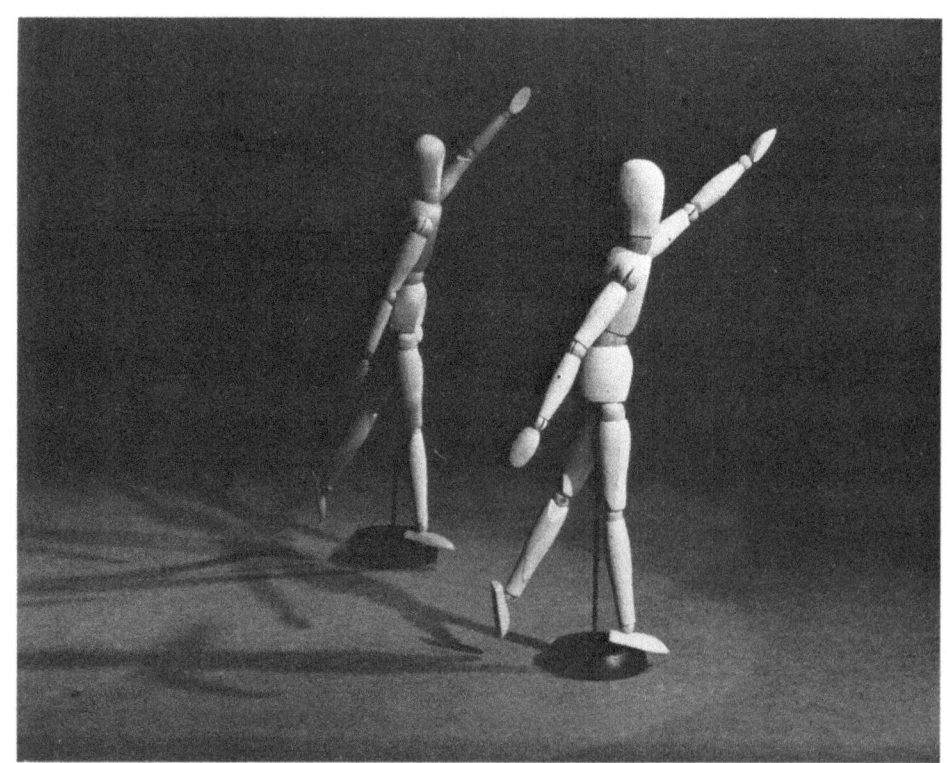

No. 1 torm, left, no. 1 ellipsoidal and no. 2 fresnel. No. 2 torm left no. 1 ellipsoidal. Box boom left, ellipsoidal. All focused to same area. (See pages 149 and 155.)

Combination of the center ceiling cove ellipsoidal with the no. 2 pipe no. 1 fresnel. The frontlight by itself is flat, but by adding the no. 2 pipe end x-light we begin to achieve a little modeling on the figures.

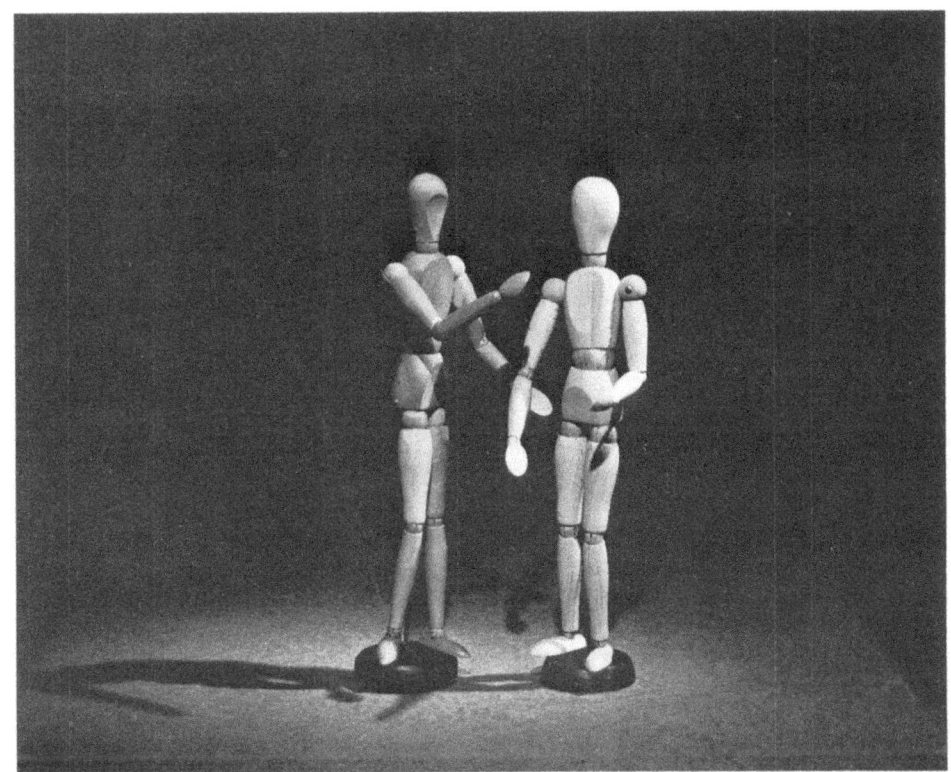

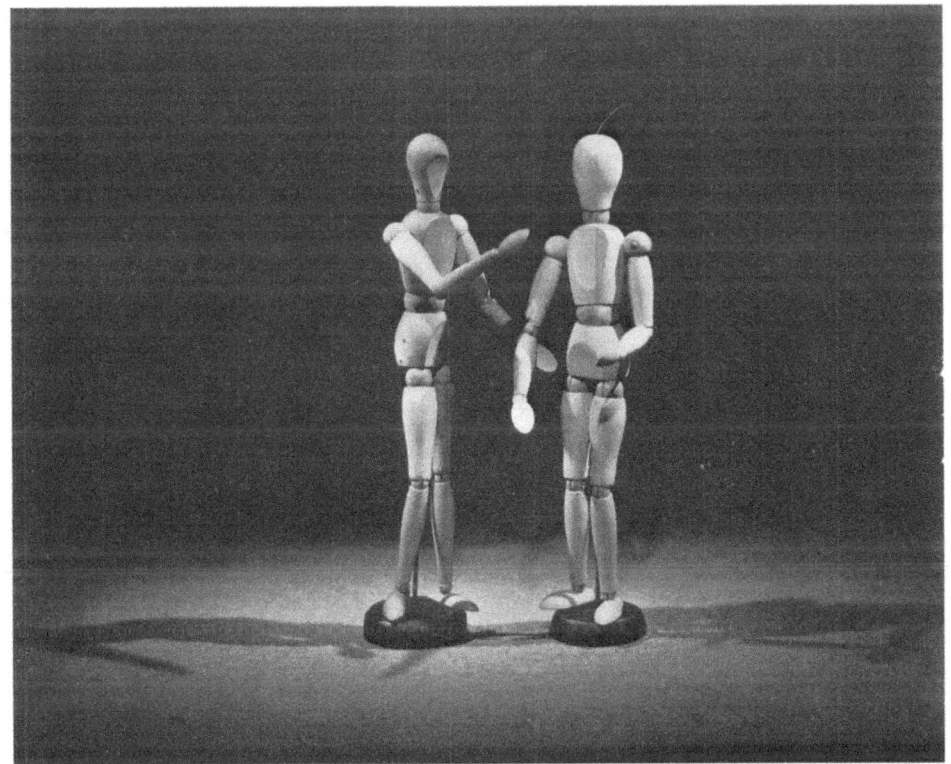

Now by adding the no. 2 pipe fresnels from both ends of the pipe (lamps no. 1 and no. 4) and taking a lower-intensity reading on the frontlight, we still have good "face" light from the front but better modeling. (See pages 142 and 148.)

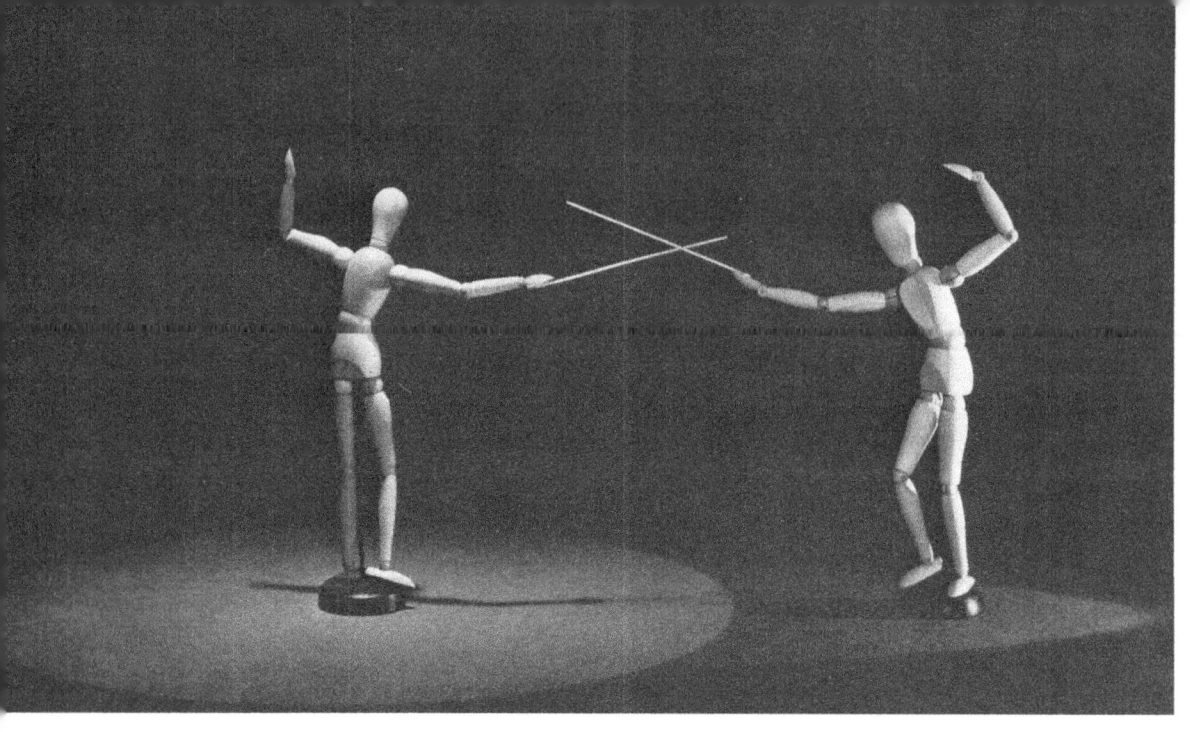

Combination. No. 1 torm left, ellipsoidal no. 4 as an uplight, hitting the back of the figure on stage left; no. 1 pipe ellipsoidal no. 3 as a downlight on the figure on stage right.

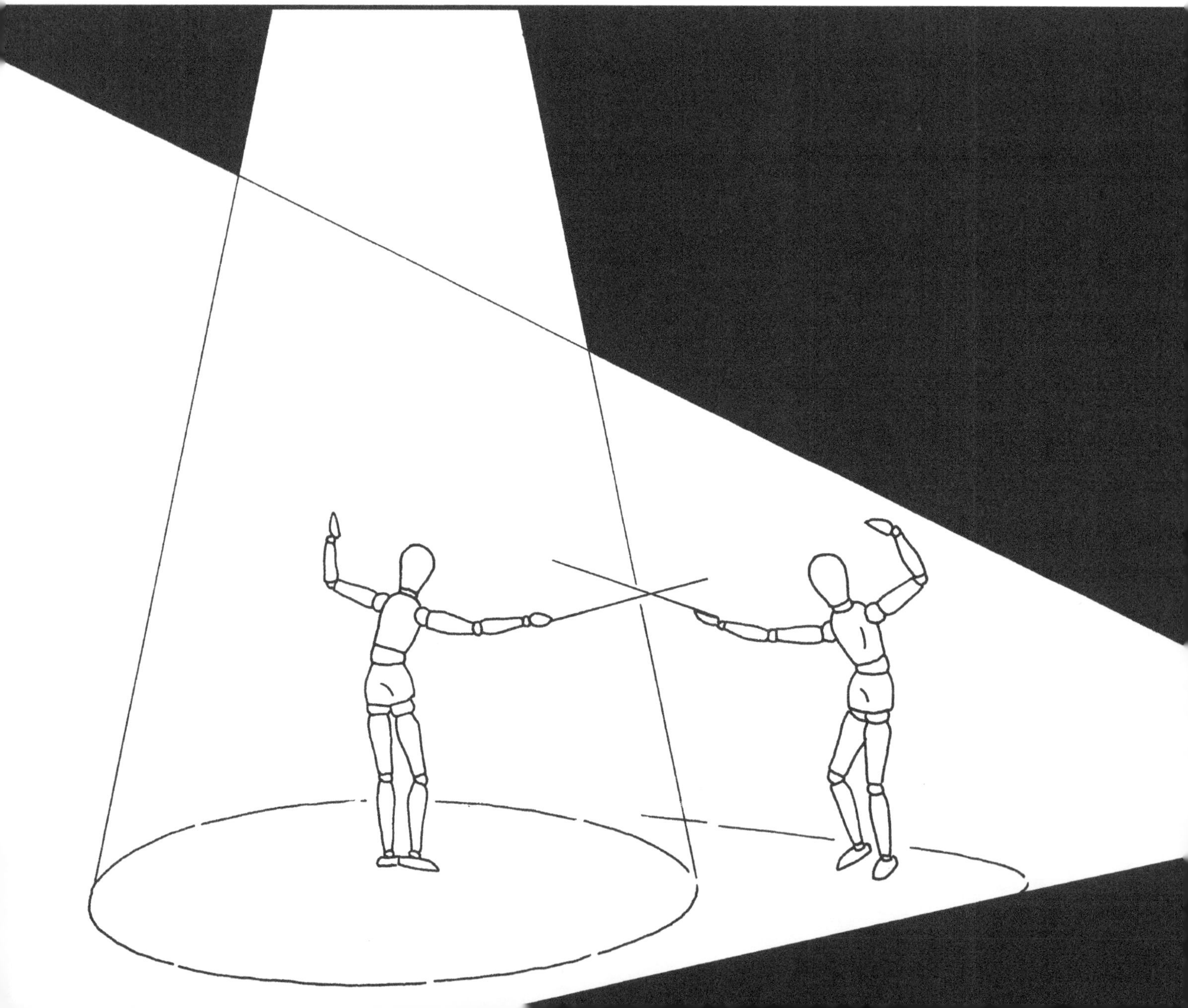

Hookup, Lighting Designer's Cue Sheets, Scene Designer's Elevation and Light Plot for "Plaza Suite"

The choice of *Plaza Suite* for examples of a hookup, cue sheet, elevation and light plot is a logical one because it gives us three different plays or situations taking place at three different times in the same location. What I have chosen to show you is the *introduction* lighting for each of the three plays — that is, the atmosphere which will start the players off on their three separate adventures.

The hookup (pages 161-166) shows which lights are connected to which dimmers. In the left-hand column are the switch numbers which correspond to the master dimmer and/or auxiliary numbers shown on the cue sheets (pages 167-170). To the right of the switch numbers are indicated the position of the lamps and the individual units which are connected to that switch, the type of lights, a general focus note, and the color medium used.

The lighting designer's cue sheet is not like the electrician's or the stage manager's. It is laid out to show what is moving in every cue, where the cue happens, and how many seconds it should take to happen. In the left-hand column are the master dimmers and their readings. *Plaza Suite*, like most Broadway shows of this time, is laid out on resistance dimmer boards, or "piano boards." The readings on intensity are the opposite of most of the more sophisticated control boards, with 3 being the higher-intensity reading and 7 being the lower-intensity.

In the right-hand column are the auxiliaries and their readings. These are preset on the masters working in the left-hand column. For instance, in Act I (page 167), master 48 controls auxiliaries 481, 483, 485, 486. Thus, when the electrician presets master 48 to full to begin the show, it will automatically bring the four auxiliaries to a reading of 5. If the master is already up or set when a cue requiring the use of an auxiliary occurs, however, then the auxiliary must be operated manually, and it is thus listed in the left-hand column with the masters. For example, in cue 3 (page 168), when the bellboy turns on the bath lights, auxiliaries 487 and 489 must be operated manually since their controlling master, 48, is already at full. The circled numbers in the cue columns are the number of seconds the cue should take to occur. What is not shown on these sheets is a "track" column, which is added on the extreme right after an accumulation of several cues, indicating what is riding in that cue from previous cues. In that way, the designer knows exactly what should be on in any given cue, as well as what is moving in the cue.

The scene designer's elevation gives a head-on view of the set, and the light plot shows where all the lights are located in the theatre. By referring to these four different charts, an idea may be formed as to what has been accomplished in the different setups for each act in terms of where the emphasis has been placed and whether it is a warm or cool or neutral scene at the top. If you can then "see" each scene, you will also see the logic of the tools of the trade and the importance of the implied discipline. In themselves these tools are not mysterious; properly controlled they can produce magic.

"PLAZA SUITE" 1968

NO. 1 BOARD HOOKUP   14 PLATE   15/3000W SWITCHBOARD

SWITCH	POSITION & UNIT NUMBER	TYPE	FOCUS NOTE	COLOR
1	BALCONY RAIL 26-30-31-36	6"X12" 750W LEKO	RIGHT	CLEAR
2	BALCONY RAIL 7-8-40-41	6"X12" 750W LEKO	RIGHT CENTER	CLEAR
3	BALCONY RAIL 22-24-28	6"X12" 750W LEKO	UP RIGHT	CLEAR
4	BALCONY RAIL 20-25-27-32	6"X12" 750W LEKO	SOFA	CLEAR
5	BALCONY RAIL 37-38-39	6"X12" 750W LEKO	X-RIGHT COOL	849
6	BOX LEFT 2-4 BOX RIGHT 1-3	6"X12" 750W LEKO	RIGHT WARM	805
7	BOX LEFT 5-6 BOX RIGHT 5-6	6"X12" 750W LEKO	CENTER WARM	805
8	BOX RIGHT 7-8	6"X12" 750W LEKO	X-SOFA	510/549
9	NO. 1 TORM RIGHT 1-5-9	6"X12" 750W LEKO	COOL X-LIGHT RIGHT TO LEFT	849
10	NO. 1 TORM RIGHT 3-7-11	6"X12" 750W LEKO	WARM X-LIGHT RIGHT TO LEFT	552
11	NO. 1 TORM RIGHT 2-6-10	6" 750W FRESNEL	WARM FAN RIGHT	552
12	NO. 1 TORM RIGHT 4-8	6" 750W FRESNEL	COOL FAN RIGHT	849
13	BALCONY RAIL 29-33	6"X12" 750W LEKO	FRONT DOOR	CLEAR
14	FOOTLIGHTS	2-50W, R20 FLOOD LAMPS PER COMPARTMENT	3 COLOR RE-PLUG	825/1 856/1 FROST

"PLAZA SUITE" 1968 (2)

NO. 2 BOARD HOOKUP   14 PLATE 15/3000W SWITCHBOARD

SWITCH	POSITION & UNIT NUMBER	TYPE	FOCUS NOTE	COLOR
15	BALCONY RAIL 6-11-15-17	6"x12" 750W LEKO	LEFT	CLEAR
16	BALCONY RAIL 12-34-35	6"x12" 750W LEKO	LEFT CENTER	CLEAR
17	BALCONY RAIL 14-19-21	6"x12" 750W LEKO	UP LEFT	CLEAR
18	BALCONY RAIL 10-13-16	6"x12" 750W LEKO	BED	552
19	BALCONY RAIL 3-4-5	6"x12" 750W LEKO	X-LEFT WARM	805
20	BOX LEFT 1-3 BOX RIGHT 2-4	6"x12" 750W LEKO	LEFT WARM	805
21	BOX LEFT 7-8	6"x12" 750W LEKO	BED	510/549
22	BOX LEFT 9-10 BOX RIGHT 9-10	6"x12" 750W LEKO	"GLITTER"	510
23	NO. 1 TORM LEFT 12 NO. 1 TORM RIGHT 12	6" 750W FRESNEL	"GLITTER"	536
24	NO. 1 TORM LEFT 1-5-9	6"x12" 750W LEKO	COOL X-LIGHT LEFT TO RIGHT	849
25	NO. 1 TORM LEFT 3-7-11	6"x12" 750W LEKO	WARM X-LIGHT LEFT TO RIGHT	552
26	NO. 1 TORM LEFT 2-6-10	6" 750W FRESNEL	WARM FAN LEFT	552
27	NO. 1 TORM LEFT 4-8	6" 750W FRESNEL	COOL FAN LEFT	849
28	AUXILIARY MASTER 281-284	—	—	—

__HOT POCKET__: AUXILIARY 101-102-103-104

"PLAZA SUITE"   1968

NO. 3 BOARD HOOK UP   14 PLATE 15/3000W SWITCHBOARD

SWITCH	POSITION & UNIT NUMBER	TYPE	FOCUS NOTE	COLOR
29	1ST PIPE 15-17-19-21	6" 750W FRESNEL	ALCOVE	552
30	1ST PIPE 13-16-18-22	6" 750W FRESNEL	UP RIGHT	552
31	1ST PIPE 12-14-20-23	6" 750W FRESNEL	"COLORS" RIGHT	510
32	2ND PIPE 11-12-23-24	6"x12" 750W LEKO	RIGHT	CLEAR
33	2ND PIPE 15-16-21-22	6" 750W FRESNEL	SOFA	CLEAR
34	AUXILIARY MASTER, 341-344	—	—	—
35	2ND PIPE 5-6-19-20	6"x12" 750W LEKO	CENTER	CLEAR
36	2ND PIPE 1-2-13-14	6"x12" 750W LEKO	LEFT	CLEAR
37	1ST PIPE 5-7-9-11	6" 750W FRESNEL	UP LEFT	552
38	1ST PIPE 2-4-6	6" 750W FRESNEL	BED	552
39	2ND PIPE 3-4-9-10	6" 750W FRESNEL	BED	CLEAR
40	1ST PIPE 1-3-8-10	6" 750W FRESNEL	"COLORS" LEFT	536
41	AUXILIARY MASTER 411-414	—	—	—
42	NO. 2 TORM LEFT 4-5-6-7	6"x12" 750W LEKO	BATHROOM WINDOWS	CLEAR

④

"PLAZA SUITE" 1968

NO. 4 BOARD HOOKUP   12 PLATE 5/6000W SWITCHBOARD

SWITCH	POSITION & UNIT NUMBER	TYPE	FOCUS NOTE	COLOR
43	3RD PIPE 1-4-7-10-13	10" 750W BEAM PROJ.	SUN	805
44	3RD PIPE 2-5-8-11-14	10" 750W BEAM PROJ.	COOL	849
45	3RD PIPE 3-6-9-12-15	10" 750W BEAM PROJ.	AIR	CLEAR
46	NO. 2 TORM RIGHT 5-7-9-11 NO. 3 TORM LEFT 3-4-7-8	10" 750W BEAM PROJ.	SUNSET	510/549
47	NO. 2 TORM RIGHT 4-6-8-10 NO. 3 TORM LEFT 1-2-5-6	6"x12" 750W LEKO	COOL	849/1
48	AUXILIARY MASTER 481-492	—	—	—
49	4th PIPE X-RAY NO. 2 TORM LEFT 1, NO. 2 TORM RIGHT 1	300W R-40 FLOOD 16" 1000W SCOOP	BACKDROP WHITE	FROST
50	4th PIPE X-RAY NO. 2 TORM LEFT 2, NO. 2 TORM RIGHT 2	300W R-40 FLOOD 16" 1000W SCOOP	BACKDROP LIGHT BLUE	849 849/1
51	4th PIPE X-RAY NO. 2 TORM LEFT 3, NO. 2 TORM RIGHT 3	300W R-40 FLOOD 16" 1000W SCOOP	BACKDROP DARK BLUE	857 857/1
52	GROUND ROW	300W QUARTZ FROSTED	BACKDROP WHITE	FROST DIFUSER
53	GROUND ROW	300W QUARTZ FROSTED	BACKDROP ORANGE	505
54	GROUND ROW	300W QUARTZ FROSTED	BACKDROP GREEN	521

"PLAZA SUITE" 1968

⑤

MASTER 28 4 PLATE · 750W AUXILIARY BOARD (8 PLATE)

SWITCH	POSITION & UNIT NUMBER	TYPE	FOCUS NOTE	COLOR
281	BALCONY RAIL 9	6"x12" 750W LEKO	BATHROOM DOOR	CLEAR
282	BALCONY RAIL 12	6"x12" 750W LEKO	BATHROOM DOOR	CLEAR
283	BALCONY RAIL 18	6"x12" 750W LEKO	CLOSET	CLEAR
284	BALCONY RAIL 23	6"x12" 750W LEKO	CLOSET	CLEAR

#2 BOARD HOT POCKET 4 PLATE · 750W AUXILIARY BOARD (8 PLATE)

SWITCH	POSITION & UNIT NUMBER	TYPE	FOCUS NOTE	COLOR
101	2ND PIPE 7	6" 750W FRES.	"COLORS"	510
102	2ND PIPE 8	6" 750W FRES.	"COLORS"	536
103	2ND PIPE 17	6" 750W FRES.	"COLORS"	536
104	2ND PIPE 18	6" 750W FRES.	"COLORS"	510

MASTER 34 4 PLATE · 750W AUXILIARY BOARD (8 PLATE)

SWITCH	POSITION & UNIT NUMBER	TYPE	FOCUS NOTE	COLOR
341	1A PIPE 5	6"x12" 750W LEKO	UP RIGHT CENTER	CLEAR
342	1A PIPE 6	6"x12" 750W LEKO	ALCOVE	CLEAR
343	1A PIPE 7	6"x12" 750W LEKO	ALCOVE	CLEAR
344	1A PIPE 8	6"x12" 750W LEKO	ENTRY DOOR	CLEAR

MASTER 41

SWITCH	POSITION & UNIT NUMBER	TYPE	FOCUS NOTE	COLOR
411	1A PIPE 1	6"x12" 750W LEKO	BATHROOM DOOR	CLEAR
412	1A PIPE 2	6"x12" 750W LEKO	BED	CLEAR
413	1A PIPE 3	6"x12" 750W LEKO	CLOSET	CLEAR
414	1A PIPE 4	6"x12" 750W LEKO	WINDOW	CLEAR

"PLAZA SUITE"   1968

MASTER 48   12 PLATE 500W AUXILIARY BOARD

SWITCH	POSITION & UNIT NUMBER	TYPE	FOCUS	COLOR
481	HALL 1	6" 500W FRES.	WARM	805
482	HALL 2	6" 500W FRES.	COOL	849
483	HALL 3	6" 500W FRES.	WARM	805
484	HALL 4	6" 500W FRES.	COOL	849
485	HALL 5	BACKING STRIP		FROST
486	HALL 6	BACKING STRIP		FROST
487	BATHROOM 1	6" 500W FRES.	WARM	805
488	BATHROOM 2	6" 500W FRES.	COOL	849
489	BATHROOM 3	6" 500W FRES.	WARM	805
490	BATHROOM 4	6" 500W FRES.	COOL	849
491	BATHROOM 5	BACKING STRIP		FROST
492	BATHROOM 6	BACKING STRIP		FROST

NOTES:

THE 800 NUMBERS IN THE COLOR COLUMN REPRESENT ROSCOLENE PLASTIC COLOR MEDIUM.

THE 500 NUMBERS REPRESENT CINEMOID PLASTIC COLOR MEDIUM.

ACT I "PLAZA SUITE"   NEW YORK 1968

PRE-SET

    9 →7   FAN ON
   12 →7   CLOSET INKY ON
   24 →7   HALL BRACKET ON
   31 →6
   37 →5   AUX. 481 →5
   40 →7   483 →5
   42 →5   485 →5
   44 →7   486 →5
   46 →5
   47 →5
   48 →FULL
   50 →5
   52 ⎫
   53 ⎬ FULL
   54 ⎭

PRE-SET WITH SWITCHES OFF:
13 →6
29 →3
30 →FULL
32 →3   AUXILIARY PRE-SETS FOR
34 →FULL   LATER CUES:
38 →3   281 →5
                                    282 →5
                                    283 →5
                                    284 →5

                                    344 →3

                                    411 →3

ACT I "PLAZA SUITE" N.Y. 1968

CUE 1   BELLBOY TURNS ON LIVING ROOM LIGHTS

SNAP   FIXTURES ON
        13 →6
        29 →3
        30 →FULL } ON SWITCH
        32 →3
        34 →FULL   344 →3

CUE 2   BELLBOY TURNS ON BEDROOM LIGHTS

SNAP   FIXTURES ON
        37 →FULL
        38 →3 — ON SWITCH

FOLLOW
  ③   15 →7
        20 →3
        41 →FULL   411 →3

CUE 3   BELLBOY TURNS ON BATH LIGHTS

BUMP   487 →3
        489 →3

FOLLOW
  ⑩   3 →5
        6 →3
        10 →5
        11 →5
        16 →3
        21 →5
        33 →5
        35 →5
        44 →FULL
        46 →3
        341 →3
        FAN OUT

ACT II "PLAZA SUITE" NEW YORK 1968

PRE-SET

- 10 →5
- 11 →5
- 29 →3
- 30 →FULL
- 31 →5
- 32 →3
- 33 →3
- 34 →FULL
- 35 →5
- 36 →5
- 37 →5
- 38 →5
- 39 →5
- 41 →FULL
- 42 →5
- 43 ⎫
- 44 ⎬ FULL
- 45 ⎭
- 46 →5
- 47 ⎫
- 48 ⎪
- 49 ⎬ FULL
- 50 ⎪
- 52 ⎪
- 53 ⎭

HALL BRACKET ON
CLOSET INKY ON

AUXILIARY PRE-SET:
- 104 →3

- 341 ⎫ FULL
- 344 ⎭

- 411 →5
- 413 ⎫ FULL
- 414 ⎭

- 481 →5
- 482 →3
- 483 →5
- 484 →3

- 489 →3
- 490 →3
- 491 →3
- 492 →3

CUE 13   CURTAIN ½ WAY UP

(3)
- 17 →3
- 20 →5
- 25 →5

ACT III   "PLAZA SUITE"   NEW YORK 1968

PRE-SET

```
    23 →5                HALL BRACKET ON
    24 →5                CLOSET INKY ON
    27 →5                AUXILIARY PRE-SET:
    30 →3                    341  ⎫
    31 →5                    342  ⎬ FULL
    32 →5                    343  ⎭
    34 →3                    344
    36 →5
    37 →3                    411 →3
    38 →3                    412 →5
    40 →5                    413 →3
    41  ⎫                    414 →3
    42  │
    44  │                    481 →5
    45  ⎬ FULL              482 →5
    47  │                    483 →5
    48  │                    484 →5
    49  │                    485 →5
    50  ⎭                    486 →5
RE-PLUG 51 →5                489 →3
    52  ⎫                    490 →3
    53  ⎬ FULL              491 →3
    54  ⎭                    492 →3
```

CUE 18   CURTAIN ½ WAY UP

   ⑤ 18 →3
       20 → FULL
       25 →3
       28 →2

FOLLOW

       13 →5 — LAG
  ⑮ 15 →3
       16 →5
       19 →5
       21 →5

"Plaza Suite"
Elevation
Drawn by Oliver Smith

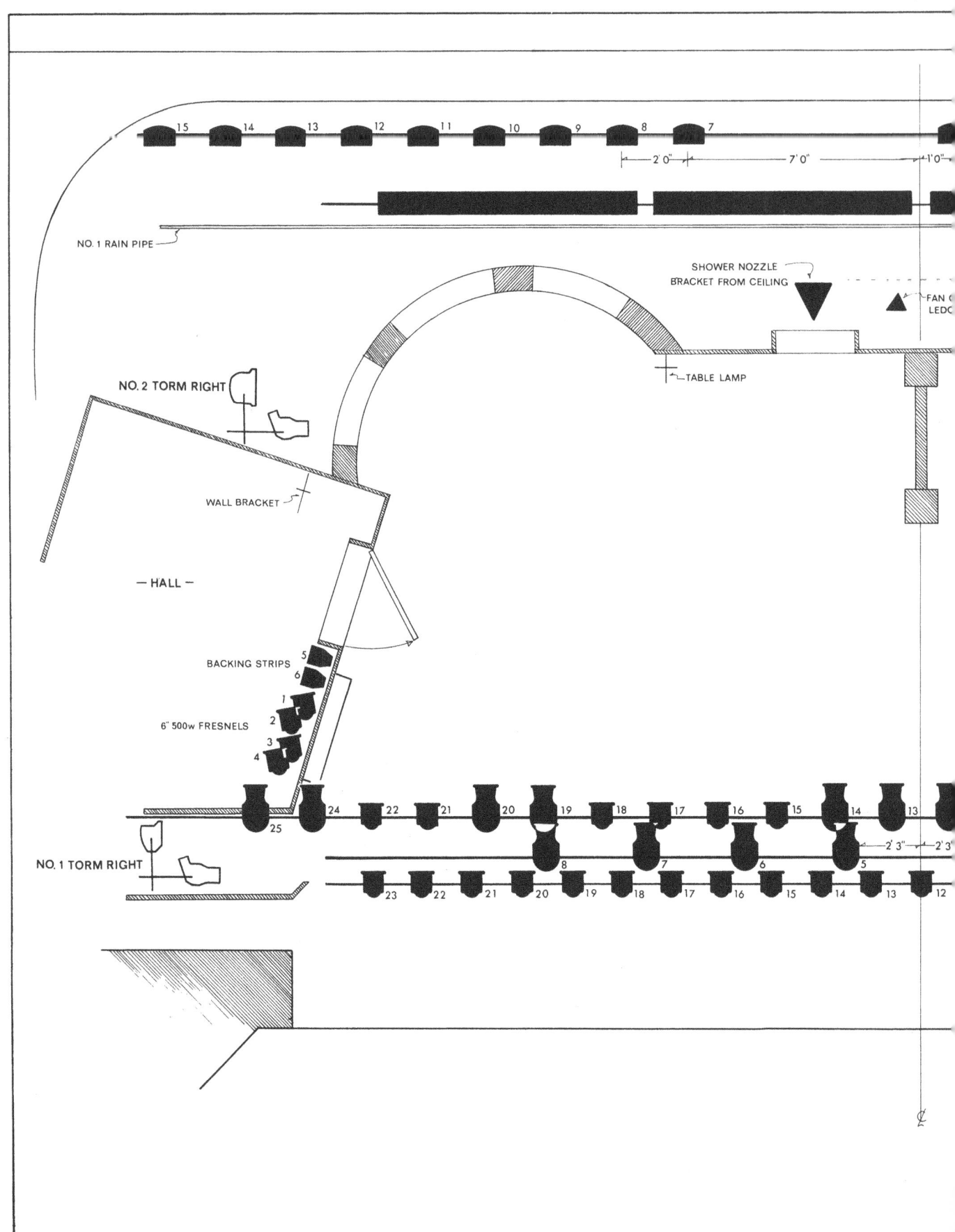

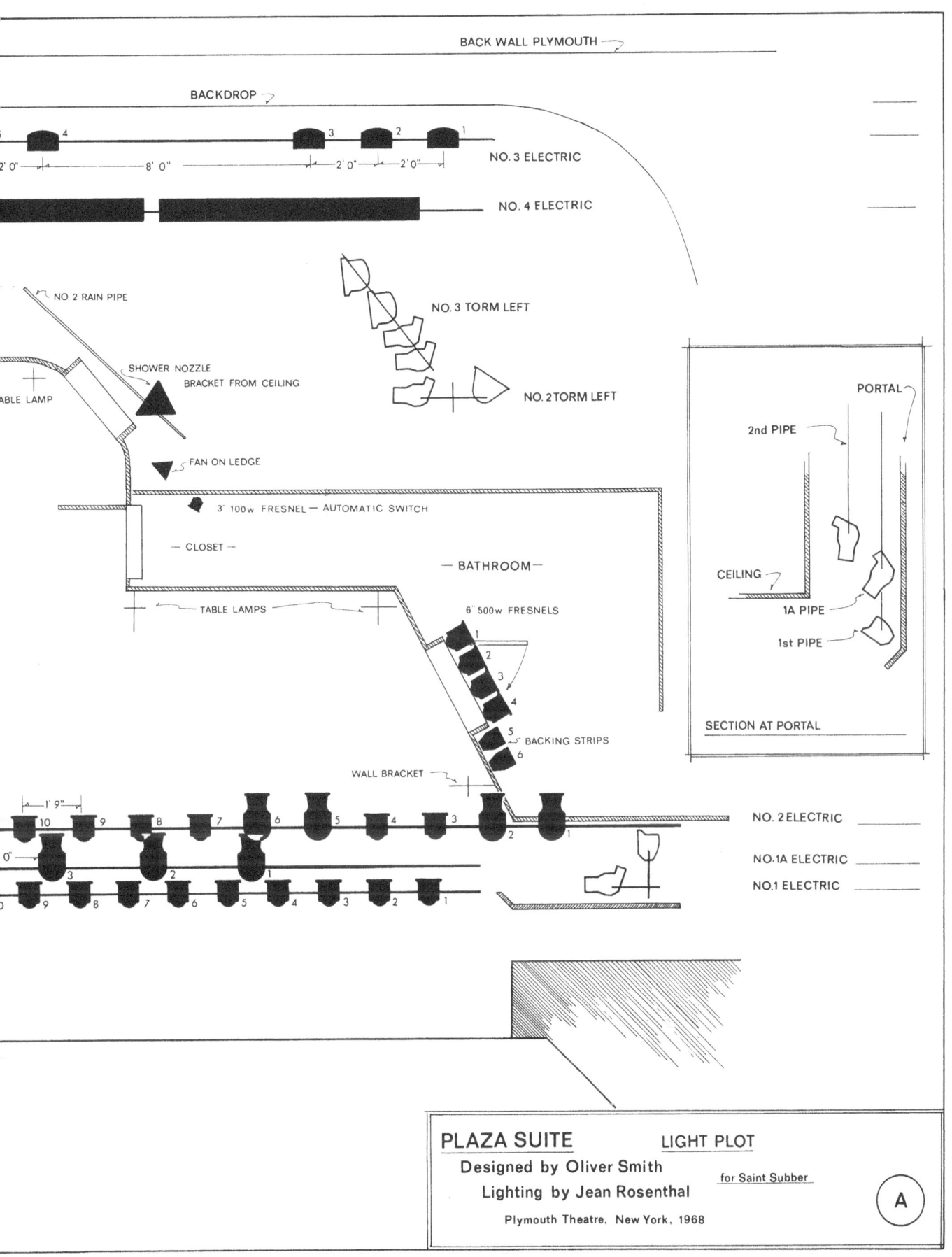

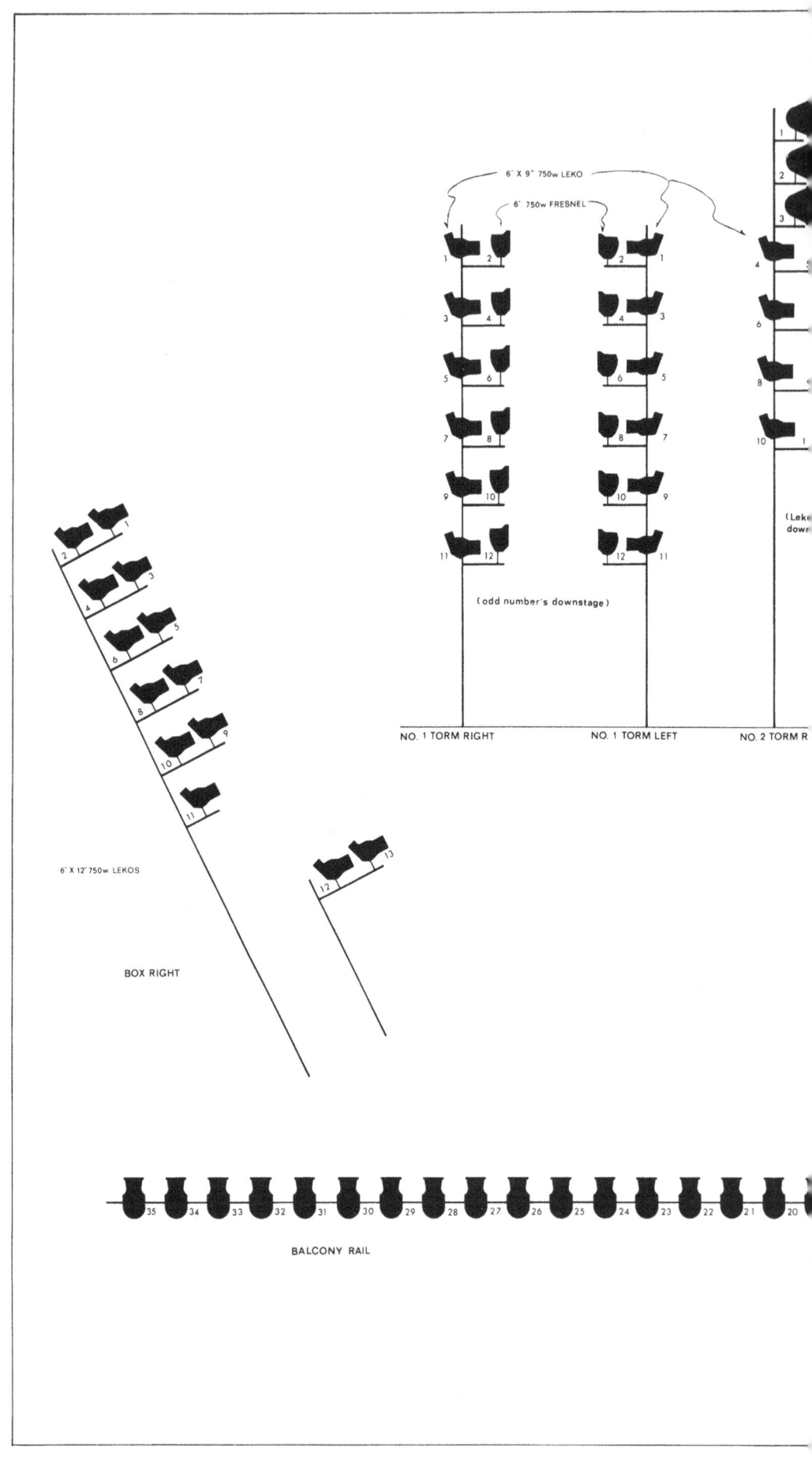

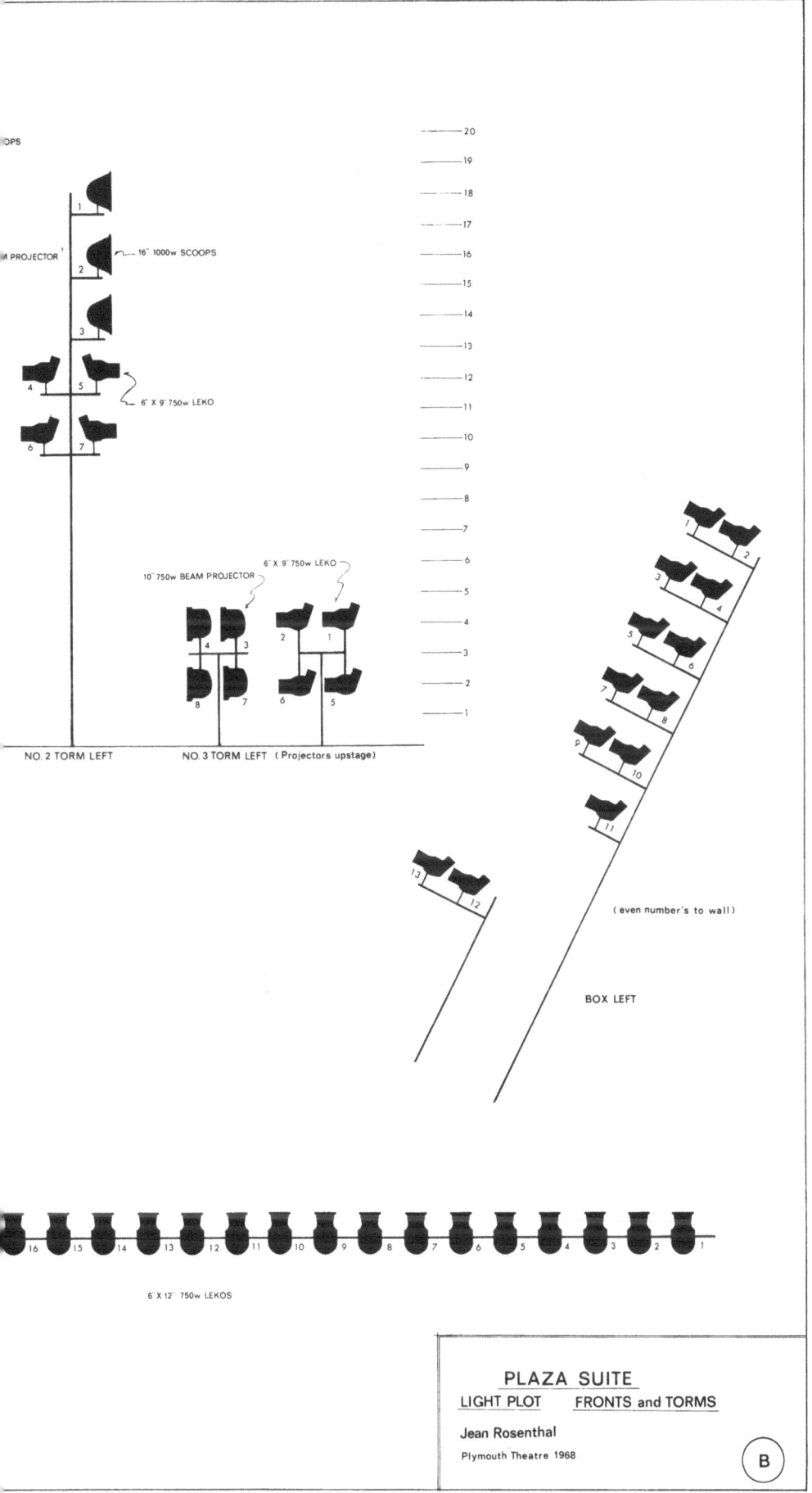

Hookup, Focus Chart and Light Plot for "Hello, Dolly!"

The hookup for *Hello, Dolly!* (pages 181-188) follows the same procedure as the hookup for *Plaza Suite*. The general focusing intentions shown in the "focus note" column of the hookup are transferred to the focus charts (pages 189-197), as a reminder of your intentions.

Technical translation of ideas into specifics begins with the focus chart. This should be thought out and prepared in advance so that the lighting designer does not keep extensive stagehands sitting on the tops of ladders while he or she thinks.

Your grid notes on paper (page 189) match the grid you will mark off on the theatre stage. The first show portal is best as your point of departure for the grid as it remains consistent in terms of hanging the rest of the show. (The house curtains vary in distance from the first set of lines in different theatres.) From the number one show portal line — 0" — one-foot increments are the most useful, running straight upstage to the last drop or cyclorama. Cross-stage runs from center — 0" — to right proscenium and center to left proscenium. (For dance stages two-foot increments are usually sufficient.)

On the focus chart — only a partial chart is shown here — the lamp numbers are listed in numerical order for each pipe in a column on the left-hand side of the page. The circuit number which controls the lamp is shown next to the lamp number on the left above a slash line. In the space to the right are the general focus notes transferred from the hookup. These are shown underlined. Additional notes are made while you are focusing.

Terms vary for the various accepted light patterns, but the ones that turn up most often and are generally understood provide a shorthand readily understandable by electricians and stage managers. Of these the most useful are:

WASH — bathing a certain section of the stage with an even field of light, using a circuit of two or more lights.
X-WASH — to achieve this even field, the lights cross specifically from left to right, or right to left. Used for frontlight, tormentor or pipe positions.

DOWNLIGHTS — can be one or more overhead pipes and are focused straight down, evenly spaced all across the stage or in singles. A full stage pattern can be controlled on an auxiliary board to work both ways. Viewed from the front, downlights create matching patterns of parallel beams.

BACKLIGHT — upstage downlight, focused to tip downstage, used in most cases with parallel beams. Purpose: to backlight whatever is downstage of the light.

SLIT — from the tormentor position, can be in any bay; although usually the farthest downstage, sometimes the farthest upstage (making a narrow path between, for example, a scrim and a drop). A slit focuses straight across and lands unseen in the opposite bay. Hence a "slit" of light.

POOL — a loose term which means too many different things in different places to different people. Essentially it means exactly what it sounds like — a pool of light which does not blend with any other light. Can be a backlight, a downlight or a couple of tight area lights that land in the same spot. Pools are usually round and small within the floor pattern.

For focusing, the stage is marked off with carpenter's chalk or masking tape into the grid pattern. One cross-stage marking at the first portal line downstage (or below it, if room allows) and one at mid-stage are sufficient for sighting your positions on the stage.

With a ground plan of the show to refer to, much of the focusing can be done with no scenery onstage, unless levels are involved. If a drop you wish to avoid is 18 feet upstage, you mark the floor and either cut the light off at that point with shutters or land off the drop at that point with the whole lamp.

For a show with platforms and levels the floor is marked in terms of levels rather than in feet, with identifying letters at each level. If the levels change for different acts, a separate ground plan will be needed for each one and the focus chart will record the act for which any given light is focused. (For example: lamp no. 3 on 2nd pipe focused on B level, Act II position.)

Shows with many drops may be focused without bringing the drops in, although cut borders (such as the foliage borders in *Swan Lake*) must be checked to make sure the lights are going past and not hitting them directly. Levels, however, should be in place when focusing. Guesswork is more time-consuming than having the levels moved on and offstage.

A turntable presents a different problem. You had best come armed with a marked cloth tape which you tack down above and below the turntable. The stop positions on the table are rarely set before the lighting designer gets the stage for focusing, and the turntable rarely just sits there in one position while you work. If you have your cloth tape you can hope to rescue the tape when a piece of scenery sitting on the table is inadvertently whirled away from you.

As you do your focusing, you make notations on your focus chart, starting with the hot spot, indicating shutters for the lekos, and indicating whether the fresnels should be on soft, half or sharp focus and the beam projectors on flood, half or sharp. (The leko is usually on sharp and need be noted only if it is not.) The final column of notes is for color and this is the only chance the designer has for checking *both* circuiting and color before lighting the show. So this is the time to catch mistakes if you do not wish to live with them for quite a while.

The samples from the focus chart of *Hello, Dolly!* are chosen to illustrate each position of major concern. Torms and ladders are shown all on one side, with some of the opposite side to show matching patterns. As with *Plaza Suite*, the light plot indicates the lamp's relative relationship to the ground plan of the show.

Following the light plot for *Hello, Dolly!* is the light plot for the Martha Graham Dance Company. This is included because it illustrates the use of minimal equipment for maximum effect.

"HELLO DOLLY" 1963

NO. 1 BOARD HOOKUP   14 PLATE 15/3000W SWITCHBOARD

SWITCH	POSITION & UNIT NUMBER	TYPE	FOCUS NOTE	COLOR
1	2ND BALCONY 1-13-14-26	8"x10" 750W LEKO	LEFT & RIGHT WARM	9-60
2	2ND BALCONY 5-9-18-22	8"x10" 750W LEKO	CENTER WARM	9-60
3	1ST BALCONY 10-15-20-25	6"x12" 750W LEKO	CENTER WARM	553
4	1ST BALCONY 3-14-21-32	6"x12" 750W LEKO	RUNWAY WARM	9-60
5	BOX LEFT 11-13 BOX RIGHT 11-13	6"x12" 750W LEKO	CENTER WARM	9-60
6	BOX LEFT 7-9-12	6"x12" 750W LEKO	X-LIGHT WARM	553
7	BOX RIGHT 7-9-12	6"x12" 750W LEKO	X-LIGHT WARM	553
8	1ST BALCONY 1-2-5-6	6"x12" 750W LEKO	NEUTRAL LEFT	CLEAR
9	1ST BALCONY 29-30-33-34	6"x12" 750W LEKO	NEUTRAL RIGHT	CLEAR
10	AUX. MASTER 83-84-85-86	—	—	—
11	1ST BALCONY 9-17-18-26	8"x10" 750W LEKO	HARMONIA STEPS & CENTER	CLEAR
12	NO. 1 TORM LEFT 2-4-6	6"x12" 750W LEKO	X-LIGHT WARM	553
13	NO. 1 TORM RIGHT 2-4-6	6"x12" 750W LEKO	X-LIGHT WARM	553
14	NO. 2 TORM LEFT 10-11 NO. 2 TORM RIGHT 10-11	6"x12" 750W LEKO	CENTER WARM	9-60

"HELLO DOLLY" ② 1963

NO. 2 BOARD HOOKUP   14 PLATE   15/3000W SWITCHBOARD

SWITCH	POSITION & UNIT NUMBER	TYPE	FOCUS NOTE	COLOR
15	NO. 2 TORM LEFT 1-4-5	8" 1000W FRESNEL	MOON LEFT TO RIGHT	9-29
16	NO. 2 TORM RIGHT 1-4-5	8" 1000W FRESNEL	MOON RIGHT TO LEFT	9-29
17	AUX. MASTER 87-88-89-90	—	—	—
18	NO. 1 LADDER LEFT 1-4-7	10" 750W BEAM PROJ.	MOON LEFT TO RIGHT	9-29
19	NO. 1 LADDER RIGHT 1-4-7	10" 750W BEAM PROJ.	MOON RIGHT TO LEFT	9-29
20	AUX. MASTER 91-92-93-94	—	—	—
21	1ST PIPE 3-6-21-24	6"X12" 750W LEKO & 6" 750W FRES.	CENTER COOL	543
22	1ST PIPE 7-11-16-20	6" 750W FRESNEL	DROP WASH	FROST
23	1ST PIPE 9-14-18	6"X12" 750W LEKO	HARMONIA STEPS	CLEAR
24	2ND PIPE 4-5-8	6"X12" 750W LEKO	CENTER X-LIGHT LEFT TO RIGHT	553
25	2ND PIPE 17-20-21	6"X12" 750W LEKO	CENTER X-LIGHT RIGHT TO LEFT	553
26	1ST PIPE 5-10-17-22	6"X12" 750W LEKO	DOWNLIGHT "A"	CLEAR
27	AUX. MASTER 95-96-97-98	—	—	—
28	4TH PIPE 9-11-14-16	10" 750W BEAM PROJ.	BACKLIGHT COOL	541

"HELLO DOLLY"   1963

③

NO. 3 BOARD HOOKUP   14 PLATE 15/3000W SWITCHBOARD

SWITCH	POSITION & UNIT NUMBER	TYPE	FOCUS NOTE	COLOR
29	2ND BALCONY 2-12-15-25	8"x10" 750W LEKO	LEFT & RIGHT COOL	543
30	2ND BALCONY 8-11-16-19	8"x10" 750W LEKO	CENTER COOL	543
31	1ST BALCONY 7-12-23-28	6"x12" 750W LEKO	CENTER COOL	543
32	1ST BALCONY 4-13-22-31	6"x12" 750W LEKO	RUNWAY COOL	517
33	BOX LEFT 8-10 BOX RIGHT 8-10	6"x12" 750W LEKO	CENTER COOL	9-29
34	BOX LEFT 2-4-6	6"x12" 750W LEKO	COOL X-LIGHT LEFT TO RIGHT	9-29
35	BOX RIGHT 2-4-6	6"x12" 750W LEKO	COOL X-LIGHT RIGHT TO LEFT	9-29
36	BOX LEFT 1-3-5	6"x12" 750W LEKO	RUNWAY LEFT TO RIGHT	536
37	BOX RIGHT 1-3-5	6"x12" 750W LEKO	RUNWAY RIGHT TO LEFT	536
38 ↕	AUX. MASTER 99-100-101-102 AUX. MASTER 103-104-105-106	— —	— —	— —
39	NO. 1 TORM LEFT 1-3-5	6"x12" 750W LEKO	COOL X-LIGHT LEFT TO RIGHT	9-29
40	NO. 1 TORM RIGHT 1-3-5	6"x12" 750W LEKO	COOL X-LIGHT RIGHT TO LEFT	9-29
41 ↕	NO. 1 TORM LEFT & RIGHT 7 NO. 1 TORM LEFT & RIGHT 8	6x12 750W LEKO 6x12 750W LEKO	X-LIGHT X-LIGHT	540 536
42	NO. 2 TORM LEFT 9-12 NO. 2 TORM RIGHT 9-12	6"x12" 750W LEKO	CENTER COOL	517

NOTE: ↕ = DOUBLE THROW SWITCH

"HELLO DOLLY" 1963

NO. 4 BOARD HOOKUP   14 PLATE 15/3000W SWITCHBOARD

SWITCH	POSITION & UNIT NUMBER	TYPE	FOCUS NOTE	COLOR
43	NO. 2 TORM LEFT 2-3-6	8" 1000W FRESNEL	SUN LEFT TO RIGHT	553
44	NO. 2 TORM RIGHT 2-3-6	8" 1000W FRESNEL	SUN RIGHT TO LEFT	553
45	NO. 2 TORM LEFT 7-8 2ND PIPE 13-14	6"x12" 750W LEKO	NEUTRAL CORNER LEFT	CLEAR
46	NO. 2 TORM RIGHT 7-8 2ND PIPE 11-12	6"x12" 750W LEKO	NEUTRAL CORNER RIGHT	CLEAR
47	NO. 1 LADDER LEFT 2-5-8	10" 750W BEAM PROJ.	WARM BEAM	553
48	NO. 1 LADDER RIGHT 2-5-8	10" 750W BEAM PROJ.	WARM BEAM	553
49	NO. 1 LADDER LEFT 3-6 3RD PIPE 14-17	6"x12" 750W LEKO	NEUTRAL CORNER LEFT	536
50	NO. 1 LADDER RIGHT 3-6 3RD PIPE 9-12	6"x12" 750W LEKO	NEUTRAL CORNER RIGHT	536
51	1ST PIPE 4-12-15-23	6"x12" 750W LEKO 6" 750W FRES.	CENTER WARM	9-60
52	2ND PIPE 1-2-3	6"x12" 750W LEKO	ENDS - EXTREME LEFT TO RIGHT	CLEAR
53	2ND PIPE 22-23-24	6"x12" 750W LEKO	ENDS - EXTREME RIGHT TO LEFT	CLEAR
54	2ND PIPE 7-10-15-18	6"x12" 750W LEKO	BACKLIGHT "A"	553
55	2ND PIPE 6-9-16-19	6"x12" 750W LEKO	BACKLIGHT "B"	CLEAR
56	4TH PIPE 6-10-15-19	10" 750W BEAM PROJ.	BEAM WARM	553

"HELLO DOLLY"

1963

(5)

NO. 5 BOARD HOOKUP   14 PLATE 15/3000W SWITCHBOARD

SWITCH	POSITION & UNIT NUMBER	TYPE	FOCUS NOTE	COLOR
57	3RD PIPE 2-5-20-24	6"x12" 750W LEKO	CENTER WARM	9-60
58	3RD PIPE 1-6-21-25	6"x12" 750W LEKO	CENTER COOL	543
59 ↑	4th PIPE 3-5-20-22	6x12 750W LEKO	CENTER X-LIGHT	543
59 ↓	AUX. MASTER 107-108-109-110-111-112	—	—	—
60	5th PIPE 1-2-4-5	6"x12" 750W LEKO	X-LIGHT CENTER	536
61	3RD PIPE 11-15	6"x12" 750W LEKO	BACKLIGHT "A"	536
62	3RD PIPE 3-8-18-23	6"x12" 750W LEKO	BACKLIGHT "B"	541
63	3RD PIPE 10-13-16	6"x12" 750W LEKO	DOWNLIGHT "A"	CLEAR
64	3RD PIPE 4-7-19-22	6"x12" 750W LEKO	DOWNLIGHT "B"	CLEAR
65	6th PIPE 1-6-12	14" 500W SCOOPS	PINK CYC	9-115
66	6th PIPE 2-7-11	14" 500W SCOOPS	PINK CYC	540
67	6th PIPE 5-8	14" 500W SCOOPS	BACKLIGHT COURTROOM & DESERTED STORE	FROST
68 ↑	5th PIPE BORDERLIGHT	R-40 300W FL.	WHITE	FROST
68 ↓	AUX. MASTER 113-114-115-116-117-118	—	—	—
69 ↑	5th PIPE BORDERLIGHT	R-40 300W FL.	PINK	9-115
69 ↓	4th PIPE 7-12-18	14" 500W SCOOP	GRAND CENTRAL	CLEAR
70 ↑	5th PIPE BORDERLIGHT	R-40 300W FL.	BLUE	540
70 ↓	4th PIPE 8-13-17	14" 500W SCOOP	WHITE CYC (BL)	540

NOTE: ↑↓ = DOUBLE THROW SWITCH

"HELLO DOLLY" 1963

(6)

NO. 6 BOARD HOOKUP   12 PLATE 5000W SWITCHBOARD

SWITCH	POSITION & UNIT NUMBER	TYPE	FOCUS NOTES	COLOR
71	2ND BALCONY 3-6-7-20-21-24	8"x10" 750W LEKO	FULL STAGE WASH	CLEAR
72	1ST PIPE 1-2 4TH PIPE 1-2-4	8" 1000W FRESNEL	RING LEFT	553
73	1ST PIPE 25-26 4TH PIPE 21-23-24	8" 1000W FRESNEL	RING RIGHT	553
74	NO. 3 TORM LEFT 1-3-5 NO. 3 TORM RIGHT 1-3-5	14" 500W SCOOP	ENDS LEFT & RIGHT	9-115
75	NO. 3 TORM LEFT 2-4-6 NO. 3 TORM RIGHT 2-4-6	14" 500W SCOOP	ENDS LEFT & RIGHT	543
76	6TH PIPE 3-4-9-10	14" 500W SCOOP	CENTER	510
77	7TH PIPE BORDERLIGHT	300W R-40 FLOOD	BLUE	541
78	7TH PIPE BORDERLIGHT	300W R-40 FLOOD	MEDIUM BLUE	532
79	7TH PIPE BORDERLIGHT	300W R-40 FLOOD	PINK	9-115
80	GROUND ROW	300W R-40 FLOOD	WHITE	FROST
81	GROUND ROW	300W R-40 FLOOD	PINK	9-115
82	GROUND ROW	300W R-40 FLOOD	LIGHT BLUE	540

NOTE:

THE 500 NUMBERS IN THE COLOR COLUMN REPRESENT CINEMOID PLASTIC COLOR MEDIUM.

THE 9-00 NUMBERS REPRESENT ROSCOLENE PLASTIC COLOR MEDIUM.

"HELLO DOLLY"   1963

AUX. HOOKUP   3 - 8 PLATE 750W AUXILIARY BOARDS

MASTER	SWITCH	POSITION & UNIT NO.	TYPE	FOCUS NOTE	COLOR
10	83	2ND BALCONY 4	10"x14" 750W LEKO	LEFT	9-60
	84	1ST BALCONY 11	8"x10" 750W LEKO	LEFT	536
	85	1ST BALCONY 24	8"x10" 750W LEKO	RIGHT	9-60
	86	2ND BALCONY 23	10"x14" 750W LEKO	RIGHT	536
17	87	NO. 2 TORM LEFT 13	6"x12" 750W LEKO	HARMONIA	9-60
	88	NO. 2 TORM RIGHT 13	6"x12" 750W LEKO	AND	9-60
	89	NO. 2 TORM LEFT 14	6"x12" 750W LEKO	LIVING	543
	90	NO. 2 TORM RIGHT 14	6"x12" 750W LEKO	STATUES	543
20	91	NO. 1 LADDER LEFT 9	6"x12" 750W LEKO	X-LIGHT &	9-115
	92	NO. 1 LADDER RIGHT 9	6"x12" 750W LEKO	SHADOWS & ABOVE	9-115
	93	NO. 1 LADDER LEFT 10	6"x12" 750W LEKO	HOTEL &	540
	94	NO. 1 LADDER RIGHT 10	6"x12" 750W LEKO	HAT SHOP	540
27	95	1ST PIPE 8	6"x12" 750W LEKO	DOWNLIGHT "B" L	553
	96	1ST PIPE 13	6"x12" 750W LEKO	DOWNLIGHT "B" ¢	CLEAR
	97	1ST PIPE 19	6"x12" 750W LEKO	DOWNLIGHT "B" R	553
	98	5th PIPE 3	6"x12" 750W LEKO	HARMONIA	536
↑ 38	99	1ST BALCONY 8	8"x10" 750W LEKO	FEED STORE TOP L	553
	100	1ST BALCONY 16	8"x10" 750W LEKO	SCRIM WASH - HARMON	540
	101	1ST BALCONY 19	8"x10" 750W LEKO	SCRIM WASH - HARMON	540
	102	1ST BALCONY 27	8"x10" 750W LEKO	FEED STORE TOP R	553
38 ↓	103	2ND BALCONY 10	10"x14" 750W LEKO	"BUTTERFLYS"	CLEAR
	104	2ND BALCONY 17	10"x14" 750W LEKO	"BUTTERFLYS"	CLEAR
	105				
	106				

"HELLO DOLLY"   1963

⑧

AUX. HOOKUP   12 PLATE 500W AUXILIARY BOARD

MASTER	SWITCH	POSITION	TYPE
↓ 59	107	HARMONIA FLAT	BRACKETS
	108	HARMONIA FLAT	RAILING
	109	HARMONIA STEPS	2 - FIGURE FIXTURES
	110	HARMONIA DINING UNIT LEFT	6 - 3 VOLT LAMPS
	111	HARMONIA DINING UNIT RIGHT	6 - 3 VOLT LAMPS
	112	HARMONIA DINING UNIT L & R	CHANDELIERS (WORK CABLE)
↓ 68	113	RUNWAY	FOOTS
	114	LIVING STATUES FRAME	BRACKETS
	115	HOTEL FLAT	3 - FIXTURES
	116	HARMONIA SCRIM	LOW VOLTAGE LAMPS AT BRACKETS
	117	NO. 2 ADJUSTABLE PORTAL	BRACKETS
	118	JUDGES STAND	FIXTURE (WORK CABLE)

NOTE: THE NUMBERS UNDER THE COLOR HEADING REPRESENT PLASTIC COLOR MEDIUM COLORS. THE 9-00 NUMBERS ARE ROSCOLENE PLASTIC COLORS, THE 500 NUMBERS ARE CINEMOID PLASTIC COLORS.

THE ARROWS (↓↑) IN THE MASTER SWITCH COLUMN REPRESENT THE POSITION OF THE DOUBLE THROW SWITCH BEING USED TO CONTROL THAT PARTICULAR MASTER SWITCH.

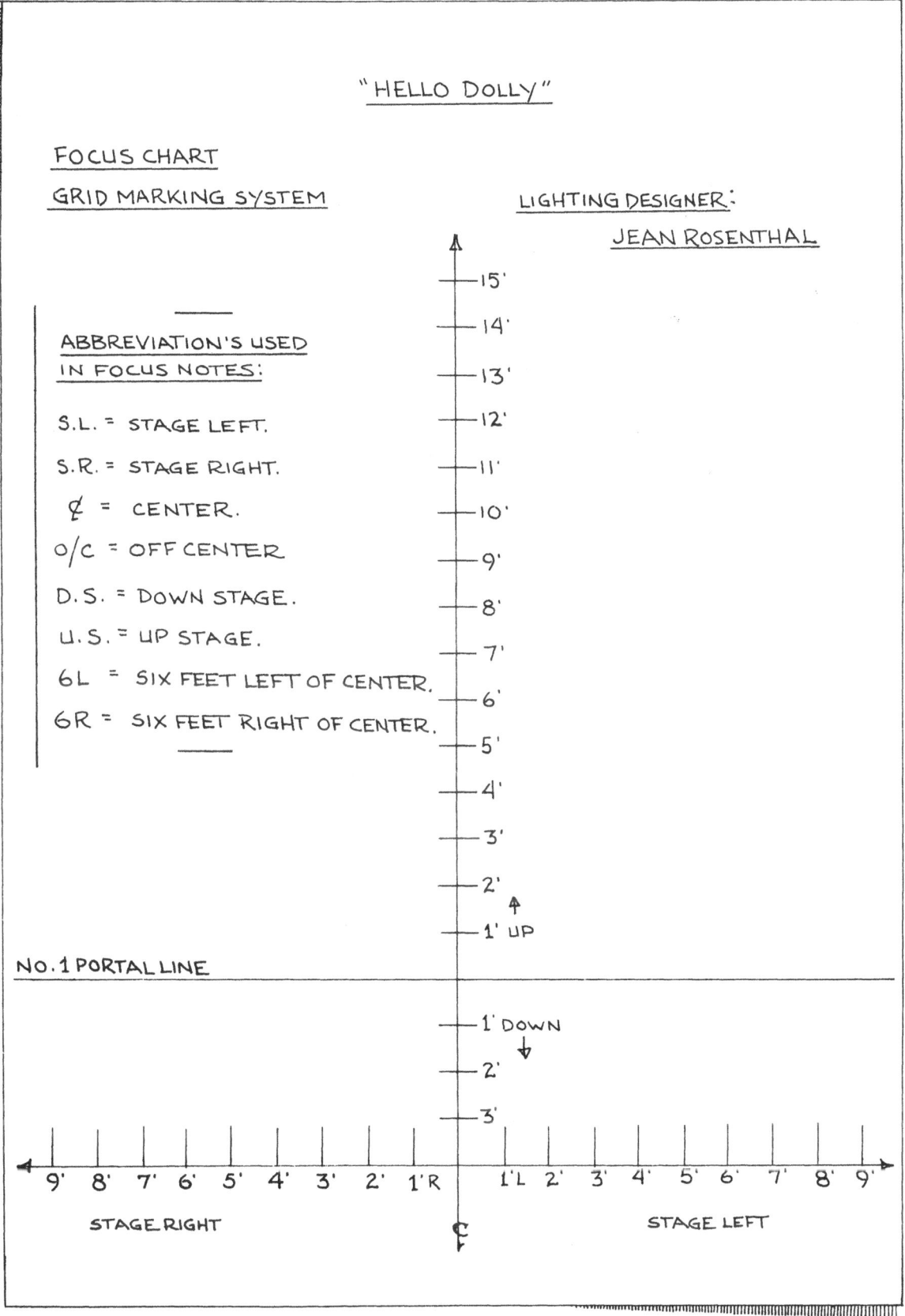

	FOCUS CHART	"HELLO DOLLY"	
SWITCH / UNIT	1ST BALCONY		COLOR
8/1	NEUTRAL LEFT - 13L AT 1UP - S.L. OFF PORTAL - S.R. TO 6L - D.S. OUT OF PIT - TOP TO 8FT. HI.		CLEAR
8/2	NEUTRAL LEFT - 12L AT 0 - S.L. OFF PORTAL - S.R. TO 6L - D.S. OUT OF PIT - TOP TO TOP OF HARMONIA UNIT.		CLEAR
4/3	RAMP WARM - 12L ON RAMP - S.L. OFF PORTAL - D.S. TO RAMP EDGE - U.S. OFF HOUSE.		9-60
32/4	RAMP COOL - 11L ON RAMP - S.L. OFF PORTAL - D.S. TO RAMP EDGE - U.S. OFF HOUSE.		517
8/5	NEUTRAL LEFT - 11L AT 0 - S.L. OFF PORTAL - D.S. OUT OF PIT - S.R. TO 6L - TOP TO TOP OF HARMONIA UNIT.		CLEAR
8/6	NEUTRAL LEFT - 12L AT 0 - S.L. OFF PORTAL - S.R. TO 6L - D.S. OUT OF PIT - TOP TO TOP OF HARMONIA UNIT.		CLEAR
31/7	CENTER COOL - 4L AT 1 DOWN - S.L. TO 10L - S.R. TO 10R - D.S. OUT OF PIT - TOP TO FINGER TIPS (7FT. HI).		543
99/38↑ /8	FEED STORE TOP LEFT - FRAME TO UPPER TOP LEFT LEVEL - BOTTOM OFF LOWER LEVEL - ANGLE/TOP TO BACK WALL - L & R OFF WALLS.		553
11/9	HARMONIA STEPS & CENTER - 4TH STEP UP - S.R. CUT TO STEPS - S.L. OFF S.L. UNIT - D.S. TO EDGE OF STAGE - TOP TO TOP RAILING.		CLEAR
3/10	CENTER WARM - 4L AT 0 - S.L. TO 10L - S.R. TO 10R - D.S. OUT OF PIT - TOP TO FINGER TIPS (7FT. HI).		553
84/10 /11	LEFT - HOT AT S.L. HARMONIA TABLE - FRAME TO INSIDE S.L. HARMONIA UNIT.		CLEAR
31/12	CENTER COOL - 2L AT 0 - S.L. AT 10L - S.R. TO 10R - D.S. OUT OF PIT - TOP TO FINGER TIPS (7FT. HI).		543
32/13	RAMP COOL - 3L ON RAMP - OFF PORTALS R & L - D.S. TO EDGE OF RAMP - TOP OFF HOUSE U.S.		517
4/14	RAMP WARM - 4L ON RAMP - OFF PORTALS R & L - D.S. TO EDGE OF RAMP - TOP OFF HOUSE U.S.		9-60
3/15	CENTER WARM - 2L AT 0 - S.L. TO 10L - S.R. TO 10R - D.S. OUT OF PIT - TOP TO FINGER TIPS (7FT. HI).		553
100/38↑ /16	HARMONIA SCRIM WASH - COVERS S.L. & L O/C OF DROP - OFF PORTAL AT TOP.		540

FOCUS CHART		"HELLO DOLLY"	
SWITCH / UNIT	BOX LEFT		COLOR
36 / 1	RUNWAY LEFT TO RIGHT - 11L ON RAMP - D.S. TO EDGE OF RAMP - S.L. TO EDGE OF RAMP - S.R. OUT OF HOUSE - U.S. OFF MIKES.		536
34 / 2	COOL X-LIGHT LEFT TO RIGHT - ¢ AT 1 UP - D.S. OFF #1 PORTAL RIGHT.		9-29
36 / 3	RUNWAY LEFT TO RIGHT - 5L ON RAMP - D.S. TO EDGE OF RAMP - S.R. OFF PROSC. & OUT OF HOUSE - U.S. OFF MIKES.		536
34 / 4	COOL X-LIGHT LEFT TO RIGHT - 6R AT 0 - D.S. TO EDGE OF STAGE - S.R. OFF PORTAL.		9-29
36 / 5	RUNWAY LEFT TO RIGHT - 1R ON RAMP - D.S. TO EDGE OF RAMP - S.R. OFF PROSC. & OUT OF HOUSE - U.S. TO 2 UP.		536
34 / 6	COOL X-LIGHT LEFT TO RIGHT - 9L AT 2 DOWN - D.S. TO EDGE OF STAGE - TOP OFF S.R. HOUSE.		9-29
6 / 7	X-LIGHT WARM - 4R AT 0 - D.S. OUT OF PIT - U.S. TO JUST ABOVE #2 PORTAL - TOP OFF S.R. PORTALS.		553
33 / 8	CENTER COOL - ¢ AT 0 - D.S. TO EDGE OF STAGE - OFF S.R. PORTAL - U.S. OFF S.R. HOUSE.		9-29
6 / 9	X-LIGHT WARM - ¢ AT 0 - D.S. OUT OF PIT - U.S. TO #2 PORTAL R - TOP OFF S.R. PORTALS.		553
33 / 10	CENTER COOL - 3L AT 0 - D.S. TO EDGE OF STAGE - OFF S.R. PORTAL & S.R. HOUSE.		9-29
5 / 11	CENTER WARM - ¢ AT 0 - D.S. OUT OF PIT - U.S. OFF #2 PORTAL - TOP OFF S.R. PORTALS.		9-60
6 / 12	X-LIGHT WARM - 5L AT 0 - D.S. OUT OF PIT - U.S. JUST ABOVE #2 PORTAL - TOP OFF S.R. PORTALS		553
5 / 13	CENTER WARM - 4L AT 0 - D.S. OUT OF PIT - U.S. ANGLE SIDE & TOP OFF #2 PORTAL R.		9-60

NOTE: ALL LEKO'S ARE SHARP FOCUS UNLESS OTHERWISE NOTED IN THIS SHOW.

SWITCH/UNIT	NO. 1 TORM LEFT	COLOR
39/1	COOL X-LIGHT LEFT TO RIGHT - 6R AT 2 DOWN - D.S. OUT OF PIT - U.S. TO 0 (#1 PORTAL) - TOP OFF S.R. MASKING.	9-29
12/2	X-LIGHT WARM - 6R AT 2 DOWN - D.S. OUT OF PIT - U.S. TO 0 (#1 PORTAL) - TOP OFF S.R. MASKING.	553
39/3	COOL X-LIGHT LEFT TO RIGHT - ¢ AT 2 DOWN - D.S. OUT OF PIT - U.S. TO 0 (#1 PORTAL) - TOP OFF MASKING S.R.	9-29
12/4	X-LIGHT WARM - ¢ AT 3 DOWN - D.S. OUT OF PIT - U.S. TO 0 (#1 PORTAL) - TOP OFF MASKING S.R.	553
39/5	COOL X-LIGHT LEFT TO RIGHT - 9L AT 3 DOWN - D.S. OUT OF PIT - U.S. TO 0 (#1 PORTAL).	9-29
12/6	X-LIGHT WARM - 9L AT 3 DOWN - D.S. OUT OF PIT - U.S. TO 0 (#1 PORTAL).	553
41↑/7	X-LIGHT - ¢ AT 3 DOWN - SLIT - D.S. OFF R PROSC. - U.S. TO 0 (#1 PORTAL) - TOP OPEN.	540
41↓/8	X-LIGHT - ¢ AT 3 DOWN - SLIT - D.S. OFF R PROSC. - U.S. TO 0 (#1 PORTAL) - TOP OPEN.	536

SWITCH/UNIT	NO. 1 TORM RIGHT (8th LAMP NOT SHOWN HERE)	COLOR
40/1	COOL X-LIGHT RIGHT TO LEFT - 9R AT 2 DOWN - D.S. OUT OF PIT - U.S. TO 0 (#1 PORTAL) - TOP OFF MASKING S.L.	9-29
13/2	X-LIGHT WARM - 9R AT 2 DOWN - D.S. OUT OF PIT - U.S. TO 0 (#1 PORTAL) - TOP OFF MASKING S.L.	553
40/3	COOL X-LIGHT RIGHT TO LEFT - 5L AT 2 DOWN - D.S. OUT OF PIT - U.S. TO 0 (#1 PORTAL) - TOP OFF MASKING S.L.	9-29
13/4	X-LIGHT WARM - 5L AT 3 DOWN - D.S. OUT OF PIT - U.S. TO 0 (#1 PORTAL) - TOP OFF MASKING S.L. - SOFT FOCUS.	553
40/5	COOL X-LIGHT RIGHT TO LEFT - ¢ AT 2 DOWN - D.S. OUT OF PIT - U.S. TO 0 (#1 PORTAL) - TOP OFF MASKING S.L. - SOFT FOCUS.	9-29
13/6	X-LIGHT WARM - ¢ AT 3 DOWN - D.S. OUT OF PIT - U.S. TO 0 (#1 PORTAL).	553
41↑/7	X-LIGHT - ¢ AT 3 DOWN - D.S. OFF S.L. PROSC. - U.S. TO 0 (#1 PORTAL) - TOP OPEN. SLIT	540

FOCUS CHART   "HELLO DOLLY"

SWITCH / UNIT	NO. 1 LADDER LEFT	COLOR
18 / 1	MOON LEFT TO RIGHT - 5R AT 9UP - FLOOD FOCUS.	9-29
47 / 2	WARM BEAM - 4R AT 9UP - FLOOD FOCUS.	553
49 / 3	NEUTRAL CORNER LEFT - 10L AT 10UP - OFF HOUSE U.S.L. - OFF #2 PORTAL L.	536
18 / 4	MOON LEFT TO RIGHT - 1L AT 10UP - FLOOD FOCUS.	9-29
47 / 5	WARM BEAM - 5L AT 10UP - FLOOD FOCUS.	553
49 / 6	NEUTRAL LEFT TO RIGHT - 15L AT 10UP - OFF HOUSE U.S.L. - OFF #2 PORTAL L D.S.	536
18 / 7	MOON LEFT TO RIGHT - 10L AT 10UP - FLOOD FOCUS.	9-29
47 / 8	WARM BEAM - 10L AT 10UP - FLOOD FOCUS.	553
91 / 20 / 9	X-LIGHT ABOVE HOTEL & HAT SHOP - 4R AT 11UP - D.S. TO 10UP - U.S. X 15UP - TOP OF R FIRE ESCAPE.	9-115
93 / 20 / 10	SHADOWS - 7R AT 8UP - U.S. OFF S.R. HOUSE - D.S. TAKE BURN OFF PORTAL L.	540

SWITCH / UNIT	NO. 1 LADDER RIGHT (1ST 5 LAMPS ONLY)	COLOR
19 / 1	MOON RIGHT TO LEFT - 5L AT 9UP - FLOOD FOCUS.	9-29
48 / 2	WARM BEAM - 4L AT 9UP - FLOOD FOCUS.	553
50 / 3	NEUTRAL CORNER RIGHT - 10R AT 10UP - U.S. OFF U.S.R. HOUSE - D.S. OFF #2 PORTAL R.	536
19 / 4	MOON RIGHT TO LEFT - 1R AT 10UP - FLOOD FOCUS.	9-29
48 / 5	WARM BEAM - 5R AT 10UP - FLOOD FOCUS. (FAVOR D.S.)	553

SWITCH/UNIT	1st PIPE	COLOR
72/1	RING LEFT - 10L AT 3UP - ½ FOCUS.	553
72/2	RING LEFT - 7L AT 3UP - ½ FOCUS.	553
21/3	CENTER COOL - 7L AT 6UP - S.L. TO 10L - U.S. TO 12UP - S.R. AND D.S. OPEN.	543
51/4	CENTER WARM - 7L AT 6UP - S.L. TO 10L - U.S. TO 10UP - S.R. & D.S. OPEN.	9-60
26/5	DOWNLIGHT "A" - STRAIGHT DOWN - NO CUTS - U.S. LANDS AT 8UP - D.S. LANDS AT 2 DOWN - S.R. LANDS AT 8L & S.L. AT 17L.	CLEAR
21/6	CENTER COOL - 3L AT 6UP - ½ FOCUS.	543
22/7	DROP WASH - FLOOD INTO S.L. SIDE OF GRAND CENTRAL DROP - 10L AT 8UP.	FROST
95/27/8	DOWNLIGHT "B" LEFT - STRAIGHT DOWN - BOTTOM LANDS AT 2 DOWN.	553
23/9	HARMONIA STEPS - 2R AT 7UP - NO CUTS.	CLEAR
26/10	DOWNLIGHT "A" - STRAIGHT DOWN - NO CUTS - BOTTOM LANDS AT 2 DOWN.	CLEAR
22/11	DROP WASH - FLOOD INTO ¢ & L O/C OF GRAND CENTRAL DROP - 3L AT 8UP.	FROST
51/12	CENTER WARM - 3R AT 7UP - ½ FOCUS.	9-60
96/27/13	DOWNLIGHT "B" CENTER - STRAIGHT DOWN - BOTTOM LANDS AT 2 DOWN.	CLEAR
23/14	HARMONIA STEPS - 6 STEPS UP (FRAME INSIDE STAIRS WITH SIDES - TOP & BOTTOM OPEN (¢ AT 15UP - SIDES CUT 2L & 2R).	CLEAR
51/15	CENTER WARM - 3L AT 7UP - ½ FOCUS.	9-60
22/16	DROP WASH - FLOOD INTO R O/C OF GRAND CENTRAL DROP - 3R AT 8UP.	FROST

FOCUS CHART	"HELLO DOLLY"	
SWITCH / UNIT	2ND PIPE	COLOR
52 / 1	ENDS - EXTREME LEFT TO RIGHT - 4L AT 3UP - D.S. TO 0 - U.S. TO 7UP (BETWEEN #1 & #2 PORTALS) OFFSTAGE LANDS AT 8L.	CLEAR
52 / 2	ENDS - EXTREME LEFT TO RIGHT - ¢ AT 3UP - D.S. TO 0 - U.S. TO 7UP - S.R. TO 10R (BETWEEN #1 & #2 PORTALS).	CLEAR
52 / 3	ENDS - EXTREME LEFT TO RIGHT - 4R AT 3UP - D.S. TO 0 - U.S. TO 7UP - (BETWEEN #1 & #2 PORTAL) - S.R. TO 10R.	CLEAR
24 / 4	CENTER X-LIGHT LEFT TO RIGHT - (FEED STORE) - 5L AT 14UP - ANGLE D.S. FROM 10'6" UP TO 11' UP AT 9L.	553
24 / 5	CENTER X-LIGHT LEFT TO RIGHT - (FEED STORE) - ¢ AT 14UP - SAME CUTS AS #4.	553
55 / 6	BACKLIGHT "B" - 12L AT 3 DOWN - U.S. LANDS AT 4 UP - NO CUTS.	CLEAR
54 / 7	BACKLIGHT "A" - 9L AT 0 - U.S. LANDS AT 5UP - NO CUTS.	553
24 / 8	¢ X-LIGHT LEFT TO RIGHT - (FEED STORE) - 5L AT 15UP - D.S. TO 10'8" - U.S. TO 21'10" - S.R. TO ¢ - S.L. TO 11'6".	553
55 / 9	BACKLIGHT "B" - 5L AT 0 - U.S. LANDS AT 5UP - NO CUTS.	CLEAR
54 / 10	BACKLIGHT "A" - 4L AT 1 DOWN - U.S. LANDS AT 5UP.	553
46 / 11	NEUTRAL CORNER RIGHT - 12R AT 4UP - U.S. CUT TO 7UP - D.S. TO 0 · (BETWEEN #1 & #2 PORTAL).	CLEAR
46 / 12	NEUTRAL CORNER RIGHT - 14R AT 4UP - U.S. TO 7UP - D.S. TO 0 (BETWEEN #1 & #2 PORTAL).	CLEAR
45 / 13	NEUTRAL CORNER LEFT - 13L AT 4UP - U.S. TO 7UP - D.S. TO 0 (BETWEEN #1 & #2 PORTAL).	CLEAR
45 / 14	NEUTRAL CORNER LEFT - 12L AT 4UP - U.S. TO 7UP - (#2 PORTAL LINE) - D.S. TO 0 (#1 PORTAL LINE).	CLEAR
54 / 15	BACKLIGHT "A" - 4R AT 0 - NO CUTS - D.S. LANDS AT EDGE - U.S. LANDS AT 5 UP.	553
55 / 16	BACKLIGHT "B" - 4R AT 0 - NO CUTS - D.S. LANDS AT EDGE OF STAGE - U.S. LANDS AT 5UP.	CLEAR

FOCUS CHART	"HELLO DOLLY"	
UNIT SWITCH	3RD PIPE	COLOR
58/1	CENTER COOL - 6L AT 8UP - U.S. TO 12UP - D.S. TO 3UP - SIDES OPEN.	543
57/2	CENTER WARM - 6L AT 8UP - U.S. TO 12UP - D.S. TO 3UP - SIDES OPEN.	9-60
62/3	BACKLIGHT "B" - 12L AT 5UP - U.S. LANDS AT 12UP - D.S. CUT BURN OFF PORTAL.	541
64/4	DOWNLIGHT "B" - STRAIGHT DOWN - D.S. TO 4UP - U.S. OFF HOUSE - S.R. LANDS AT 11L - OFF PORTAL FROM SIDE.	CLEAR
57/5	CENTER WARM - 3L AT 7UP - U.S. TO 12 UP. NO OTHER CUTS.	9-60
58/6	CENTER COOL - 2L AT 6UP - D.S. TO 2UP - U.S. TO 11UP - SIDES OPEN.	543
64/7	DOWNLIGHT "B" - STRAIGHT DOWN - D.S. LANDS AT 4UP - U.S. OFF HOUSE (13½ UP) - NO OTHER CUTS.	CLEAR
62/8	BACKLIGHT "B" - 6L AT 6UP - U.S. LANDS AT 12UP - NO CUTS.	541
50/9	NEUTRAL CORNER RIGHT - 11R AT 10UP - D.S. TO 2UP - U.S. OFF WHITE CYC (12UP) - TOP OFF R PORTAL.	536
63/10	DOWNLIGHT "A" - STRAIGHT DOWN - D.S. LANDS AT 4UP - U.S. TO 13UP - SIDES OPEN.	CLEAR
61/11	BACKLIGHT "A" - 4L AT 6UP - U.S. LANDS AT 13UP - NO CUTS.	536
50/12	NEUTRAL CORNER RIGHT - 12R AT 10UP - U.S. OFF WHITE CYC - TOP OFF R PORTAL.	536
63/13	DOWNLIGHT "A" - STRAIGHT DOWN - D.S. LANDS AT 2UP.	CLEAR
49/14	NEUTRAL CORNER LEFT - 11L AT 9UP - U.S. OFF WHITE CYC (12UP) - TOP OFF PORTAL LEFT.	536
61/15	BACKLIGHT "A" - 4R AT 6UP - TAKE BURN OFF PORTAL D.S.	536
63/16	DOWNLIGHT "A" - STRAIGHT DOWN - BOTTOM LANDS AT 4UP D.S. - U.S. CUT TO 13½ UP.	CLEAR

FOCUS CHART	"HELLO DOLLY"	
SWITCH / UNIT	4th PIPE	COLOR
72/1	RING LEFT - 10L AT 8UP - ½ FOCUS.	553
72/2	RING LEFT - 5L AT 7UP - ½ FOCUS.	553
59↑/3	CENTER X-LIGHT LEFT & RIGHT - 7L AT 10UP - S.L. LANDS AT 10L - D.S. OPEN - U.S. CUTS OFF WHITE CYC AT 12½ UP.	543
72/4	RING LEFT - ₵ AT 7UP - ½ FOCUS.	553
59↑/5	CENTER X-LIGHT LEFT & RIGHT - 1L AT 10UP - D.S. OPEN - U.S. TO 12½ UP (OFF WHITE CYC).	543
56/6	WARM BEAM - 10L AT 5UP - FLOOD FOCUS.	553
69↓/7	GRAND CENTRAL - BACKLIGHT S.L. SIDE OF DROP - WATCH BORDER BEHIND.	CLEAR
70↓/8	WHITE CYC BLUE FLOOD - TIP STRAIGHT DOWN ⌒	540
28/9	BACKLIGHT COOL - 7L AT 6UP - FLOOD FOCUS.	541
56/10	WARM BEAM - 4L AT 5UP - FLOOD FOCUS.	553
28/11	BACKLIGHT COOL - 2L AT 6UP - U.S. LANDS AT 8UP - FLOOD FOCUS.	541
69↓/12	GRAND CENTRAL - BACKLIGHT ₵ OF DROP - WATCH BORDER BEHIND.	CLEAR
70↓/13	WHITE CYC BLUE FLOOD - STRAIGHT DOWN ⌒ WATCH BORDER U.S.	540/540 & FROST
28/14	BACKLIGHT COOL - 2R AT 6UP - FLOOD FOCUS.	541
56/15	WARM BEAM - 4R AT 5UP - FLOOD FOCUS.	553
28/16	BACKLIGHT COOL - 7R AT 6UP - FLOOD FOCUS.	541

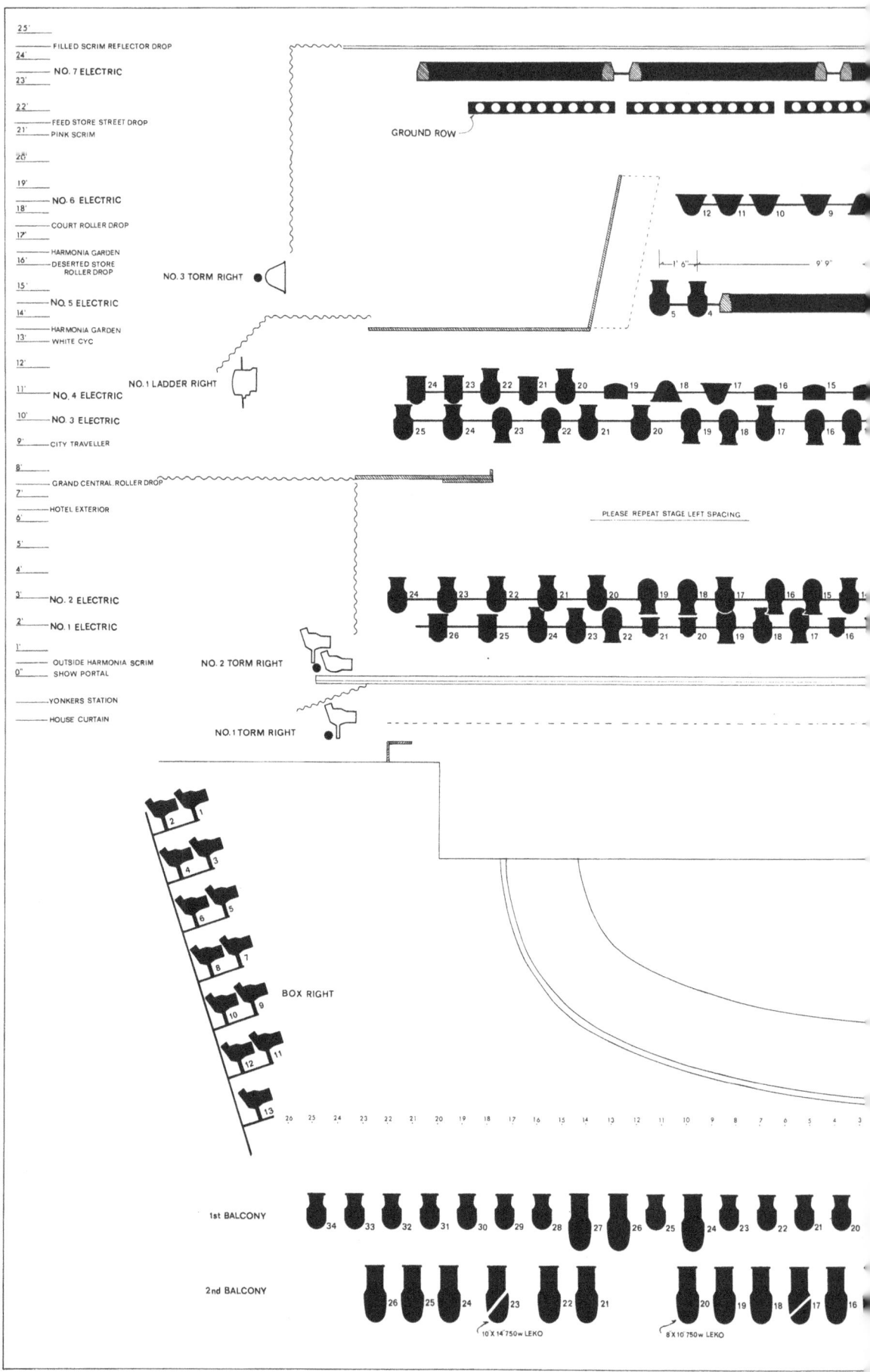

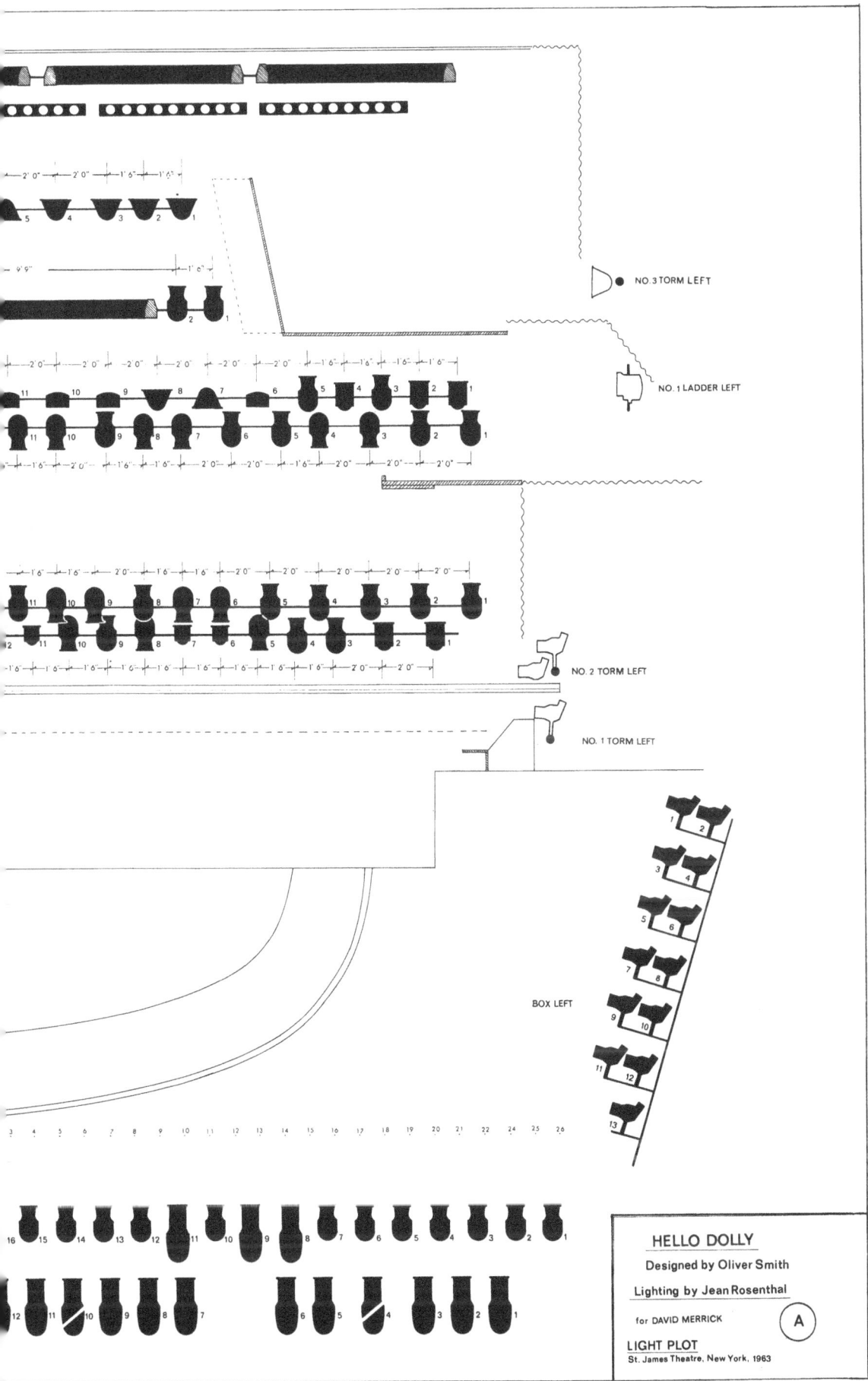

HELLO DOLLY

Designed by Oliver Smith

Lighting by Jean Rosenthal

for DAVID MERRICK (A)

LIGHT PLOT
St. James Theatre, New York, 1963

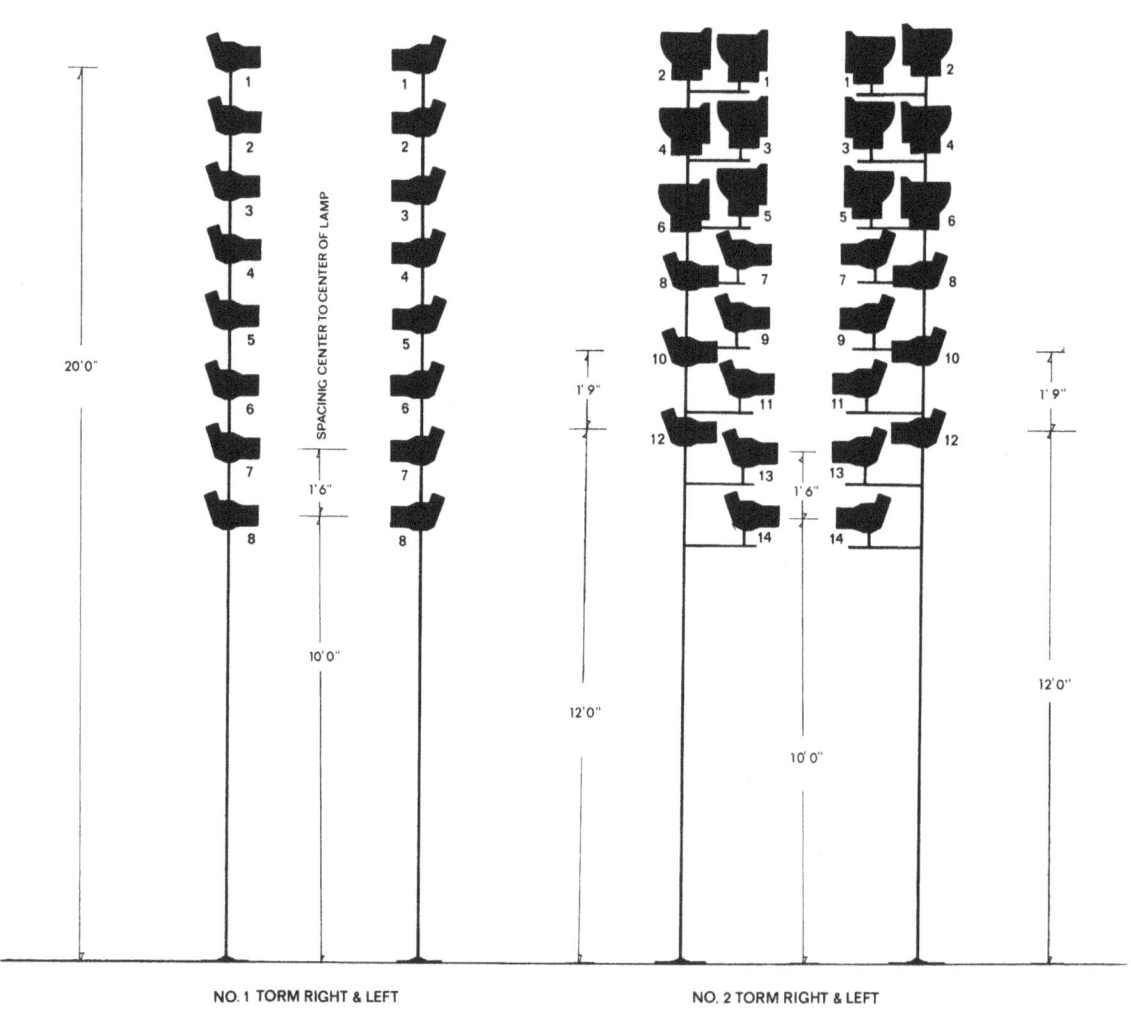

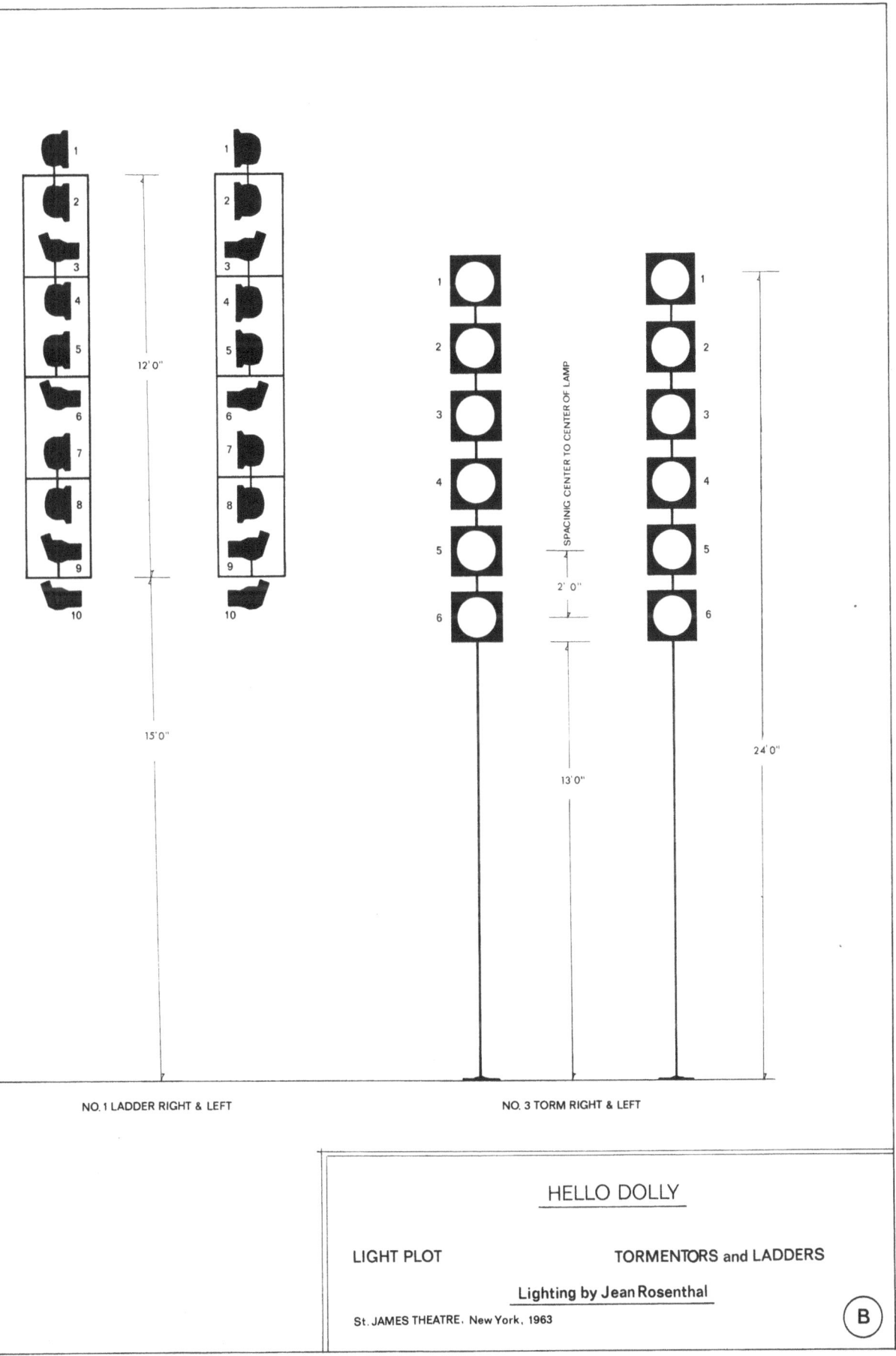

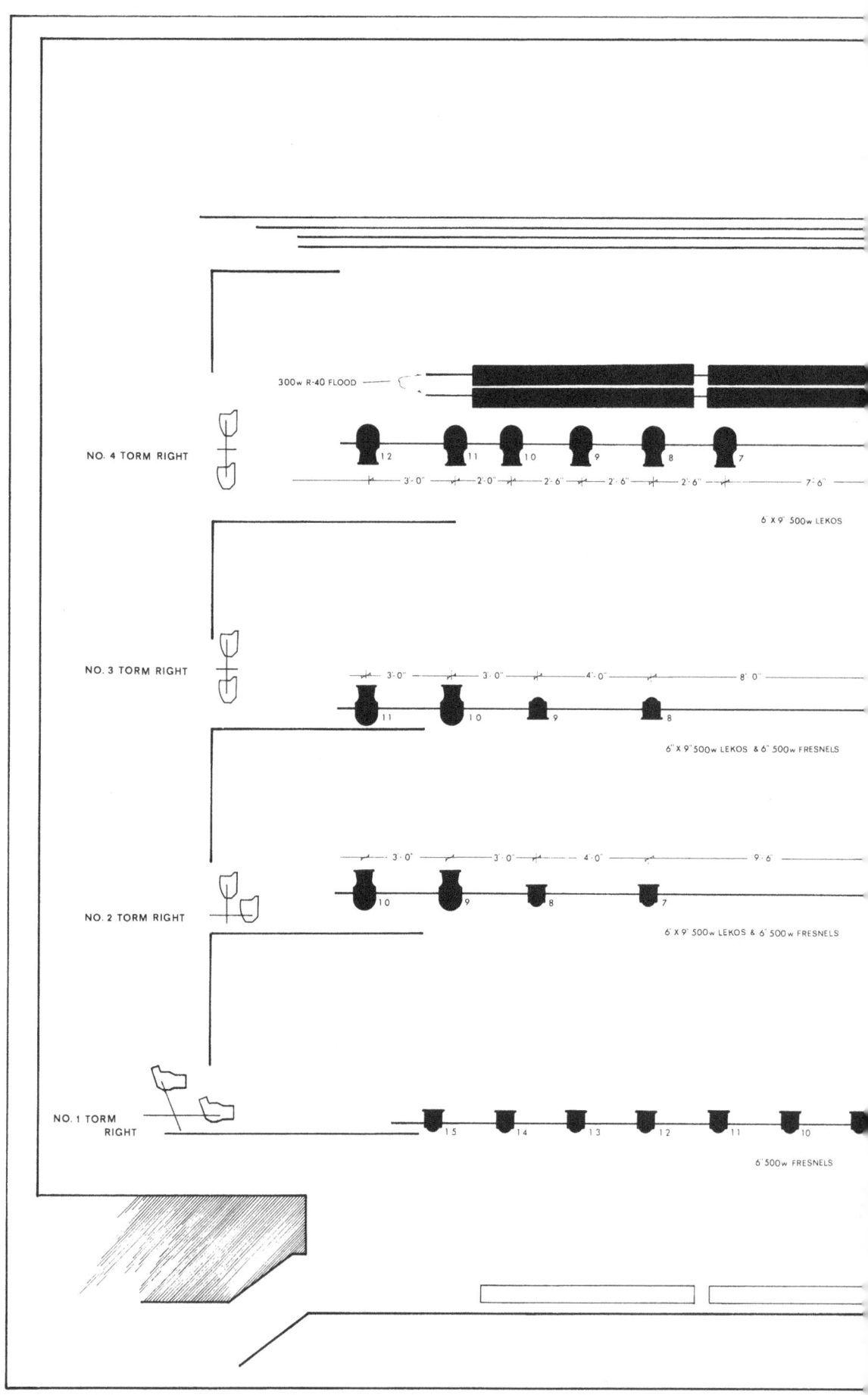

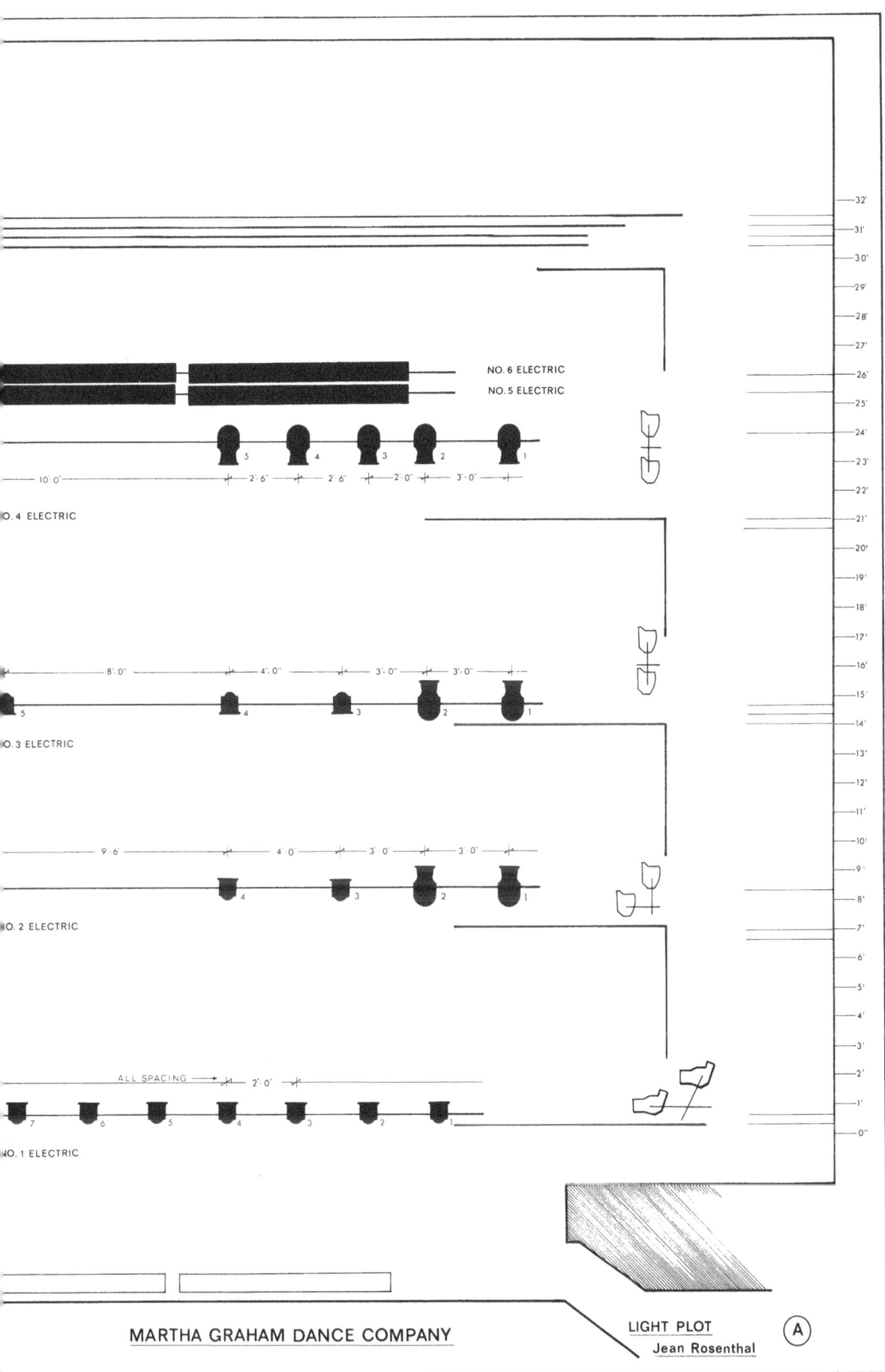

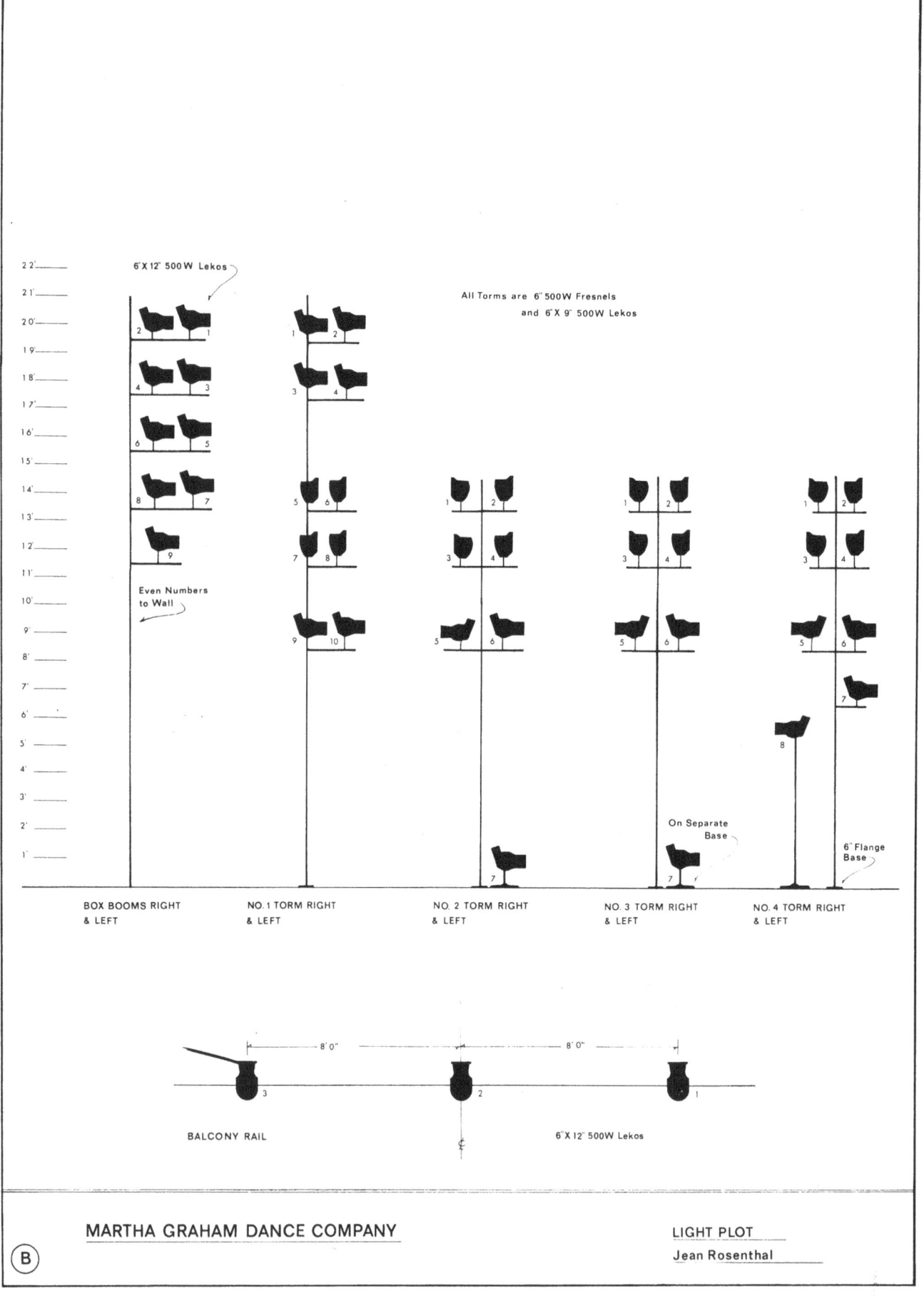

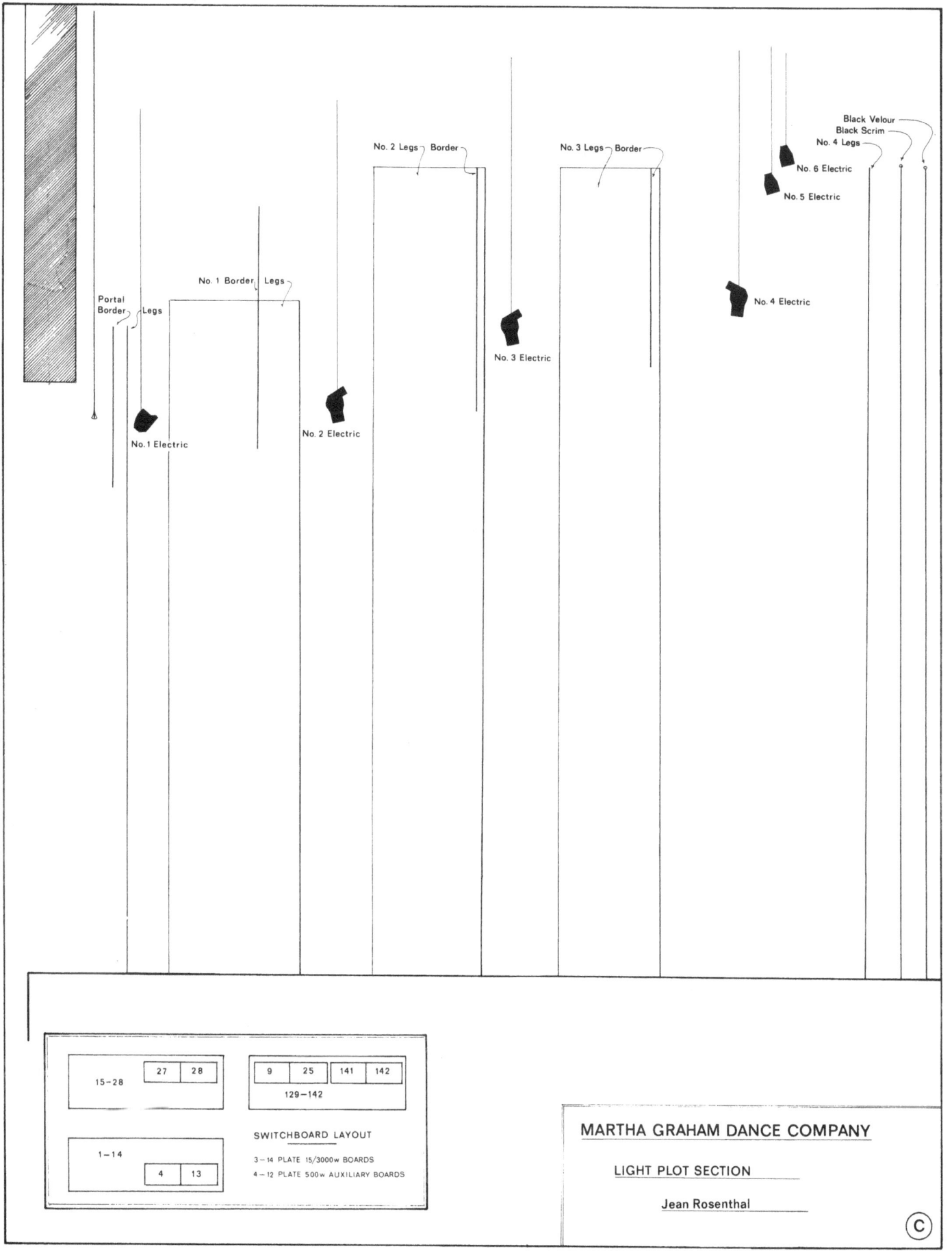

Appendix. Lighting by Jean Rosenthal

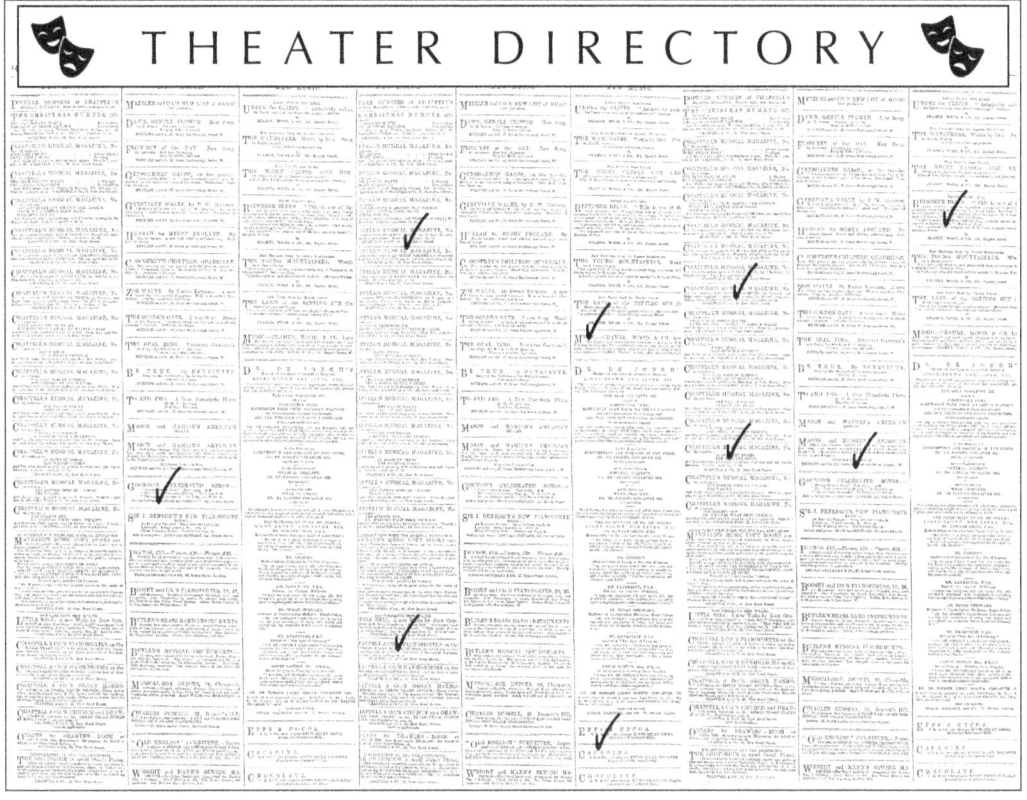

The archives of the performing arts have been kept, in the past, in a sketchy and random manner. Consistent records are available through the Research Libraries at Lincoln Center only for the past few years. The achievements of Jean Rosenthal's career were checked with the available sources. When dates were disputed, the source considered most reliable was used. If no verification of her participation in a remembered event could be found, that event was omitted. Unless she is specifically credited for other functions, Jean Rosenthal did the lighting for all the performances listed here.

Early Nonlighting Credits

Miscellaneous Productions

"LA BELLE HÉLÈNE" (pre-Broadway tryout, Westport County Playhouse, July 1941)
Choreography: Demetrios Vilan and Felicia Sorel
Costumes: Karinska
Director and designer: Stewart Chaney
General production supervisor: Jean Rosenthal
Music: Herbert Kingsley (Offenbach and A. P. Herbert)

"HAMLET" (Nov. 10, 1936)
Director: Leslie Howard, in collaboration with John Houseman
Mime for players: Agnes de Mille
Music: Virgil Thomson
Sets and costumes: Stewart Chaney
Assistant stage manager: Jean Rosenthal

NEIGHBORHOOD PLAYHOUSE
Jean Rosenthal was staff lecturer, Oct. 5, 1937 to May 16, 1938, on theatres, scenery, costumes, lighting, modes of production, and style of technique. She was on the faculty, Oct. 1, 1940 to May 14, 1941, as production advisor.

WPA FEDERAL THEATRE PROJECTS: Unit 891, Maxine Elliott Theatre
Jean Rosenthal was production assistant, 1936-1937. Projects included *Horse Eats Hat*, by the Orson Welles-John Houseman Unit.

The Mercury Theatre, Inc.

Jean Rosenthal was a member of the board and production and lighting manager, but was not credited in the program as lighting designer.

"THE CRADLE WILL ROCK" (opened at the Mercury, Dec. 5, 1937; moved to the Windsor Theatre, Jan. 3, 1938)
    Book, music and lyrics: Marc Blitzstein
    Staging: Marc Blitzstein
    Production supervisor: Jean Rosenthal

"DANTON'S DEATH" by Georg Büchner (opened Nov. 2, 1938)
    Producer: Orson Welles
    Production manager: Jean Rosenthal
    Songs: Marc Blitzstein
    With Orson Welles, Joseph Cotten, Martin Gabel, Arlene Francis, Vladimir Sokoloff

"FIVE KINGS," chronicle plays of Shakespeare, adapted by Orson Welles (opened March 20, 1939; played Philadelphia, Boston, Washington; closed out of town)
    Costumes: Millia Davenport
    Production supervisor: Jean Rosenthal
    Scenery: James Morcom

"HEARTBREAK HOUSE" by George Bernard Shaw (opened April 25, 1938)
    Costumes: Millia Davenport
    General stage director: Jean Rosenthal
    Setting: John Koenig
    Staging: Orson Welles
    With Geraldine Fitzgerald, Brenda Forbes, Orson Welles, Mady Christians, Vincent Price, George Coulouris

"JULIUS CAESAR" by William Shakespeare (opened Nov. 10, 1937)
    Music: Marc Blitzstein
    Production: Orson Welles
    Production manager: Jean Rosenthal
    Setting: Samuel Leve

"NATIVE SON" by Paul Green and Richard Wright (opened March 24, 1941)
    Presented by Orson Welles and John Houseman, in association with Bern Bernard
    Production supervisor: Jean Rosenthal*
    With Canada Lee, Ray Collins, Everett Sloane

"THE SHOEMAKER'S HOLIDAY" by Thomas Dekker (opened Jan. 1, 1938)
    Costumes: Millia Davenport
    Music: Lehman Engel
    Production: Orson Welles
    Production manager: Jean Rosenthal
    Scenery: Samuel Leve

"TOO MUCH JOHNSON" by William Gillette (tryout, Stony Creek, Conn., August 1938; never produced in New York)

Dance

A Holiday Dance Festival (Dec. 26-31, 1939)

Produced by Frances Hawkins in association with Jean Rosenthal, at the St. James Theatre.†

Sai Shoki — A Set of Korean Dances

*A newspaper notice credits her with lighting.
†This probably marks the beginning of Jean Rosenthal's professional relationship with George Balanchine and Lincoln Kirstein, which continued until 1957.

Carmalita Maracci — A Set of Spanish Dances

The American Ballet Caravan

"AIR AND VARIATION"
　　Choreography: William Dollar
　　Music: J. S. Bach ("The Goldberg Variations")
　　Costumes: Eudokia Mironowa

"BILLY THE KID"
　　Choreography: Eugene Loring
　　Music: Aaron Copland
　　Costumes: Jared French

"CHARADE, OR THE DEBUTANTE" (premiere Dec. 26, 1939)
　　Choreography: Lew Christensen
　　Music: American melodies arranged by Trude Rittman
　　Costumes: Alvin Colt

"CITY PORTRAIT" (premiere Dec. 28, 1939)
　　Choreography: Eugene Loring
　　Music: Henry Brant
　　Costumes: Forrest Thayr, Jr.

"FILLING STATION"
　　Choreography: Lew Christensen
　　Music: Virgil Thomson
　　Costumes: Paul Cadmus

"PROMENADE" (revival)
　　Choreography: William Dollar
　　Music: Maurice Ravel ("Les Valses Nobles et Sentimentales")
　　Costumes: Horace Vernet

"SERENADE," see under New York City Ballet

American Ballet (formerly American Ballet Caravan)

Latin American Tour, 1941. Miss Rosenthal did not go on the tour, but prepared the lighting in advance.

Ballet International (Marquis de Cuevas Company)

"CONSTANTIA" (Oct. 16, 1944)
　　Choreography: William Dollar
　　Music: Frédéric Chopin (Piano Concerto in F Minor)
　　Decor: Horace Armistead
　　Costumes: Grace Houston

"THE MUTE WIFE" (Nov. 22, 1944)
　　Choreography: Antonia Cobos
　　Music: Niccolò Paganini ("Perpetual Motion")
　　Decor and costumes: Rico Lebrun

"SEBASTIAN" (Oct. 31, 1944)
　　Choreography: Edward Caton
　　Music: Gian Carlo Menotti
　　Scenery: Oliver Smith
　　Costumes: Milena

Martha Graham*

"ACROBATS OF GOD" (April 27, 1960)
    Music: Carlos Surinach
    Scenery: Isamu Noguchi

"ALCESTIS" (April 29, 1960)
    Music: Vivian Fine
    Scenery: Isamu Noguchi

"AMERICAN DOCUMENT" (1938; lit by Jean Rosenthal in December 1939)
    Music: Ray Green
    Costumes: Edythe Gilfond

"APPALACHIAN SPRING" (Oct. 30, 1944)
    Music: Aaron Copland
    Scenery: Isamu Noguchi
    Costumes: Edythe Gilfond

"THE ARCHAIC HOURS" (April 11, 1969)†
    Music: Eugene Lester
    Scenery: Marion Kinsella

"ARDENT SONG" (March 18, 1954)
    Music: Alan Hovhaness

"CANTICLE FOR INNOCENT COMEDIANS" (April 22, 1952)
    Music: Thomas Ribbink
    Scenery: Frederick Kiesler

"CAVE OF THE HEART" (May 10, 1946)
    Music: Samuel Barber
    Scenery: Isamu Noguchi
    Costumes: Edythe Gilfond

"CELEBRATION" (1934; lit by Jean Rosenthal in 1939)
    Music: Louis Horst

"CHRONICLE" (Dec. 20, 1936)
    Music: Wallingford Riegger
    Scenery: Isamu Noguchi

"CIRCE" (Sept. 6, 1963)
    Music: Alan Hovhaness
    Scenery: Isamu Noguchi

"CLYTEMNESTRA" (April 1, 1958)
    Music: Halim El-Dabh
    Scenery: Isamu Noguchi

"COLUMBIAD" (Dec. 27, 1939)
    Music: Louis Horst
    Scenery: Philip Stapp
    Costumes: Edythe Gilfond

*Unless otherwise credited, all costumes for Martha Graham productions were designed by Miss Graham, and all choreography was by her.

†This was J. R.'s last creative work, and it was performed at the New York City Center. It is interesting to note that on Feb. 20, 21, and 22, 1930, at the same theatre, then called the Mecca Auditorium, the Neighborhood Playhouse and the Cleveland Symphony Orchestra presented *A Pagan Poem* by Charles Martin Loeffler, directed by Irene Lewissohn, danced by Martha Graham and Charles Weidman. Listed on the program was:

    Assistant Stage Manager: Jean Rosenthal

She was then a student at the Neighborhood Playhouse. Her first credit and her last, and a vast body of her work in dance and opera, were performed here.

"CORTEGE OF EAGLES" (Feb. 21, 1967)
    Music: Eugene Lester
    Scenery: Isamu Noguchi

"DANCING GROUND" (Feb. 24, 1967)
    Music: Ned Rorem
    Scenery: Jean Rosenthal

"DARK MEADOW" (Jan. 23, 1946)
    Music: Carlos Chávez
    Scenery: Isamu Noguchi
    Costumes: Edythe Gilfond

"DEATHS AND ENTRANCES" (July 1943; lit by Jean Rosenthal later in the season)
    Music: Hunter Johnson
    Scenery: Arch Lauterer
    Costumes: Edythe Gilfond

"DEEP SONG" (1937; lit by Jean Rosenthal in December 1939)
    Music: Henry Cowell

"DIVERSION OF ANGELS" (premiere Aug. 13, 1948, American Dance Festival, Connecticut College Palmer Auditorium, New London)
    Music: Norman dello Joio
    Scenery: Isamu Noguchi
    Costumes: Oliver Gray

"EL PENITENTE" (1940; lit at a later time by Jean Rosenthal)
    Music: Louis Horst
    Scenery: Arch Lauterer
    Costumes: Edythe Gilfond

"EMBATTLED GARDEN" (April 3, 1958)
    Music: Carlos Surinach
    Scenery: Isamu Noguchi

"EPISODES: PART I" (May 14, 1959)
    Music: Anton von Webern
    Scenery: David Hays
    Costumes: Karinska

"ERRAND INTO THE MAZE" (Feb. 28, 1947)
    Music: Gian Carlo Menotti
    Scenery: Isamu Noguchi

"EVE OF ANGUISH" (Jan. 22, 1950)
    Music: Vincent Persichetti
    Scenery: Henry Kurth
    Costumes: Fred Cunning

"EVERY SOUL IS A CIRCUS" (Dec. 27, 1939)
    Music: Paul Nordoff
    Scenery: Philip Stapp
    Costumes: Edythe Gilfond

"FRONTIER" (1935; lit by Jean Rosenthal in December 1939)
    Music: Louis Horst
    Scenery: Isamu Noguchi

"GOSPEL OF EVE" (Jan. 23, 1950)
    Music: Paul Nordoff
    Scenery: Oliver Smith
    Costumes: Miles White

"HÉRODIADE" (Oct. 30, 1944)
    Music: Paul Hindemith
    Scenery: Isamu Noguchi
    Costumes: Edythe Gilfond

"IMAGINED WING" (Oct. 30, 1944)
    Music: Darius Milhaud
    Scenery: Isamu Noguchi
    Costumes: Edythe Gilfond

"JUDITH" (Jan. 4, 1950)
    Music: William Schuman
    Scenery: Charles Hyman, William Sherman, Isamu Noguchi

"THE LADY OF THE HOUSE OF SLEEP" (May 30, 1968)
    Music: Robert Starer
    Scenery: Ming Cho Lee

"LAMENTATION" (1930; Jean Rosenthal lit a later revival in December 1939)
    Music: Zoltán Kodály

"LEGEND OF JUDITH" (Oct. 25, 1962)
    Music: Mordecai Seter
    Scenery: Dani Karavan

"LETTER TO THE WORLD" (August 1940; lit at a later time by Jean Rosenthal)
    Music: Hunter Johnson
    Scenery: Arch Lauterer
    Costumes: Edythe Gilfond

"A LOOK AT LIGHTNING" (March 5, 1962)
    Music: Halim El-Dabh
    Scenery: Ming Cho Lee

"NIGHT JOURNEY" (May 3, 1947)
    Music: William Schuman
    Scenery: Isamu Noguchi

"ONE MORE GAUDY NIGHT" (April 20, 1961)
    Music: Halim El-Dabh
    Scenery: Jean Rosenthal

"PART REAL—PART DREAM" (Nov. 3, 1965)
    Music: Mordecai Seter
    Scenery: Dani Karavan

"PHAEDRA" (March 4, 1962)
    Music: Robert Starer
    Scenery: Isamu Noguchi

"THE PLAIN OF PRAYER" (May 29, 1968)
    Music: Eugene Lester
    Scenery: Jean Rosenthal

"PRIMITIVE MYSTERIES" (1931; lit by Jean Rosenthal in December 1939)
    Music: Louis Horst

"PUNCH AND THE JUDY" (August 1941; lit at a later time by Jean Rosenthal)
    Music: Robert McBride
    Scenery: Arch Lauterer
    Costumes: Charlotte Trowbridge

"SALEM SHORE" (Dec. 26, 1943)
    Music: Paul Nordoff
    Scenery: Arch Lauterer
    Costumes: Edythe Gilfond

"SAMSON AGONISTES" (March 6, 1962; a new version of *Visionary Recital*)
    Music: Robert Starer
    Scenery: Rouben Ter-Arutunian

"SARABANDE" (1934; second of four solos in work called *Transitions*. Jean Rosenthal lit a later revival, probably in December 1939)
    Music: Lehman Engel

"SECULAR GAMES" (Aug. 17, 1962; American Dance Festival, Connecticut College)
    Music: Robert Starer
    Scenery: Jean Rosenthal

"SERAPHIC DIALOGUE" (May 8, 1955)
    Music: Norman dello Joio
    Scenery: Isamu Noguchi

"A TIME OF SNOW" (*Heloise and Abelard*; May 25, 1968)
    Music: Norman dello Joio
    Scenery: Rouben Ter-Arutunian

"THE TRIUMPH OF SAINT JOAN" (Dec. 5, 1951)
    Music: Norman dello Joio
    Scenery: Frederick Kiesler

"TWO PRIMITIVE CANTICLES" (1931; lit by Jean Rosenthal in December 1939)
    Music: Heitor Villa-Lobos

"VISIONARY RECITAL" (April 16, 1961)
    Music: Robert Starer
    Scenery: Rouben Ter-Arutunian

"VOYAGE" (May 17, 1953; new version, *Theatre For a Voyage*, May 5, 1955)
    Music: William Schuman
    Scenery: Isamu Noguchi
    Costumes: Edythe Gilfond

"THE WITCH OF ENDOR" (Nov. 2, 1965)
    Music: William Schuman
    Scenery: Ming Cho Lee

Ballet Society (1946-1948)
Lighting and technical director: Jean Rosenthal

"BLACKFACE" (May 18, 1947)
    Choreography: Lew Christensen
    Music: Carter Herman
    Costumes and decor: Robert Drew

"CAPRICORN CONCERTO" (March 22, 1948)
    Choreography: Todd Bolender
    Music: Samuel Barber
    Costumes and decor: Esteban Francés

"DIVERTIMENTO" (Jan. 13, 1947)
    Choreography: George Balanchine
    Music: Alexei Haieff
    (Performed in practice clothes, no set)

"ÉLÉGIE" (April 28, 1948)
    Choreography: George Balanchine
    Music: Igor Stravinsky

"THE FOUR TEMPERAMENTS" (Nov. 20, 1946; later moved into New York City Ballet Repertory)
    Choreography: George Balanchine
    Music: Paul Hindemith
    Costumes and decor: Kurt Seligmann

"HIGHLAND FLING" (March 26, 1947)
    Choreographer: William Dollar
    Music: Stanley Bate
    Costumes and decor: David Ffolkes

"THE MINOTAUR" (March 26, 1947)
    Choreography: John Taras
    Music: Elliott Carter
    Costumes and decor: Joan Junyer

"ORPHEUS" (April 4, 1948; later moved into New York City Ballet repertory)
    Choreography: George Balanchine
    Music: Igor Stravinsky
    Costumes and decor: Isamu Noguchi

"PASTORELA" (Jan. 13, 1947)
    Choreography: Lew Christensen
    Music: Paul Bowles
    Costumes and decor: Alvin Colt
    Book: José Martínez

"PUNCH AND THE CHILD" (Nov. 12, 1947)
    Choreography: Fred Danieli
    Music: Richard Arnell
    Costumes and decor: Horace Armistead

"RENARD" (The Fox; Jan. 13, 1947)
    Choreography: George Balanchine
    Music: Igor Stravinsky
    Costumes and decor: Esteban Francés

"THE SEASONS" (May 18, 1947)
    Choreography: Merce Cunningham
    Music: John Cage
    Costumes and decor: Isamu Noguchi

"SERENADE" (November 1948; see under New York City Ballet)

"THE SPELLBOUND CHILD" (Nov. 20, 1946)
    Choreography: George Balanchine
    Music: Maurice Ravel
    Costumes and decor: Aline Bernstein
    Poem: Colette

"SYMPHONIE CONCERTANTE" (Nov. 12, 1947; later moved into New York City Ballet repertory)
    Choreography: George Balanchine
    Music: Wolfgang Amadeus Mozart
    Costumes and decor: James Stewart Morcom

"SYMPHONY IN C" (March 22, 1948; later moved into New York City Ballet repertory)
    Choreography: George Balanchine
    Music: Georges Bizet

"THE TRIUMPH OF BACCHUS AND ARIADNE" (Feb. 9, 1948)
    Choreography: George Balanchine
    Music: Vittorio Rieti
    Costumes and decor: Corrado Cagli

"ZODIAC" (March 26, 1947)
  Choreography: Todd Bolender
  Music: Rudi Revil
  Costumes and decor: Esteban Francés

José Limón and Company*

"THE MOOR'S PAVANNE" (August 1949; Connecticut College, Palmer Auditorium, New London; December 1949, New York City Center; now in American Ballet Theatre Reportory)
  Choreography: José Limón
  Costumes: Pauline Lawrence

"RITMO JONDO" (April 15, 1953; Alvin Theatre, New York, Dance Festival season)
  Choreography: Doris Humphrey
  Music: Carlos Surinach
  Scenery: Jean Rosenthal (after painting by Charles Oscar)

New York City Ballet (1948-1957)
Lighting and technical director: Jean Rosenthal

"AFTERNOON OF A FAUN"† (May 14, 1953; also in repertory of Jerome Robbins, Ballets U.S.A.)
  Choreography: Jerome Robbins
  Music: Claude Debussy
  Costumes: Irene Sharaff
  Set: Jean Rosenthal

"AGE OF ANXIETY" (Feb. 26, 1950)
  Choreography: Jerome Robbins
  Music: Leonard Bernstein (based on W. H. Auden's poem)
  Decor: Oliver Smith
  Costumes: Irene Sharaff

"A LA FRANÇAIX" (Sept. 11, 1951)
  Choreography: George Balanchine
  Music: Jean Françaix ("Serenade for Small Orchestra")

"ALLEGRO BRILLANTE" (March 1, 1956)
  Choreography: George Balanchine
  Music: Pëtr Ilich Tchaikovsky (from the unfinished Third Piano Concerto)

"APOLLO" (Revival, Nov. 15, 1951)
  Choreography: George Balanchine
  Music and book: Igor Stravinsky

"LE BAISER DE LA FÉE" (Nov. 28, 1950)
  Choreography: George Balanchine
  Music and book: Igor Stravinsky
  Costumes and scenery: Alicia Halicka

"BALLADE" (Feb. 14, 1952)
  Choreography: Jerome Robbins

*Jean Rosenthal lit several seasons for José Limón, mostly in dance festivals at Connecticut College or in New York City.

†At this printing, Jean Rosenthal's decor and lighting have been added to the repertory of the Royal Ballet, Covent Garden, London. The first performance was Dec. 14, 1971.

Music: Claude Debussy ("Six Epigraphes Antiques")
Costumes and scenery: Boris Aronson

"BAYOU" (Feb. 21, 1952)
Choreography: George Balanchine
Music: Virgil Thomson
Costumes and scenery: Dorothea Tanning

"BOURRÉE FANTASQUE" (Dec. 1, 1949)
Choreography: George Balanchine
Music: Emmanuel Chabrier
Costumes: Karinska
Lighting and scenery: Jean Rosenthal

"THE CAGE" (June 14, 1951)
Choreography: Jerome Robbins
Music: Igor Stravinsky (Concerto Grosso in D for Strings)
Costumes: Ruth Sobotka
Decor and lighting: Jean Rosenthal

"CAKEWALK" (June 12, 1951)
Choreography: Ruthanna Boris
Music: Louis Moreau Gottschalk, arranged and orchestrated by Hershy Kay
Costumes and decor: Robert John Drew

"CAPRICCIO BRILLANTE" (June 7, 1951)
Choreography: George Balanchine
Music: Felix Mendelssohn
Costumes: Karinska

"CARACOLE" (Feb. 19, 1952; restaged 1956 as *Divertimento No. 15,* which see)
Choreography: George Balanchine
Music: Wolfgang Amadeus Mozart (Divertimento No. 15, K. 287)
Decor: James Stewart Morcom
Costumes: Christian Bérard

"CARD GAME" (Revival; Feb. 15, 1951)
Choreography: George Balanchine
Music and book: Igor Stravinsky
Costumes and decor: Irene Sharaff

"CON AMORE" (June 9, 1953)
Choreography: Lew Christensen
Music: Gioacchino Rossini
Libretto: James Graham-Lujan
Scenery and costumes: James Bodrero (physical production borrowed from San Francisco Ballet Company; new scenery and costumes in 1954 by Esteban Francés)

"THE CONCERT" (March 6, 1956; revived and restaged. See Jerome Robbins' Ballets U.S.A.)
Choreography: Jerome Robbins
Music: Frédéric Chopin
Costumes: Irene Sharaff
Decor and lighting: Jean Rosenthal

"CONCERTO BAROCCO"* (Oct. 11, 1948)
Choreography: George Balanchine
Music: Johann Sebastian Bach (Concerto in D Minor for Two Violins)
Costumes and decor: Eugene Berman (restaged in 1951 with cyclorama and black practice clothes)

"CONCERTINO" (Dec. 30, 1952)
Choreography: George Balanchine

Music: Jean Françaix
Costumes: Karinska

"DIVERTIMENTO" (1948 revival; originally done for Ballet Society)
Choreography: George Balanchine
Music: Alexei Haieff
Performed in practice costumes, no sets

"DIVERTIMENTO NO. 15" (Dec. 19, 1956; restaging of *Caracole*)
Choreography: George Balanchine
Music: Wolfgang Amadeus Mozart
Scenery: James Stewart Morcom
Costumes: Karinska

"THE DUEL" (Feb. 24, 1950)
Choreography: William Dollar
Music: Raffaello de Banfield
Costumes: Robert Stevenson

"FANFARE" (June 2, 1953)†
Choreography: Jerome Robbins
Music: Benjamin Britten
Costumes and scenery: Irene Sharaff
Jean Rosenthal did the lighting, although not credited on the program.

"FILLING STATION" (May 12, 1953 revival; premiere by Ballet Caravan, Hartford, Conn., Jan. 6, 1938)
Choreography: Lew Christensen
Music: Virgil Thomson
Book: Lincoln Kirstein
Scenery and costumes: Paul Cadmus

"FIREBIRD" (Nov. 27, 1949)
Choreography: George Balanchine
Music: Igor Stravinsky
Costumes and decor: Marc Chagall

"THE FILLY" (or *A Stableboy's Dream*; May 19, 1953)
Choreography: Todd Bolender
Music: John Colman
Scenery and costumes: Peter Larkin

"THE FIVE GIFTS" (Jan. 20, 1953)
Choreography: William Dollar
Music: Ernest Dohnanyi
Costumes: Esteban Francés

"THE FOUR TEMPERAMENTS" (Oct. 25, 1948; originally done for Ballet Society)
Choreography: George Balanchine
Music: Paul Hindemith
Costumes and decor: Kurt Seligmann (Scenery and costumes discarded in favor of practice clothes and plain backdrop in November 1951.)

"LA GLOIRE" (Feb. 26, 1952)
Choreography: Anthony Tudor
Music: Ludwig van Beethoven (Overtures to "Egmont" and "Coriolanus," and the "Leonora" Overture No. 3)
Decor: Gaston Longchamp
Costumes: Robert Fletcher

*Performed at New York City Center the night New York City Ballet was born.
†First performance Coronation Night, Elizabeth II of England.

"THE GUESTS" (Jan. 20, 1949)
    Choreography: Jerome Robbins
    Music: Marc Blitzstein
"HARLEQUINADE PAS DE DEUX" (Dec. 16, 1952)
    Choreography: George Balanchine
    Music: Richard Drigo
    Costumes: Karinska
"ILLUMINATIONS" (March 2, 1950)
    Choreography: Frederick Ashton
    Music: Benjamin Britten (poems by Arthur Rimbaud set to music)
    Costumes and decor: Cecil Beaton
"INTERPLAY" (Dec. 23, 1952; also in repertory of American Ballet Theatre)
    Choreography: Jerome Robbins
    Music: Morton Gould
    Scenery and costumes: Irene Sharaff
"IVESIANA" (Sept. 14, 1954)
    Choreography: George Balanchine
    Music: Charles Ives
"JEUX d'ENFANTS" (Nov. 22, 1955)
    Choreography: George Balanchine, Barbara Milberg, Francisco Moncion
    Music: Georges Bizet
    Scenery and costumes: Esteban Francés
"JINX" (Nov. 24, 1949; premiere by Dance Players, New York City, April 24, 1942)
    Choreography: Lew Christensen
    Music: Benjamin Britten (Variations on a Theme by Frank Bridge)
    Costumes and decor: George Bockman
"JONES BEACH" (March 9, 1950)
    Choreography: George Balanchine and Jerome Robbins
    Music: Juriaan Andriessen (Berkshire Symphonies)
    Costumes: Jantzen
"KALEIDOSCOPE" (Dec. 18, 1952)
    Choreography: Ruthanna Boris
    Music: Dmitri Kabalevsky
    Costumes: Alvin Colt
    Decor and lighting: Jean Rosenthal (decor not credited)
"LADY OF THE CAMELLIAS" (Feb. 28, 1951)
    Choreography: Anthony Tudor
    Music: Giuseppe Verdi
    Costumes and decor: Cecil Beaton
"LILAC GARDEN" (Nov. 30, 1951; revival)
    Choreography: Anthony Tudor
    Music: Ernest Chausson
    Decor: Horace Armistead
    Costumes: Karinska
"THE MASQUERS" (March 29, 1957; no lighting credited on premiere, Jan. 29, 1957)
    Choreography: Todd Bolender
    Music: Francis Poulenc (Sextet for Wind Instruments and Piano)
    Scenery and costumes: David Hays
"MAZURKA, FROM A LIFE FOR THE TSAR" (Nov. 30, 1950)
    Choreography: George Balanchine
    Music: Mikhail Glinka

"METAMORPHOSES" (Nov. 25, 1952)
    Choreography: George Balanchine
    Music: Paul Hindemith (Variations on Themes of Carl Maria von Weber)
    Decor and lighting: Jean Rosenthal (decor not credited)
    Costumes: Karinska

"THE MIRACULOUS MANDARIN" (Sept. 6, 1951)
    Choreography: Todd Bolender
    Music: Béla Bartók
    Decor and costumes: Alvin Colt

"MOTHER GOOSE SUITE" (Nov. 1, 1948)
    Choreography: Todd Bolender
    Music: Maurice Ravel
    Costumes: André Derain

"THE NUTCRACKER" (Feb. 2, 1954)
    Choreography: George Balanchine
    Music: Pëtr Ilich Tchaikovsky
    Scenery: Horace Armistead
    Costumes: Karinska
    Masks: Vlady
    Lighting and production: Jean Rosenthal

"ONDINE" (Dec. 9, 1949)
    Choreography: William Dollar
    Music: Antonio Vivaldi
    Decor and costumes: Horace Armistead

"OPUS 34" (Jan. 19, 1954)
    Choreography: George Balanchine
    Music: Arnold Schönberg
    Costumes: Esteban Francés
    Decor and lighting: Jean Rosenthal

"ORPHEUS" (Oct. 11, 1948)*
    Choreography: George Balanchine
    Music: Igor Stravinsky
    Decor and costumes: Isamu Noguchi

"PAS DE DEUX ROMANTIQUE" (March 3, 1950)
    Choreography: George Balanchine
    Music: Carl Maria von Weber
    Costumes: Robert Stevenson

"PAS DE DIX" (Nov. 9, 1955)
    Choreography: George Balanchine
    Music: Alexander Glazounov
    Costumes: Esteban Francés

"PAS DE TROIS" (Feb. 18, 1951; revival)
    Choreography: George Balanchine
    Music: Leon Minkus
    Costumes: Karinska

"PAS DE TROIS (II)" (March 1, 1955)
    Choreography: George Balanchine
    Music: Mikhail Glinka
    Costumes: Karinska

"PASTORALE" (Feb. 14, 1957)
    Choreography: Francisco Moncion

*Performed the night the New York City Ballet was born. Originally presented by Ballet Society.

Music: Charles Turner
Scenery: David Hays
Costumes: Ruth Sobotka

"PICNIC AT TINTAGEL" (Feb. 28, 1952)
Choreography: Frederick Ashton
Music: Sir Arnold Bax (The Garden of Fand)
Costumes and decor: Cecil Beaton

"THE PIED PIPER" (Dec. 4, 1951)
Choreography: Jerome Robbins
Music: Aaron Copland (Concerto for Clarinet and String Orchestra)

"THE PRODIGAL SON" (Feb. 23, 1950)
Choreography: George Balanchine
Music: Sergei Prokofiev
Costumes and decor: Georges Roualt (added the following season)

"QUARTET" (Feb. 18, 1954)
Choreography: Jerome Robbins
Music: Sergei Prokofiev
Scenery: Jean Rosenthal
Costumes: Karinska

"ROMA" (Feb. 23, 1955)
Choreography: George Balanchine
Music: Georges Bizet (Roma Suite)
Scenery and costumes: Eugene Berman

"SCOTCH SYMPHONY" (Nov. 11, 1952)
Choreography: George Balanchine
Music: Felix Mendelssohn
Scenery: Horace Armistead
Women's costumes: Karinska
Men's costumes: David Ffolkes

"SERENADE" (Oct. 18, 1948)
Choreography: George Balanchine
Music: Pëtr Ilich Tchaikovsky (Serenade in C Major for String Orchestra)

"SOUVENIRS" (Nov. 15, 1955)
Choreography: Todd Bolender
Music: Samuel Barber
Scenery and costumes: Rouben Ter-Arutunian

"THE STILL POINT" (March 13, 1956)
Choreography: Todd Bolender
Music: Claude Debussy (String Quartet) transcribed for orchestra by Frank Black

"SWAN LAKE" (Act II; Nov. 19, 1957)
Choreography: George Balanchine (after Lev Ivanov)
Music: Pëtr Ilich Tchaikovsky
Decor and costumes: Cecil Beaton

"SYLVIA: PAS DE DEUX" (Dec. 1, 1950)
Choreography: George Balanchine
Music: Léo Delibes
Costumes: Karinska

"SYMPHONY CONCERTANTE" (1948 revival; originally done for Ballet Society)
Choreography: George Balanchine
Music: Wolfgang Amadeus Mozart (Sinfonia Concertante in E Flat Major for Violins and Viola)
Costumes and decor: James Stewart Morcom

"SYMPHONY IN C" (Nov. 11, 1948)*
    Choreography: George Balanchine
    Music: Georges Bizet

"TIMETABLE" (January 1949)
    Choreography: Anthony Tudor
    Music: Aaron Copland
    Costumes and decor: James Stewart Morcom

"TYL EULENSPIEGEL" (Nov. 14, 1951)
    Choreography: George Balanchine
    Music: Richard Strauss
    Costumes and decor: Esteban Francés

"THE UNICORN, THE GORGON, AND THE MANTICORE" (Feb. 15, 1957)
    Choreography: John Butler
    Music and libretto: Gian Carlo Menotti
    Scenery and lighting: Jean Rosenthal
    Costumes: Robert Fletcher

"LA VALSE" (Feb. 20, 1951)
    Choreography: George Balanchine
    Music: Maurice Ravel ("Valses Nobles et Sentimentales," and "La Valse")
    Costumes: Karinska
    Decor and lighting: Jean Rosenthal (decor not credited)

"VALSE FANTAISIE" (Jan. 6, 1953)
    Choreography: George Balanchine
    Music: Mikhail Glinka
    Costumes: Karinska

"WESTERN SYMPHONY" (Sept. 7, 1954)
    Choreography: George Balanchine
    Music: Hershy Kay (Symphony based on American folk themes)
    Scenery: John Boyt (added Feb. 27, 1955)
    Costumes: Karinska (added Feb. 27, 1955)

"WILL O' THE WISP" (Jan. 13, 1953)
    Choreography: Ruthanna Boris
    Music: Virgil Thomson
    Scenery and costumes: Dorothea Tanning

The New York City Center Dance Theatre (December 1949)

Lighting designer and production director: Jean Rosenthal

Companies: Charles Weidman
              José Limón
              Dudley-Maslow-Bales Trio

Artists: Valerie Bettis
        Nina Fonaroff
        Eve Gentry
        Katherine Litz
        Iris Mabry
        Merce Cunningham
        Peter Hamilton

*Performed the night New York City Ballet was born.

The Bethsabee De Rothschild Foundation Presents American Dance (Alvin Theatre, April 14-26, 1953)

Lighting designer and production director: Jean Rosenthal

Choreographers: Martha Graham
José Limón and Doris Humphrey
Merce Cunningham
Pearl Lang
May O'Donnell
Nina Fonaroff

The Bethsabee De Rothschild Foundation Presents American Dance (ANTA Theatre, May 3-22, 1955)

Lighting designer and production director: Jean Rosenthal

Choreographers: Martha Graham
John Butler
Pearl Lang
José Limón and Doris Humphrey
Valerie Bettis
Anna Sokolow
Janet Collins
Ann Halprin
Pauline Koner
Paul Draper
Daniel Nagrin
Iris Mabry

Jerome Robbins' Ballets: U.S.A. (1961 season, ANTA Theatre)

Lighting designer and production supervisor: Jean Rosenthal

"AFTERNOON OF A FAUN" (October 1961; see under New York City Ballet)

"THE CAGE" (October 1961; see under New York City Ballet)

"THE CONCERT" First performance, Festival of Two Worlds, Spoleto, Italy [lighting done "on paper"] June 8, 1958; Alvin Theatre, Sept. 4, 1958 and ANTA Theatre, October 1961 [as revised and restaged from New York City Ballet, which see]
Choreography: Jerome Robbins
Music: Frédéric Chopin
Scenery: Saul Steinberg
Costumes: Irene Sharaff

"EVENTS" (October 1961)
Choreography: Jerome Robbins
Music: Robert Prince
Decor: Ben Shahn
Costumes: Ray Diffen

"INTERPLAY" (see under New York City Ballet)

"NEW YORK EXPORT, OPUS JAZZ" (lit "on paper" for Festival of Two Worlds, Spoleto, Italy, June 1958; Alvin Theatre 1958, ANTA Theatre 1961)
Choreography: Jerome Robbins

  Music: Robert Prince
  Scenery: Ben Shahn
  Costumes: Ben Shahn and Florence Klotz

"3 × 3" (October 1958 and September 1961)
  Choreography: Jerome Robbins
  Music: George Auric (Wind Trio)
  Scenery: Jean Rosenthal
  Costumes: Irene Sharaff

American Ballet Theatre

"AT MIDNIGHT" (1968)
  Choreography: Eliot Feld
  Music: Gustav Mahler
  Decor: Leonard Baskin
  Costumes: Stanley Simmons

"BILLY THE KID" (April 29, 1960)
  Choreography: Eugene Loring
  Music: Aaron Copland
  Scenery: Jared French

"BLUEBEARD" (April 19, 1960)
  Choreography: Michel Fokine
  Music: Jacques Offenbach, arranged by Antal Dorati
  Scenery and costumes: Marcel Vertès

"THE CATHERINE WHEEL" (Dec. 7, 1967)
  Choreography: Michael Smuin
  Music: Timothy Thompson
  Scenery: Oliver Smith
  Costumes: Stanley Simmons

"CAPRICHOS" (May 5, 1960)
  Choreography: Herbert Ross
  Music: Béla Bartók ("Contrasts for Violin, Clarinet and Piano")
  Costumes: Helene Pons

"CHOPIN CONCERTO" (April 19, 1960)
  Choreography: William Dollar
  Music: Frédéric Chopin
  Costumes: Karinska

"THE COMBAT" (May 2, 1960)
  Choreography: William Dollar
  Music: Raffaelo de Banfield
  Scenery and costumes: Georges Wakhevitch

"DANSES CONCERTANTES" (Oct. 10, 1967)
  Choreography: Kenneth MacMillan
  Music: Igor Stravinsky
  Scenery and costumes: Nicholas Georgiadis

"DARK ELEGIES" (Revival; 1965)
  Choreography: Antony Tudor
  Music: Gustav Mahler
  Scenery and costumes: Nadia Benois

"DIALOGUES" (April 26, 1960)
  Choreography: Herbert Ross
  Music: Leonard Bernstein

Scenery: Jean Rosenthal
Costumes: Florence Klotz

"FALL RIVER LEGEND" (April 25, 1960)
Choreography: Agnes de Mille
Music: Morton Gould
Costumes: Miles White
Scenery: Oliver Smith

"LA FILLE MAL GARDÉE" (April 29, 1960)
Choreography: Dauberval, restaged by Dimitri Romanoff
Music: Wilhelm Hertel
Scenery and costumes: Sergei Soudeikine

"THE FOUR MARYS" (March 23, 1961)
Choreography: Agnes de Mille
Music: Trude Rittmann
Scenery: Oliver Smith
Costumes: Stanley Simmons

"THE FRAIL QUARRY" (Tally-Ho; April 2, 1965)
Choreography: Agnes de Mille
Music: Christoph Willibald Gluck
Scenery and costumes: Motley

"GARTENFEST" (Dec. 18, 1968)
Choreography: Michael Smuin
Music: Wolfgang Amadeus Mozart
Scenery: Jack Brown
Costumes: Marcos Paredes

"GISELLE" (April 21, 1960)
Choreography: Jean Coralli
Music: Adolphe Adam
Scenery and costumes: Eugene Berman

"GRAND PAS" (1961; Broadway)
Choreography: George Balanchine
Music: Alexander Glazounov
Costumes: Karinska and Tom Lingwood

"HARBINGER" (May 11, 1967)
Choreography: Eliot Feld
Music: Sergei Prokofiev
Scenery: Oliver Smith
Costumes: Stanley Simmons

"INTERPLAY" (Spring 1961; also in repertory of New York City Ballet)
Choreography: Jerome Robbins
Music: Morton Gould
Decor: Oliver Smith
Costumes: Irene Sharaff

"JARDIN AUX LILAS" (May 2, 1960)
Choreography: Antony Tudor
Music: Ernest Chausson
Scenery and costumes: Hugh Stevenson

"JUDGMENT OF PARIS" (April 30, 1960)
Choreography: Antony Tudor
Music: Kurt Weill
Sets and costumes: Lucinda Ballard

"LADY FROM THE SEA" (April 20, 1960)
Choreography: Brigit Cullberg

    Music: Knudage Riisager
    Scenery and costumes: Kerstin Hedeby

"THE MOOR'S PAVANNE" (July 1969; originally, Limón Company, Connecticut Dance Festival, 1951)
    Choreography: José Limón
    Music: Henry Purcell
    Costumes: Pauline Lawrence

"LES NOCES" (March 30, 1965)
    Choreography: Jerome Robbins
    Music: Igor Stravinsky
    Scenery: Oliver Smith
    Costumes: Irene Sharaff

"PAS ET LIGNES" (May 19, 1960)
    Choreography: Serge Lifar
    Music: Claude Debussy ("Petite Suite")

"PAS DE QUATRE" (April 28, 1960)
    Choreography: Anton Dolin
    Music: Cesare Pugni
    Costumes: after Chalon

"PILLAR OF FIRE" (April 19, 1960)
    Choreography: Antony Tudor
    Music: Arnold Schönberg
    Scenery and costumes: Jo Mielziner

"RODEO" (April 22, 1960)
    Choreography: Agnes de Mille
    Music: Aaron Copland
    Scenery: Oliver Smith
    Costumes: Motley

"RICERCARE" (Jan. 25, 1966)
    Choreography: Glen Tetley
    Music: Mordecai Seter
    Scenery and costumes: Rouben Ter-Arutunian

"SARGASSO" (March 24, 1965)
    Choreography: Glen Tetley
    Music: Ernst Křenek
    Decor and costumes: Rouben Ter-Arutunian

"SERENADE FOR SEVEN" (April 26, 1960)
    Choreography: Herbert Ross
    Music: Leonard Bernstein
    Decor: Jean Rosenthal
    Costumes: Florence Klotz

"LES SYLPHIDES" (April 1960)
    Choreography: Michel Fokine
    Music: Frédéric Chopin
    Scenery: Eugene Dunkel, after Jean Corot

"SWAN LAKE" (1967)
    Choreography: Petipa — Lev Ivanov, as staged by David Blair
    Music: Pëtr Ilich Tchaikovsky
    Scenery: Oliver Smith
    Costumes: Freddy Wittop

"THE WIND IN THE MOUNTAINS" (March 18, 1965)
    Choreography: Agnes de Mille
    Music: Laurence Rosenthal

Decor: Jean Rosenthal
Costumes: Stanley Simmons

Kansas City Performing Arts Foundation (Purcell Festival)

"FAERIE QUEEN" (May 1966)
    Choreography: Marina Svetlova
    Music: Henry Purcell
    Scenery and costumes: Peter Hall

Opera

Individual Productions

"ROSALINDA" (operetta adapted from *Die Fledermaus* by Johann Strauss; Oct. 28, 1942; The New Opera Company, Forty-fourth Street Theatre, New York)
    Staging: Felix Brentano
    Choreography: George Balanchine
    Settings: Oliver Smith

"THE CONSUL" by Gian Carlo Menotti (March 15, 1950). Produced by Efrem Zimbalist, Jr., and Chandler Cowles, at the Barrymore Theatre. Voted Best Musical of 1949-50 by the New York Drama Critics Circle.
    Staging: Gian Carlo Menotti
    Dream choreography: John Butler
    Settings: Horace Armistead
    With Patricia Neway and Marie Powers

The New Opera Company (five-week season from Nov. 3, 1942)

"THE BAT" by Johann Strauss

"FAIR AT SOROCHINSK" by Modest Moussorgsky

"MACBETH" by Giuseppe Verdi

"THE OPERA CLOAK" by Walter Damrosch

"THE QUEEN OF SPADES" by Pëtr Ilich Tchaikowsky

"LA VIE PARISIENNE" by Jacques Offenbach

Ballet Society

"THE MEDIUM" and "THE TELEPHONE" by Gian Carlo Menotti (opened at the Heckscher Theatre Feb. 18, 1947; moved to Broadway May 1, 1947)
    Director: Gian Carlo Menotti
    Costumes and decor: Horace Armistead
    Lighting and technical direction: Jean Rosenthal
    With Marie Powers

"FAR HARBOUR" by Baldwin Bergersen (produced at Hunter College, Jan. 22, 1948)
    Text and direction: William Archibald

Scenery and costumes: Horace Armistead
Lighting and technical direction: Jean Rosenthal

New York City Opera (1951 season)
Lighting director: Jean Rosenthal

"AÏDA" by Giuseppe Verdi

"LA BOHÈME" by Giacomo Puccini

"CAVALLERIA RUSTICANA" by Pietro Mascagni and "PAGLIACCI" by Ruggiero Leoncavallo

"CARMEN" by Georges Bizet

"DON GIOVANNI" by Wolfgang Amadeus Mozart

"MANON" by Jules Massenet

"THE MARRIAGE OF FIGARO" by Wolfgang Amadeus Mozart

"DIE MEISTERSINGER" by Richard Wagner

"RIGOLETTO" by Giuseppe Verdi

"DER ROSENKAVALIER" by Richard Strauss

"SALOME" by Richard Strauss

"TOSCA" by Giacomo Puccini

"LA TRAVIATA" by Giuseppe Verdi

"WOZZECK" by Alban Berg

New York City Opera (1953 season)
Production consultant and lighting: Jean Rosenthal

"AMAHL AND THE NIGHT VISITORS" by Gian Carlo Menotti

"BLUEBEARD'S CASTLE" by Béla Bartók

"LA CENERENTOLA" by Gioacchino Rossini

"THE CONSUL" by Gian Carlo Menotti

"FALSTAFF" by Giuseppe Verdi

"FAUST" by Charles Gounod

"HANSEL AND GRETEL" by Engelbert Humperdinck

"L'HEURE ESPAGNOLE" by Maurice Ravel

"THE MEDIUM" by Gian Carlo Menotti

"DIE MEISTERSINGER" by Richard Wagner

"REGINA" by Marc Blitzstein

"TURANDOT" by Giacomo Puccini

"WOZZECK" by Alban Berg

"THE TENDER LAND" by Aaron Copland (April 1, 1954)
    Director: Jerome Robbins
    Scenery: Oliver Smith
    Costumes: John Boyt
    Choreography: John Butler

Lyric Opera of Chicago (1953)

"I PURITANI" by Vencinzo Bellini
   With Maria Callas

New York City Center Light Opera Company

"THE BEGGAR'S OPERA" by John Gay (March 13, 1957)
   Staging: Richard Baldridge
   Musical staging: John Heawood
   Setting: Watson Barratt

"DIE FLEDERMAUS" by Johann Strauss (May 19, 1954)
   Libretto: Haffner and Genée (based on a German comedy by Roderich Bendix)
   Staging: Glenn Jordan
   Choreography: Robert Pagent

"THE SAINT OF BLEECKER STREET" by Gian Carlo Menotti (Dec. 27, 1954)
   Production: Chandler Cowles
   Staging: Gian Carlo Menotti
   Scenery and costumes: Robert Randolph

Dallas Civic Opera (1957-1969)

In addition to lighting, Jean Rosenthal was production manager, 1957, 1958, 1959, and production director, 1960-1969.

"ITALIAN GIRL IN ALGIERS" by Gioacchino Rossini (1957; revived in 1958, American stage debut of Teresa Berganza)
   Direction, costumes, scenery: Franco Zeffirelli
   With Giulietta Simionato

"JULIUS CAESAR" by George Frederick Handel (Fall 1965; original production with Kansas City Performing Arts Foundation, May 1965)
   Direction: Luciana Novaro
   Scenery: Gianni Polidori
   Costumes: Peter Hall

"LUCIA DI LAMMERMOOR" by Gaetano Donizetti (1959)
   Direction, scenery, costumes: Franco Zeffirelli
   With Maria Callas

"MACBETH" by Giuseppe Verdi (Fall 1966; revived, Fall 1967, with Alexis Minotis directing)
   Direction: Luciana Novaro
   Scenery and costumes: Peter Hall

"MEDEA" by Luigi Cherubini (1958; revived in 1959 and 1967)
   Direction: Alexis Minotis
   Costumes and scenery: Yanni Tsarouchis
   With Maria Callas, Jon Vickers, Nicola Zaccaria, Teresa Berganza

"OTELLO" by Giuseppe Verdi (1962; revived in 1968 with Carlo Maestrini directing)
   Direction: John Houseman
   Costumes and scenery: Attilio Colonnello
   With Mario del Monaco, Ilva Ligabue, Ramon Vinay

"TOSCA" by Giacomo Puccini (Fall 1965)
 Direction: John Houseman
 Scenery and costumes: Peter Hall
 With Renata Tebaldi, Giuseppe Taddei, F. Tagliavini

Kansas City Performing Arts Foundation
Production director: Jean Rosenthal, 1965-1968

"DIDO AND AENEAS"* by Henry Purcell (May 1966)
 Direction: Ellis Rabb
 Scenery: Oliver Smith
 Costumes: Peter Hall

"JULIUS CAESAR" by George Frederick Handel (May 1965; see also Dallas Civic Opera)
 Direction: Luciana Novaro
 Scenery: Gianni Polidori
 Costumes: Peter Hall

"ORPHEUS IN THE UNDERWORLD" by Jacques Offenbach (1967)
 Direction: Ellis Rabb
 Costumes: Hal C. George
 Scenery: Peter Hall

The American National Opera Company (for U.S. tour; premiere September 1967, Clowes Hall, Butler University, Indianapolis)

"FALSTAFF" by Giuseppe Verdi
 Director and conductor: Sarah Caldwell
 Scenery: Oliver Smith
 Costumes: Lewis Brown

"TOSCA" by Giacomo Puccini
 Director: Sarah Caldwell
 Costumes and scenery: Rudolph Heinrich

Metropolitan Opera Company at Lincoln Center

"CARMEN" by Georges Bizet (Dec. 15, 1967)
 Director: Jean-Louis Barrault
 Scenery and costumes: Jacques Dupont
 With Grace Bumbry and Justino Diaz

"HANSEL AND GRETEL" by Engelbert Humperdinck (Nov. 6, 1967)
 Director: Nathaniel Merrill
 Scenery and costumes: Robert O'Hearn

 *Dido was presented on a double bill with *The Faerie Queen, A Ballet*. Music by Henry Purcell in a New Edition by Nicola Rescigno
 Choreographer: Marina Svetlova
 Scenery and costumes: Peter Hall
 With Margot Fonteyn and Attilio Labis

"LUISA MILLER" by Giuseppe Verdi (Feb. 8, 1968)
  Director: Nathaniel Merrill
  Scenery and costumes: Attilio Colonnello
  With Montserrat Caballé, Richard Tucker, Sherrill Milnes

"MARTHA" by Friedrich von Flotow (Dec. 31, 1967)
  Director: Nathaniel Merrill
  Scenery: Oliver Smith
  Costumes: Motley

"ROMÉO ET JULIETTE" by Charles Gounod (Sept. 19, 1967)
  Director: Paul-Émile Deiber
  Designer: Rolf Gérard
  With Franco Corelli and Mirella Freni

Plays

"ALL'S WELL THAT ENDS WELL" by William Shakespeare (1959 season of The American Shakespeare Festival Theatre)
  Director: John Houseman
  Scenery: Will Steven Armstrong
  Costumes: Dorothy Jeakins
  Music: Herman Chessid

"THE BALLAD OF THE SAD CAFE" by Edward Albee, adapted from Carson McCullers (produced by Lewis Allen and Ben Edwards, Oct. 30, 1963)
  Director: Alan Schneider
  Scenery: Ben Edwards
  Costumes: Jane Greenwood
  With Colleen Dewhurst

"BAREFOOT IN THE PARK" by Neil Simon (produced by Saint Subber, Oct. 23, 1963)
  Director: Mike Nichols
  Scenery: Oliver Smith
  Costumes: Donald Brooks
  With Elizabeth Ashley, Mildred Natwick, Robert Redford, Kurt Kasznar

"BECKET" by Jean Anouilh, translated by Lucienne Hill (produced by David Merrick, Oct. 5, 1960)
  Staging: Peter Glenville
  Production designer: Oliver Smith
  Costumes: Motley
  With Laurence Olivier and Anthony Quinn

"CALIGULA" by Albert Camus, adapted by Justin O'Brien (produced by Chandler Cowles, Charles Bowden and Ridgely Bullock, Feb. 16, 1960)
  Staging: Sidney Lumet
  Settings and costumes: Will Steven Armstrong
  With Kenneth Haigh and Colleen Dewhurst

"CAESAR AND CLEOPATRA" by George Bernard Shaw (revived by Richard Aldrich and Richard Myers in association with Julius Fleischmann, Dec. 21, 1949)
  Staging: Cedric Hardwicke
  Settings and costumes: Rolf Gérard
  With Cedric Hardwicke, Lilli Palmer, Arthur Treacher

"THE CHINESE PRIME MINISTER" by Enid Bagnold (produced by Roger L. Stevens in association with Lyn Austin and Victor Samrock, Jan. 2, 1964)
  Director: Joseph Anthony

Scenery: Oliver Smith
Costumes: Valentina
With Margaret Leighton, Alan Webb, Peter Donat

"THE CLIMATE OF EDEN" by Moss Hart, based on Edgar Mittelholzer's novel *Shadows Move Among Them* (produced by Joseph M. Hyman and Bernard Hart, Nov. 13, 1952)
Staging: Moss Hart
Scenery: Frederick Fox
Costumes: Kenn Barr
With Isobel Elsom, Rosemary Harris, Earle Hyman

"THE COUNTRY WIFE" by William Wycherly (produced by Repertory Theatre of Lincoln Center, Dec. 9, 1965)
Director: Robert Symonds
Scenery and costumes: James Hart Stearns
Associate designer: James F. Göhl
Costume supervisor: Deirdre Cartier

"THE DARK AT THE TOP OF THE STAIRS" by William Inge (produced by Saint-Subber and Elia Kazan, Dec. 5, 1957)
Staging: Elia Kazan
Setting: Ben Edwards
Costumes: Lucinda Ballard
With Teresa Wright, Pat Hingle, Eileen Heckart

"DAUGHTER OF SILENCE" by Morris L. West, adapted from his novel (produced by Richard Halliday, Nov. 30, 1961)
Staging: Vincent J. Donehue
Settings: Oliver Smith
Costumes: Helene Pons and Oliver Smith
With Emlyn Williams

"DEAR LIAR" by Jerome Kilty, adapted from the correspondence of Mrs. Patrick Campbell and George Bernard Shaw (produced by Guthrie McClintic in association with Sol Hurok, March 17, 1960)
Staging: Jerome Kilty
Decor: Donald Oenslager
Costumes: Cecil Beaton
With Katharine Cornell and Brian Aherne

"THE DISENCHANTED" by Budd Schulberg and Harvey Breit, based on the novel by Budd Schulberg (produced by William Darrid and Eleanor Saidenberg, Jan. 3, 1958)
Staging: David Pressman
Settings: Ben Edwards
Costumes: Ann Roth
With Jason Robards, Jr., Rosemary Harris, George Grizzard

"THE DUCHESS OF MALFI" by John Webster (produced by Phoenix Theatre in association with John Houseman, March 19, 1957)
Staging: Jack Landau
Festival stage: Rouben Ter-Arutunian
Production and lighting: Jean Rosenthal
Costumes: Saul Bolasni
With Earle Hyman, Hurd Hatfield, Joseph Wiseman, Jacqueline Brookes

"THE EXERCISE" by Lewis John Carlino (produced by Lyn Austin, Oliver Smith, Jay J. Cohen and Leslie J. Staro, April 24, 1968)
Director: Alfred Ryder
Scenery: Oliver Smith
With Anne Jackson

"FREAKING OUT OF STEPHANIE BLAKE" by Richard Chandler (produced by Cheryl Crawford and Carl Schaeffer, Oct. 30, 1967)
    Director: Michael Kahn
    Scenery: Ben Edwards
    Costumes: Jeanne Button
    With Jean Arthur

"A GIFT OF TIME" by Garson Kanin, based on *Death of a Man* by Lael Tucker Wertenbaker (produced by William Hammerstein in association with David Shaber and William Snyder, Jr., Feb. 22, 1962)
    Staging: Garson Kanin
    Settings: Boris Aronson
    Costumes: Edith Lutyens Bel Geddes
    With Henry Fonda and Olivia de Havilland

"THE GREAT SEBASTIANS" by Howard Lindsay and Russel Crouse (produced by the authors, Jan. 4, 1956)
    Staging: Bretaigne Windust
    Settings: Raymond Sovey
    Costumes: Miss Fontanne's dresses by Mainbocher
    With Alfred Lunt and Lynn Fontanne

"HAMLET" by William Shakespeare (The American Shakespeare Festival, 1958 season)
    Director: John Houseman
    Scenery: David Hays
    Costumes: Alvin Colt
    Music: Virgil Thomson

"HAMLET" by William Shakespeare (produced by Alexander H. Cohen in association with Frenman Productions, April 9, 1964)
    Director: John Gielgud
    Scenery: Ben Edwards
    Clothes: Jane Greenwood
    With Richard Burton, Alfred Drake, Hume Cronyn, Eileen Herlie

"HAPPILY EVER AFTER" by J. A. Ross (produced by George W. George and Frank Granat, March 10, 1966)
    Director: Joseph Anthony
    Scenery: Peter Larkin
    Costumes: Theoni V. Aldredge
    With Barbara Barrie

"THE HAVEN" by Dennis Hoey (produced by Violla Rubber and J. Walker, Nov. 13, 1946)
    Staging: Clarence Derwent
    Settings: William Saviter
    Costumes: Noel Taylor
    (Lighting by Jean Rosenthal, though not credited)

"HENRY IV PART I" by William Shakespeare (produced by Theatre Inc., T. Edward Hambleton and Norris Houghton, March 1, 1960)
    Staging: Stuart Vaughan
    Scenery and costumes: Will Steven Armstrong

"HENRY IV PART II" by William Shakespeare (same set-up as Part I; April 18, 1960)

"A HOLE IN THE HEAD" by Arnold Schulman (produced by Producers Theatre, Robert Whitehead, Feb. 28, 1957)
    Staging: Garson Kanin

Production design: Boris Aronson, assisted by Lisa Jalowetz and Robert Randolph
Costumes: Patton Campbell
With David Burns, Kay Medford, Paul Douglas

"INCIDENT AT VICHY" by Arthur Miller (produced by Repertory Theatre of Lincoln Center, Dec. 3, 1964)
Director: Harold Clurman
Settings: Boris Aronson
Costumes: Jane Greenwood
With David Wayne, Hal Holbrook, Joseph Wiseman

"IVANOV" by Anton Chekhov, adapted by John Gielgud, based on translation by Ariadne Nicolaeff (Tennant Productions and Alexander H. Cohen, May 3, 1966)
Director: John Gielgud
Scenery and costumes: Rouben Ter-Arutunian
With John Gielgud and Vivien Leigh

"JOY TO THE WORLD" by Allan Scott (produced by John Houseman and Wlilliam R. Katzell, March 18, 1948)
Director: Jules Dassin
Scenery: Harry Horner
Costumes: Beverly Woodner
With Marsha Hunt and Alfred Drake

"JULIUS CAESAR" by William Shakespeare (The American Shakespeare Festival, 1955)
Director: Denis Carey
Scenery: Horace Armistead
Music: Lehman Engel

"JUNIPER AND THE PAGANS" by John Patrick, based on a novel by James Norman; (opened, Boston, Dec. 10, 1959; closed, Philadelphia, Dec. 26, 1959)
Director: Robert Lewis
Scenery: Oliver Smith
Costumes: Noel Taylor
Incidental music: Lehman Engel
With David Wayne

"KING JOHN" by William Shakespeare (The American Shakespeare Festival, 1956)
Directors: John Houseman and Jack Landau
Production and lighting: Jean Rosenthal
Scenery and costumes: Rouben Ter-Arutunian
Music: Virgil Thomson

"LEDA HAD A LITTLE SWAN" by Bamber Gascoigne (produced by Claire Nichtern, March 29, 1968)
Director: Andre Gregory
Scenery: Wolfgang Roth
Costumes: Carrie Fishbein

"LORD PENGO" by S. N. Behrman, suggested by his "Days of Duveen" (produced by Paul Gregory and Amy Lynn in association with Jane Friedlander and Michael Parver, Nov. 19, 1962)
Staging: Vincent J. Donehue
Scenery: Oliver Smith
Costumes: Lucinda Ballard
With Charles Boyer and Agnes Moorehead

"LUV" by Murray Schisgal (produced by Claire Nichtern, Nov. 11, 1964)
    Director: Mike Nichols
    Settings: Oliver Smith
    Costumes: Theoni V. Aldredge
    With Anne Jackson, Eli Wallach, Alan Arkin

"MEASURE FOR MEASURE" by William Shakespeare (The American Shakespeare Festival, 1956 season, and at Phoenix Theatre, N.Y.C., 1957 season)
    Directors: John Houseman and Jack Landau
    Production and lighting: Jean Rosenthal
    Scenery and costumes: Rouben Ter-Arutunian
    Music: Virgil Thomson

"THE MERCHANT OF VENICE" by William Shakespeare (The American Shakespeare Festival, 1957 season at Phoenix Theatre, N.Y.C.)
    Director: Jack Landau
    Production and lighting: Jean Rosenthal
    Scenery: Rouben Ter-Arutunian
    Costumes: Motley
    Music: Virgil Thomson

"MUCH ADO ABOUT NOTHING" by William Shakespeare (The American Shakespeare Festival, 1957 season at the Phoenix Theatre, N.Y.C.)
    Directors: John Houseman and Jack Landau
    Production supervisor: Jean Rosenthal
    Scenery and costumes: Rouben Ter-Arutunian
    Lighting: Tharon Musser
    Dance arrangements: John Butler
    Music: Virgil Thomson

"THE NIGHT OF THE IGUANA" by Tennessee Williams (produced by Charles Bowden in association with Violla Rubber, Dec. 28, 1961)
    Staging: Frank Corsaro
    Settings: Oliver Smith
    Costumes: Noel Taylor
    With Margaret Leighton, Bette Davis, Patrick O'Neal, Alan Webb

"THE ODD COUPLE" by Neil Simon (produced by Saint-Subber, March 10, 1965)
    Director: Mike Nichols
    Settings: Oliver Smith
    Costumes: Ann Roth
    With Art Carney and Walter Matthau

"ON AN OPEN ROOF" by Avraham Inlender (produced by Ridgely Bullock, Milton Katselas and Current Productions in association with Clement Stone, Jan. 28, 1963)
    Staging: Milton Katselas
    Scenery and lighting: Jean Rosenthal
    Costumes: Florence Klotz

"ONDINE" by Jean Giraudoux, adapted by Maurice Valency (produced by the Playwrights Company, Feb. 18, 1954)
    Staging: Alfred Lunt
    Settings: Peter Larkin
    Costumes: Richard Whorf
    With Audrey Hepburn and Mel Ferrer

"OTHELLO" by William Shakespeare (The American Shakespeare Festival, 1957 season at the Phoenix Theatre, N.Y.C.)
    Director: John Houseman
    Scenery and costumes: Rouben Ter-Arutunian

Production and lighting: Jean Rosenthal
   Music: Virgil Thomson

"*PLAZA SUITE*" by Neil Simon (three one-act plays; produced by Saint-Subber, Feb. 14, 1968)
   Director: Mike Nichols
   Scenery: Oliver Smith
   Costumes: Patricia Zipprodt
   With Maureen Stapleton and George C. Scott

"*POOR BITOS*" by Jean Anouilh, translated by Lucienne Hill (produced by Harold Prince in association with Michael Codrun and Pledon Ltd., Nov. 14, 1964)
   Director: Shirley Butler
   Foreign production designer: Timothy O'Brien
   American production supervisor: Jean Rosenthal
   Costumes: Donald Brooks
   With Donald Pleasence

"*QUADRILLE*" by Noel Coward (Nov. 3, 1954)
   Staging: Alfred Lunt
   Settings and costumes: Cecil Beaton
   With Alfred Lunt, Lynn Fontanne, Brian Aherne, Edna Best, Jerome Kilty

"*RICHARD III*" by William Shakespeare (presented by Theatre Productions, Jean Rosenthal, March 27, 1943)
   Staging: George Coulouris
   Scenery and costumes: Motley
   Production and lighting: Jean Rosenthal
   Music: George Hirst
   With George Coulouris and Mildred Dunnock

"*SEVENTH TRUMPET*" by Charles Rann Kennedy (produced by Theatre Associates, Nov. 21, 1941)
   Staging: Mr. Kennedy
   Lighting and scenery: Jo Mielziner
   Production supervisor: Jean Rosenthal
   Incidental music: Horace Middleton

"*THE STAR-SPANGLED GIRL*" by Neil Simon (produced by Saint-Subber, Dec. 21, 1966)
   Director: George Axelrod
   Scenery: Oliver Smith
   Costumes: Ann Roth
   With Anthony Perkins, Connie Stevens, Richard Benjamin

"*SUNDOWN BEACH*" by Bessie Breurer (produced by Louis J. Singer as sponsor for The Actor's Studio, Sept. 7, 1948)
   Staging: Elia Kazan
   Settings: Ben Edwards
   With Julie Harris, Phyllis Thaxter, Martin Balsam, Warren Stevens, Cloris Leachman

"*THE TAMING OF THE SHREW*" by William Shakespeare (The American Shakespeare Festival, 1956 season; at the Phoenix Theatre, 1957 season)
   Director: Norman Lloyd
   Festival stage: Rouben Ter-Arutunian
   Lighting and additional decor: Jean Rosenthal
   Costumes: Dorothy Jeakins
   Music: Irwin Bazelon

"*A TASTE OF HONEY*" by Shelagh Delaney (produced by David Merrick, by arrangement with Donald Albery and Oscar Lewenstein Ltd., Oct. 4, 1960)

    Staging: Tony Richardson and George Devine
    Production designer: Oliver Smith
    Costumes: Dorothy Jeakins
    With Joan Plowright and Angela Lansbury

"THE TEMPEST" by William Shakespeare (The American Shakespeare Festival, 1955)
    Director: Denis Carey
    Scenery: Horace Armistead
    Costumes: Robert Fletcher
    Music: Ernest Bacon
    Ballet masque: George Balanchine

"THE TIME OF YOUR LIFE" by William Saroyan (revived by N.Y.C. Center Theatre Co., Jan. 19, 1955)
    Staging: Sanford Meisner
    Settings: Watson Barratt
    Costumes: Grace Houston
    With Franchot Tone, Myron McCormick, John Carradine

"WEEKEND" by Gore Vidal (produced by Saint-Subber and Lester Osterman, March 13, 1968)
    Director: Joseph Anthony
    Scenic production: Oliver Smith
    Costumes: Theoni V. Aldredge
    With Kim Hunter, John Forsythe, Rosemary Murphy

"WINESBURG, OHIO" by Christopher Sergal, based on the novel by Sherwood Anderson (produced by Yvette Schumer, S. L. Adler and the Saba Co., Feb. 5, 1958)
    Staging: Joseph Anthony
    Settings: Oliver Smith
    Costumes: Dorothy Jeakins
    With Ben Piazza, Dorothy McGuire, James Whitmore, Leon Ames

"THE WINTER'S TALE" by William Shakespeare (American Shakespeare Festival, 1958)
    Directors: John Houseman and Jack Landau
    Scenery: David Hays
    Costumes: Dorothy Jeakins
    Dances: George Balanchine
    Music and songs: Marc Blitzstein

Musicals

"THE APPLE TREE"
    Book: Sheldon Harnick and Jerry Bock, based on "The Diary of Adam and Eve" by Mark Twain, "The Lady or the Tiger" by Frank Stockton, and "Passionella" by Jules Feiffer; additional book material by Jerome Coopersmith
    Music: Jerry Bock
    Lyrics: Sheldon Harnick
    Producer: Stuart Ostrow, Oct. 18, 1966
    Director: Mike Nichols
    Additional musical staging: Herbert Ross
    Choreography: Lee Theodore
    Scenery and costumes: Tony Walton
    With Alan Alda, Barbara Harris, Larry Blyden

"BAKER STREET" (adapted from stories by Sir Arthur Conan Doyle)
    Book: Jerome Coopersmith
    Music and lyrics: Marion Grudeff and Raymond Jessel
    Producer: Alexander H. Cohen, Feb. 16, 1965
    Director: Harold Prince
    Choreography: Lee Theodore
    Settings: Oliver Smith
    Costumes: Motley
    "Diamond Jubilee Parade" by Bil Baird's Marionettes
    With Inga Swenson, Fritz Weaver, Martin Gabel

"THE BEAST IN ME" (musical revue conceived by Haila Stoddard, based on James Thurber's *Fables For Our Times*)
    Adaptation and lyrics: James Costigan
    Music: Don Elliott
    Producer: Bonard Productions, May 16, 1963
    Staging: John Lehne
    Musical staging: John Butler
    Scenery and lighting: Jean Rosenthal
    Costumes: Leo Van Witse

"CABARET" (based on John van Druten's play *I Am a Camera* and stories by Christopher Isherwood)
    Book: Joe Masteroff
    Music: John Kander
    Lyrics: Fred Ebb
    Producer: Harold Prince in association with Ruth Mitchell, Nov. 20, 1966
    Director: Harold Prince
    Dances and cabaret numbers: Ronald Field
    Scenery: Boris Aronson
    Costumes: Patricia Zipprodt
    With Joel Grey and Lotte Lenya

"CAROUSEL" (based on Ferenc Molnár's *Liliom*)
    Music: Richard Rodgers
    Lyrics: Oscar Hammerstein
    Revived by New York City Center Light Opera Company, June 2, 1954
    Staging: William Hammerstein
    Choreography: Agnes de Mille choreography restaged by Robert Pagent
    Settings: Oliver Smith
    Costumes: John Boyt

"CHEVALIER AT 77" (a musical revue produced by Alexander H. Cohen, April 1, 1965)
    With Maurice Chevalier

"THE CONQUERING HERO" (based on *Hail the Conquering Hero* by Preston Sturges)
    Book: Larry Gelbart
    Music: Moose Charlap
    Lyrics: Norman Gimbel
    Producer: Robert Whitehead and Roger L. Stevens by special arrangement with Emka Ltd., Jan. 16, 1961
    Settings: Jean Rosenthal and William Pitkin
    Costumes: Patton Campbell
    With Tom Poston, Jane Mason, Lionel Stander

"DEAR WORLD" (based on *The Madwoman of Chaillot* by Jean Giraudoux, as adapted by Maurice Valency)
    Book: Jerome Lawrence and Robert E. Lee

Music and lyrics: Jerry Herman
Producer: Alexander H. Cohen, Feb. 6, 1969
Director and choreography: Joe Layton
Scenery: Oliver Smith
Costumes: Freddy Wittop
With Angela Lansbury

"DESTRY RIDES AGAIN" (based on the story by Max Brand)
Book: Leonard Gershe
Music and lyrics: Harold Rome
Producer: David Merrick in association with Max Brown, April 23, 1959
Director and choreography: Michael Kidd
Production designer: Oliver Smith
Costumes: Alvin Colt
With Andy Griffith and Dolores Gray

"FIDDLER ON THE ROOF" (based on Sholom Aleichem's stories)
Book: Joseph Stein
Music: Jerry Bock
Lyrics: Sheldon Harnick
Producer: Harold Prince, Sept. 22, 1964
Director and choreography: Jerome Robbins
Settings: Boris Aronson
Costumes: Patricia Zipprodt
With Zero Mostel and Maria Karnilova

"A FUNNY THING HAPPENED ON THE WAY TO THE FORUM" (based on plays by Plautus)
Book: Burt Shevelove and Larry Gelbart
Music and lyrics: Stephen Sondheim
Producer: Harold Prince, May 8, 1962
Staging: George Abbott
Choreography and musical staging: Jack Cole
Settings and costumes: Tony Walton
With Zero Mostel, David Burns, Jack Gilford

"THE GAY LIFE" (suggested by Arthur Schnitzler's *Anatol*)
Book: Fay and Michael Kanin
Music and lyrics: Arthur Schwartz and Howard Dietz
Producer: Kermit Bloomgarden, Nov. 18, 1961
Staging: Gerald Freedman
Staging of musical numbers and dances: Herbert Ross
Settings: Oliver Smith
Costumes: Lucinda Ballard
With Jules Munshin, Walter Chiari, Barbara Cook, Elizabeth Allen

"THE HAPPY TIME" (based on the play by Samuel Taylor and the book by Robert Fontaine)
Book: N. Richard Nash
Music: John Kander
Lyrics: Fred Ebb
Producer: David Merrick, Jan. 18, 1968
Director, film and choreography: Gower Champion
Scenery: Peter Wexler
Costumes: Freddy Wittop
With Robert Goulet and David Wayne

"HELLO, DOLLY!" (suggested by Thornton Wilder's play *The Matchmaker*)
Book: Michael Stewart

Music and lyrics: Jerry Herman
   Producer: David Merrick, Jan. 16, 1964
   Director and choreography: Gower Champion
   Assistant director: Lucia Victor
   Scenery: Oliver Smith
   Costumes: Freddy Wittop
   With Carol Channing, David Burns, Charles Nelson Reilly, Eileen Brennan

"HOUSE OF FLOWERS"
   Book: Truman Capote
   Music: Harold Arlen
   Lyrics: Capote and Arlen
   Producer: Saint-Subber, Dec. 30, 1954
   Staging: Peter Brook
   Dances and musical numbers: Herbert Ross
   Sets and costumes: Oliver Messel
   With Pearl Bailey, Juanita Hall, Diahann Carroll

"I DO! I DO!" (based on Jan de Hartog's play *The Fourposter*)
   Book and lyrics: Tom Jones
   Music: Harvey Schmidt
   Producer: David Merrick, Dec. 5, 1966
   Director: Gower Champion
   Scenery: Oliver Smith
   Costumes: Freddy Wittop
   With Mary Martin and Robert Preston

"ILLYA DARLING" (based on the film *Never on Sunday*)
   Book: Jules Dassin
   Music: Manos Hadjidakis
   Lyrics: Joe Darion
   Producer: Kermit Bloomgarden in association with United Artists, April 11, 1967
   Director: Jules Dassin
   Dances and musical numbers: Onna White
   Scenery: Oliver Smith
   Costumes: Theoni V. Aldredge
   With Melina Mercouri and Orson Bean

"JAMAICA"
   Book: E. Y. Harburg and Fred Saidy
   Music: Harold Arlen
   Lyrics: E. Y. Harburg
   Producer: David Merrick, Oct. 31, 1957
   Staging: Robert Lewis
   Choreography: Jack Cole
   Designer: Oliver Smith
   Costumes: Miles White
   With Lena Horne and Ricardo Montalban

"JENNIE" (suggested by the biography *Laurette* by Marguerite Courtney)
   Book: Arnold Schulman
   Music and lyrics: Howard Dietz and Arthur Schwartz
   Producers: Cheryl Crawford and Richard Halliday, Oct. 17, 1963
   Director: Vincent J. Donehue
   Choreography: Matt Mattox
   Scenery: George Jenkins
   Costumes: Irene Sharaff
   With Mary Martin and George Wallace

"JUDY GARLAND AT THE PALACE" (a musical revue, staged and directed by Charles Walters, Oct. 16, 1951)
    Gowns: Irene Sharaff and Pierre Balmain

"JUDY GARLAND AT THE MET" (a musical revue, staged and choreographed by Richard Barstow, May 11, 1959)
    Scenery and costumes: Irene Sharaff
    Musical direction: Gordon Jenkins
    With Judy Garland, Alan King, John W. Bubbles

"THE KING AND I" (based on Margaret Landon's novel *Anna and the King of Siam*)
    Music: Richard Rodgers
    Lyrics: Oscar Hammerstein
    Revived by New York City Center Light Opera Company, April 18, 1956
    Staging: John Fearnley
    Choreography: Jerome Robbins choreography remounted by June Graham
    Scenery: Jo Mielziner
    Costumes: Irene Sharaff
    With Jan Clayton and Zachary Scott

"KISS ME KATE" (based on Shakespeare's *The Taming of the Shrew*. Revived by New York City Center Light Opera Company, May 9, 1956)
    Book: Bella and Samuel Spewack
    Music and lyrics: Cole Porter
    Staging: Burt Shevelove
    Scenery: Watson Barratt
    Costumes: Alvin Colt
    With Kitty Carlisle and David Atkinson

"REDHEAD"
    Book: Herbert and Dorothy Fields, Sidney Sheldon and David Shaw
    Music: Albert Hague
    Lyrics: Dorothy Fields
    Producers: Robert Fryer and Lawrence Carr, Feb. 5, 1959
    Production staging and choreography: Robert Fosse
    Designer: Rouben Ter-Arutunian
    With Gwen Verdon and Richard Kiley

"SARATOGA" (based on Edna Ferber's novel *Saratoga Trunk*)
    Book: Morton da Costa
    Music: Harold Arlen
    Lyrics: Johnny Mercer
    Producer: Robert Fryer, Dec. 7, 1959
    Staging: Morton da Costa
    Choreography: Ralph Beaumont
    Settings and costumes: Cecil Beaton
    With Carol Lawrence and Howard Keel

"SHOW BOAT" (based on the novel by Edna Ferber. Revived by the New York City Center Light Opera Company, May 5, 1954)
    Book and lyrics: Oscar Hammerstein
    Music: Jerome Kern
    Staging: William Hammerstein
    Settings: Howard Bay
    Costumes: John Boyt
    With Robert Rounseville and Burl Ives

"SHOW BOAT" (produced by Music Theatre of Lincoln Center, July 19, 1966)
    Book and lyrics: Oscar Hammerstein
    Music: Jerome Kern

Director: Lawrence Kasha
  Choreography: Ronald Field
  Scenery: Oliver Smith
  Costumes: Stanley Simmons
  With Barbara Cook, Stephen Douglass, David Wayne, Margaret Hamilton, Constance Towers, Allyn McLerie

"THE SOUND OF MUSIC" (suggested by Maria Trapp's *The Trapp Family Singers*)
  Book: Howard Lindsay and Russel Crouse
  Music: Richard Rodgers
  Lyrics: Oscar Hammerstein
  Producers: Leland Hayward, Richard Halliday, Richard Rodgers, and Oscar Hammerstein, Nov. 16, 1959
  Staging: Vincent J. Donehue
  Staging of musical numbers: Joe Layton
  Scenic production: Oliver Smith
  Costumes: Lucinda Ballard
  Miss Martin's clothes: Mainbocher
  With Mary Martin and Theo Bikel

"TAKE ME ALONG" (based on Eugene O'Neill's play *Ah, Wilderness!*)
  Book: Joseph Stein and Robert Russell
  Music and lyrics: Bob Merrill
  Producer: David Merrick, Oct. 22, 1959
  Staging: Peter Glenville
  Staging of dances and musical numbers: Onna White
  Settings: Oliver Smith
  Costumes: Miles White
  With Jackie Gleason, Walter Pidgeon, Una Merkel, Eileen Herlie, Robert Morse

"A TIME FOR SINGING" (based on Richard Llewellyn's novel *How Green Was My Valley*)
  Book and lyrics: Gerald Freedman and John Morris
  Music: John Morris
  Producer: Alexander H. Cohen, May 21, 1966
  Director: Gerald Freedman
  Choreography: Donald McKayle
  Scenery: Ming Cho Lee
  Costumes: Theoni V. Aldredge
  With Tessie O'Shea, David O'Brien, Shani Wallis

"WEST SIDE STORY" (based on a conception of Jerome Robbins from *Romeo and Juliet* by William Shakespeare)
  Book: Arthur Laurents
  Music: Leonard Bernstein
  Lyrics: Stephen Sondheim
  Producers: Robert E. Griffith and Harold Prince by arrangement with Roger L. Stevens, Sept. 26, 1957 (revived April 27, 1960 and April 8, 1964)
  Staging and choreography: Jerome Robbins
  Choreography: Peter Gennaro
  Scenic production: Oliver Smith
  Costumes: Irene Sharaff
  With Carol Lawrence, Larry Kert, Chita Rivera

Theatre Consultant Projects

FACILITY	LOCATION	CLIENT
American Shakespeare Festival Theatre	Stratford, Conn.	Edwin Howard
Bank of America, World Headquarters Building*	San Francisco, Calif.	Skidmore, Owings, Merrill
Beloit College*	Beloit, Wis.	Beloit College
Bethel College	Newton, Kansas	John A. Shaver
Birmingham-Jefferson Civic Center*	Birmingham, Ala.	Geddes, Brecher, Qualls, Cunningham
Canadian Center for the Performing Arts	Ottawa, Canada	Affleck, Desbarats, Diamakopolous, Ledensold, Sise
Charles Street Center	Baltimore, Md.	John M. Johansen
Clowes Memorial Hall, Butler University	Indianapolis, Ind.	Evans Woolen III
Dickinson College, Theatre Facilities	Carlisle, Pa.	Howell, Lewis, Shay & Associates
Indiana University, University Schools, Theatre Facilities	Bloomington, Ind.	James Associates
Ithaca Festival Theatre	Ithaca, N.Y.	Ithaca Festival Theatre
Juilliard School at Lincoln Center for the Performing Arts Alice B. Tully Hall Drama Workshop Juilliard Opera Theatre C. Michael Paul Hall	New York City	Belluschi, Catalano, Westermann
Los Angeles Music Center Dorothy B. Chandler Pavilion Ahmanson Theatre	Los Angeles, Calif.	Welton Becket & Associates
Manitoba Theatre Center	Winnipeg, Canada	Waisman, Ross, Blankstein, Coop, Gillmor, Hanna
Marymount College	Salina, Kans.	John A. Shaver
Northwestern University Fine Arts Complex*	Evanston, Ill.	Loebl, Schlossman, Bennet, Dart
Pacific Terrace Convention Center, Auditorium Building	Long Beach, Calif.	Architects Associated
Philadelphia Academy of Music Restoration	Philadelphia, Pa.	——
Place des Arts Theatre Maisonneuve Theatre Port Royal	Montreal, Canada	David & Boulva
Russell Sage College	Ithaca, N.Y.	Neils H. Larsen
St. Louis Municipal Opera	St. Louis, Mo.	Hellmuth, Obata, & Kassabaum

*Design not complete in May 1969.

San Diego Theatre*	La Jolla, Calif.	Originally Bertrand Goldberg Associates Currently Frank L. Hope & Associates
State University of New York Fine Arts Centers		
College at Albany	Albany, N.Y.	Edward D. Stone
College at Fredonia	Fredonia, N.Y.	I. M. Pei & Partners
College at Oswego	Oswego, N.Y.	Skidmore, Owings, Merrill
College at Purchase	Purchase, N.Y.	Edward Barnes
Tyrone Guthrie Theatre	Minneapolis, Minn.	Ralph Rapson
United States Military Academy, Pershing Hall, Cadet Union Building	West Point, N.Y.	Welton Becket Associates
University of Washington Central Quadrangle Development and Performing Arts Building	Seattle, Wash.	Kirk, Wallace, McKinley
Wascana Centennial Auditorium	Regina, Sask., Canada	Imuzi, Arnott, Sugiyama

Illumination Consultant Projects

LITTLE DIX BAY
  Virgin Gorda, British Virgin Islands

MAUNA KEA BEACH HOTEL
  Hawaii

PAN AMERICAN WORLD AIRWAYS TERMINAL
  John F. Kennedy Airport, New York

READER'S DIGEST
  Pleasantville, New York

Restoration — Sound and Light Consultant and Designer

BOSCOBEL RESTORATION
  Garrison, New York

Renovations

THE PLAYHOUSE Malcolm Atterbury, owner
  Albany, New York

*Design not complete in May 1969.

Sources of Marginal Quotations

APPIA, ADOLPHE. Swiss-German philosopher, artist, visionary, called "father of modern stagecraft." From *The Work of Living Art,* translated by H. D. Albright (Miami, Fla., 1969).

ARONSON, BORIS. Scene designer and artist. From a 1969 interview.

BAKER, GEORGE PIERCE. Director of Yale Drama School. From *Dramatic Technique* (Boston, 1919).

BARRYTOWN (N.Y.) *Explorer.* From a review of *Boscobel Sound and Light,* July 1964.

BERNSTEIN, LEONARD. Conductor, composer. From a letter to Lael Wertenbaker, 1971.

CALLAS, MARIA. Opera diva. From a letter to Lael Wertenbaker, 1971.

CHAMBERLAIN, DORA. Treasurer, Martin Beck Theatre.

CHUJOY, ANATOLE. Author and editor. From a letter to Alfred Knopf, 1953.

CLURMAN, HAROLD. Director, Group Theatre, drama critic. From a review of *Luv* in his *The Naked Image* (New York, 1966).

CRAIG, GORDON. English stage designer, producer and actor. From *On the Art of the Theatre* (New York, 1925).

DANCE AND DANCERS. From an article "Personality of the Month. Jean Rosenthal," October 1959.

FEDER, ABE. Lighting designer. From a profile of Feder, "The Right Light," by Joseph Wechsberg, in *The New Yorker* (Oct. 22, 1960).

GIELGUD, JOHN. Actor. From a letter to Hamish Hamilton, 1970.

GRAHAM, MARTHA. Dancer, choreographer. From a 1970 interview.

HOUSEMAN, JOHN. Producer, director, actor. From a 1970 interview.

JONES, ROBERT EDMOND. Scene designer. From *The Dramatic Imagination* (New York).

KANIN, GARSON. Playwright, director, actor, writer. From a 1969 interview.

KELLY, LAWRENCE. Manager, The Chicago Opera and The Dallas Opera. From a 1971 interview.

LANSBURY, ANGELA. Actress and musical-comedy star. From a letter to Marion Kinsella, 1971.

LEATHERMAN, LEROY. Writer. From *Martha Graham: Portrait of the Lady as an Artist* (New York, 1966).

LUNT, ALFRED. Actor, director. From a letter to Suzanne Gleaves, 1970.

MANSON, JOY. Free-lance journalist. From an unpublished article, 1967.

MARTIN, JOHN. Dance critic, *New York Times,* 1927-1962. From reviews published in the *New York Times.*

MARTIN, MARY. Singing star of, among other productions, *South Pacific, I Do! I Do!* From a letter to Lael Wertenbaker, 1970.

McCANDLESS, STANLEY. Engineer and teacher of lighting design. From *A Method of Lighting the Stage* (New York, 1954).

MONTAIGNE, MICHEL DE (1533-1592). Essayist. From *Selected Essays of Montaigne.* Charles Cotton–W. Hazlitt translation (New York, 1949).

NEWSWEEK MAGAZINE. From an article in the "Movies" section, March 3, 1969.

PHILLIPS, WENDELL K. Actor, director, teacher of acting. From a 1970 interview.

ROBERTSON, THOMAS W. (1829-1871). Actor and playwright. From an article in *Illustrated Times* of London, quoted in A. M. Nagler, *Sources of Theatrical History* (New York, 1952).

ROSENTHAL, JEAN. From letters to Dr. Pauline Rosenthal and Dr. Maurice Rosenthal: *page 12,* written from the Manumit School March 4, 1926; *page 15,* written from New Haven, December 6, 1933; *page 18,* written on "Wednesday," 1936.

ROSENTHAL, DR. PAULINE. Psychiatrist, writer, mother of J. R. From a letter to Lael Wertenbaker, 1970.

SARGEANT, WINTHROP. Writer and music critic for *The New Yorker.* From "Please, darling, bring three to seven," a profile of Jean Rosenthal in *The New Yorker,* Feb. 4, 1956.

SMITH, OLIVER. Scene designer and co-director of *American Ballet Theatre.* From a 1970 interview.

STRINDBERG, AUGUST (1849-1912). Playwright and novelist. From the Manifesto at the time of first performance of *Miss Julie* to its French audience, 1893.

VARIETY. From a review of *Boscobel,* July 1964.

VICTOR, LUCIA. Stage manager, director. From a 1970 interview.

WEST, CHRISTOPHER. Resident Producer, Royal Opera House, Covent Garden, London. From a letter to J. R., July 1950.

Index

Index of Lighting Terms

auxiliary boards, 69, 159
cues and cue sheets, 63-64, 111, 112-113, 119, 159
dimmers, 75, 126, 159-160
ellipsoidal (spotlight), 63, 125-127, 137, 140-158 *passim*
focusing and focus chart, 63, 95, 99, 113, 118, 119, 135-157 *passim*, 178-180
fresnel, 62, 135, 140-149 *passim*, 155, 156, 157, 180
hook-up, 62, 118, 119, 124, 159, 178
keylight, 69, 131
lekolite (leko), 62, 137, 180
lighting records, 63, 159-160
master boards or dimmers, 69, 159
preset, 69, 159

Index of Names

Actors' Equity, 19, 21
Adams, Franklin P., 13
Adams, Maude, 33
Afternoon of a Faun, The (Claude Debussy — Jerome Robbins), 124
Aïda (Giuseppe Verdi), 90, 91
Ailey, Alvin, 127
All's Well That Ends Well (William Shakespeare), vi
Appia, Adolphe, 55, 117
Archaic Hours (Martha Graham), viii-ix
archy and mehitabel (Don Marquis), 34
arena stage, 109
Armistead, Horace, 99
Arms and the Man (George Bernard Shaw), 12
Aronson, Boris, 33, 34, 68, 69, 72
Atkinson, Brooks, 13

Bailey, Pearl, 84
Baird, Bil, 17
Baker, George Pierce, 15, 16
Balanchine, George, 32, 117, 118, 119-125, 128, 129. *See also* specific ballets
Ballet Caravan, 120
Ballet Imperial (P. I. Tchaikovsky — George Balanchine), 128
Ballet International, 118
Ballet Russe, 13, 117
Ballet Society, 23, 25, 37, 118, 120, 127
Ballet Theatre (American), 118, 119, 127-128
Barry, Philip, 16
Barrymore, John, 18
Baum, Morton, 122
Bayreuth, Germany, 92, 101
Beaton, Cecil, 120

Becket (Jean Anouilh), 35, 63
Beerbohm-Tree, Sir Herbert, 53
Belasco, David, 30, 49, 54, 55
Ben-Hur (Lew Wallace), 54
Bérard, Christien, 120
Bernstein, Aline, 14
Bernstein, Leonard, 33, 76
Bevin, Frank, 15
Bing, Rudolph, 92, 99, 100, 101, 103
Blitzstein, Marc, quoted, 18-21
Blocks (Molly Day Thatcher), 14
Bolero (Maurice Ravel — Nijinska), 36
Boscobel, vii, 111-113
Boston Theatre, 52
Brechtian theatre, 16
Brooks, Randall, 128
Broun, Heywood, 13
Brown, John Mason, 13
Burton, Richard, 11
Butz, David, 111-112

Cage, The (Igor Stravinsky — George Balanchine), 124, 126, 128
Caldwell, Sarah, 92
Callas, Maria, 34, 97-98, 101-103
Callimachus, 45
Caracalla (Theatre), 125
Carmen (Georges Bizet), 95
Carroll, Albert, 14
Carson, Nat, 17
Cave of the Heart, The (Samuel Barber — Martha Graham), 131
Cervantes, Miguel, 45
Chagall, Marc, 120, 122-123
Chamberlain, Dora, 25
Chandler, Pavilion, 38
Chase, Lucia, 127, 129

Cherubini, Luigi, 102
Chestnut Street Opera House, 52
Chicago Opera (Lyric), 97
Chinese Prime Minister, The (Enid Bagnold), 71
Chujoy, Anatol, 120
City Center (of Music and Drama), 25, 93, 95-96, 97, 122, 123
Clayton, Dr. John, 52
Cleghorn, Sara, 12
Clurman, Harold, 31, 32
Comedians, The (Dmitri Kabalevsky — Ruthanna Boris), 124
Comedy of Errors (William Shakespeare), 47
Commedia dell'arte, 47, 107
Consul, The (Gian Carlo Menotti), 98
Corelli, Franco, 100-101
Cornell, Katharine, 15, 33
Cotten, Joseph, 17
Coulouris, George, 24
Covent Garden, 52
Cradle Will Rock, The (Marc Blitzstein), 18-21
Craig, Gordon, 55
Cuevas, Marquis de, 35
Cupid and Psyche myth, 46
Cyrano de Bergerac (Edmond Rostand), 72

Dali, Salvador, 36
Dallas Civic Opera, 101-103
Dance and Dancers, 117
Davies, Marion, 35
Davis, Bette, 34, 70
Dean, Alexander, 60
Dear Liar (Jerome Kilty — Shaw-Campbell letters), 15
Dear World (Jerome Lawrence — Robert E. Lee — Jerry Herman), 71
Death of a Man (Lael Wertenbaker), 68
de Havilland, Olivia, 68-69
Deiber, Paul-Emile, 100
Delectable History of Fortnum and Mason, 47
De Mille, Agnes, 128
de' Sommi, Leone Hebreo, 47-48, 53
Diaghilev, Sergei, 120
Dialogues on Stage Affairs (Leone Hebreo de' Sommi), 47
Dido and Aeneas (Henry Purcell), 101
Don Giovanni (W. A. Mozart), 90, 96-97
Dybbuk, The (Saloman Ansky), 13

East Lynne (Alfred Kempe), 55
Eaves Costume Company, 24
Ebert, Carl, 98
Elizabethan theatre, 65
Elliott, Laura, 13, 14
Empire Theatre, 24, 25
Encyclopaedia Britannica, 46
Endgame (Samuel Beckett), 34
L'Enfant et les Sortilèges (Maurice Ravel — George Balanchine), 120
Engel, Lehman, 20
Erechtheum, 45
Erlangers, the, 30
Ethical Culture School, 12
Euripides, 102

Faust (Charles Gounod), 90

Feder, Abe, 17, 20-22, 100
Federal Theatre Project (WPA), 17, 19-21, 56
Feld, Elliott, 127
Felsenstein, Walter, 92
Fields, Herb, 12
Fincke, William, 12
Firebird, The (Igor Stravinsky — George Balanchine), 122
Fitch, Clyde, 15
Five Kings (William Shakespeare — Orson Welles), 23
Fonda, Henry, 14, 68-69
Fontanne, Lynn, 32, 33-34
Fountainhead, The (Ayn Rand), 37
Four Methods of Lighting (Joseph Furttenbach the Elder), 50
Four Temperaments, The (Paul Hindemith — George Balanchine), 123
Francés, Estebán, 122
Francis, Arlene, 17
Friends Seminary, 13
Furttenbach, Joseph, the Elder, 47, 49, 50

Garland, Judy, 33
Garrick, David, 52
Genesis, 39
Gerard, Rolf, 95
Gielgud, John, 15, 33, 65
Gift of Time, A (Garson Kanin — Lael Wertenbaker), 68-70
Girl of the Golden West, The (David Belasco), 54
Giselle (Adolphe Adam), 127
Gleaves, Suzanne, v, 111
Götterdämmerung (Richard Wagner), 125
Graham, Martha, viii-ix, 13, 14, 17, 23, 25, 32, 35, 36, 38, 56, 117, 119, 121, 127, 128, 129-131, 180
Gran Teatro del Liceo, 125-126
Greek National Theatre, 102
Green, Paul, 23
Group Theatre, 31, 56
Guthrie, Tyrone, 32

Hamlet (William Shakespeare), 11, 17-18, 65
Hammerstein, Oscar, II, 12
Hammond, Percy, 13
Handel, George Frederick, 101
Hart, Lorenz, 12, 13
Hayes, Helen, 112-113
Heartbreak House (George Bernard Shaw), 22
Hearst, William Randolph, 35
Hello, Dolly! (Michael Stewart — Jerry Herman), 71, 76-84, 178, 180
Henry IV (William Shakespeare), 23
Henry V (William Shakespeare), 23, 64-65
Henry VI (William Shakespeare), 23
Henry Street Playhouse, 14
Hewitt, Barnard, 47
Hindemith, Paul, 120
Hippodrome (New York), 54
Hopkins, Arthur, 30, 55
Horse Eats Hat (Eugène Labiche — Edwin Denby), 17
Horst, Louis, 13, 14
House of Flowers (Truman Capote — Harold Arlen), 72

254

Houseman, John, vi, 16, 17-18, 19-25 passim, 32, 35, 56, 111-112, 120
Howard, Leslie, 11, 17-18
Hudson, Henry, 112-113

Ibsen, Hendrick, 54
I Puritani (Vincenzo Bellini), 98
Irving, Sir Henry, 53, 55
Israel (Ernest Bloch), 14
Italian Girl in Algiers (Gioacchino Rossini), 101

Jenny (Arnold Schulman — Howard Dietz and Arthur Schwartz), 112
Jones, Robert Edmond, 4, 34, 55-56, 59
Julius Caesar (William Shakespeare), 22
Julius Caesar (George Frederick Handel), 101
Julliard School of Music and Drama, 25

Kaleidoscope (Dmitri Kabalevsky — Ruthanna Boris), 124
Kane, Whitford, 17
Kanin, Garson, 32, 63, 68, 69
Karinska, Barbara, 124
Kazan, Elia, 31, 32
Kelly, Lawrence, 97-98, 101
Kennedy Airport Pan American building, 25
Keynes, Maynard, 117
Kidd, Michael, 127
Kinsella, Marion, v
Kirstein, Lincoln, 23, 32, 36, 117, 119, 120-122, 127, 129
Klaws, the, 30

La Bohème (Giacomo Puccini), 90, 95
Lansbury, Angela, 34, 62, 71
La Scala, 91
Lascaux Caves, 45
La Traviata (Giuseppe Verdi), 90, 95, 101
League of Composers, 13
Leatherbee, Charles, 14
Leatherman, Leroy, 14, 131
LeClercq, Tanaquil, 124
Leighton, Margaret, 34, 70, 71
Les Biches (Francis Poulenc — Bronislava Nijinska), 36, 117
Leve, Sam, 22
Lewisohn, Alice, 13, 14
Lewisohn, Irene, 13, 14
Lewisohn Stadium, 24
Liceo, Gran Teatro del, 125-126
Limón, José, 127
Lincoln Center, 25
Little Clay Cart (King Shudraka — translation, Arthur Wm. Ryder; adaptation, Agnes Morgan), 13
Los Angeles Music Center, 25, 38
Lunt, Alfred, 32, 33, 34
Luv (Murray Schisgal), 72
Lyceum Theatre, 52

Macbeth (William Shakespeare), 53
McCandless, Stanley, 16, 62
McCormack, Myron, 14
McHugh, Eddie, 18
MacLeish, Archibald, 21
Madame Butterfly (Giacomo Puccini), 90
Magnani, Anna, 33

Manson, Joy, 99, 100, 101
Manumit School, 12
Marcy, Helen, 24
Marquis de Cuevas ballet, 35
Markova, Alicia, 101
Marriage of Figaro (W. A. Mozart), 95
Martha's Vineyard, 26
Martin Beck Theatre, 25
Martin, John, 118, 123, 124
Martin, Mary, 33
Mask of Apollo, The (Mary Renault), 44
Mason, William, 47
Massine, Léonide, 36
Maxine Elliott Theatre, 17, 18, 19, 20
May, Elaine, 32
Médéa (Luigi Cherubini), 101-102
Medium, The (Gian Carlo Menotti), 98-99, 100
Mendelssohn, Felix, 123
Menotis, Alexis, 102
Menotti, Gian Carlo, 25, 93, 98
Mercury Theatre, 21-23, 25, 31, 36, 56
Meredith, Burgess, 23
Merrick, David, 32
Merrill, Gary, 112
Metamorphosis (Paul Hindemith — George Balanchine), 124
Method for Lighting the Stage, A (Stanley McCandless), 16
Metropolitan Opera, 91, 92, 95, 99-101, 103
Mielzner, Jo, 34, 100
Minckelers, Jean Pierre, 52
Miró, Joan, 120
Molière, Jean Baptiste, 30
Montaigne, Michel, Seigneur de, 68
Morcom, Jimmy (James Stewart), 23
Mostel, Zero, 33
Mourning Becomes Electra (Eugene O'Neill), 4
Mozart, Wolfgang Amadeus, 95. *See also specific operas*
Murdock, William, 52
Musicians Union, 20

Native Son (Richard Wright — Paul Green), 23, 25
Neighborhood Playhouse (School of the Theatre), 13-14, 47, 129
New York City Ballet, 25, 37, 118, 120-128 *passim*
New York City Center, *see* City Center
New York State Theatre, 128
Nichols, Mike, 32, 67
Nicoll, Allardyce, 47
Night of the Iguana (Tennessee Williams), 34, 70
Nijinska, Bronislava, 36
Niguchi, Isamu, 120, 124
Nolan, Willy, 36, 38
Nordheimer, Clyde, 111-112

Odd Couple, The (Neil Simon), 35
Oenslager, Donald, 15, 34
Oeri, Georgine, 62
O'Neill, Eugene, 4, 16
Opus 34 (Arnold Schönberg — George Balanchine), 124
Orpheus (Igor Stravinsky — George Balanchine), 128

255

O'Shea, Madeleine, 37
Othello (William Shakespeare), 72
Oxford Companion to the Theatre, 47

Pavlova, Anna, 13
Pearson, Heskith, 53
Phillips, Wendell K., 17, 18
Phoenix Theatre, 56
Picasso, Pablo, 117, 120
Pinero, Arthur Wing, 15, 16
Plaza Suite (Neil Simon), 67-68, 159, 178, 180
Poindexter, H. R., 101
Porcher, Nananne, 24-25, 101, 119, 125-126, 128
Powers, Marie, 101
Practica (Nicola Sabbattini), 49-50
Project no. 891 (WPA), 17
Purcell, Henry, 101

Ravel, Maurice, 120
Reader's Digest, 111
Redhead (Herbert and Dorothy Fields — Sidney Sheldon and David Shaw — Albert Hague and Dorothy Fields), 63
Renaissance Stage, The (ed. Barnard Hewitt), 47
Renault, Mary, 44
Rescigno, Nicola, 97
Return of Peter Grimm (David Belasco), 55
Richard III (William Shakespeare), 23, 24
Rigoletto (Giuseppe Verdi), 94
Robbins, Jerome, 32, 76, 127, 129
Robert-Houdin, Paul, 110
Robertson, Thomas William, 53
Rodgers, Richard, 12, 13, 76
Romeo and Juliet (William Shakespeare), 45, 72
Roméo et Juliette (Charles Gounod), 90, 100-101
Rome Opera House, 126
Rosenkavalier, Der (Richard Strauss), 96
Rosenthal, Ivan, 12
Rosenthal, Leon, 12
Rosenthal, Pauline, 11-12, 15
Royal Opera House, 125

Sabbattini, Nicola, 47, 49-50
Saint James Theatre, 25
Saint Joan (George Bernard Shaw), 5
Saint-Subber, Arnold, 32-33, 67
Salome (Richard Strauss), 90, 96
Sands, Dorothy, 14
Santini, Mr., 126, 127
Sargeant, Winthrop, 4, 63, 64
Schönberg, Arnold, 124
School of American Ballet, 120
Scotch Symphony (Felix Mendelssohn — George Balanchine), 123
Scott, George C., 67
Seldes Marion, 69
Serlio, Sebastiano, 47, 50
Seventh Trumpet, The (Charles Rann Kennedy), 71
Shakespeare, William, 4, 15, 22, 23, 30, 45, 53, 64-67, 72. See also specific plays
Shakespeare Festival (Statford, Conn.), 25
Shaw, George Bernard, 5, 12
Sherman, Hiram, 17

Shoemaker's Holiday (Thomas Dekker), 22
Shuberts, the, 30
Simon, Neil, 67
Simonson, Lee, 55-56
Smith, Oliver, 26, 33, 34, 35, 61-72 *passim*, 76-77, 100, 120, 127-128
Son et lumière, 110
Sound and Light, 110-113
Staedtische Oper, 98
Stapleton, Maureen, 67
Strasberg, Lee, 31
Strindberg, August, 54, 55
Stravinsky, Igor, 13, 120
Swan Lake (P. I. Tchaikovsky — George Balanchine), 36, 117, 127, 179

Tallchief, Maria, 117, 119
Tarrytown Explorer, 113
Tempest, The (William Shakespeare), 65-67
Ter-Aruturian, Reuben, 122
Terry, Walter, 123
Théâtre de la Foire de Saint Germain, 102
Theatre Guild, 14, 23, 33, 55
Theatre Production Service, 24-25, 37
Theatre Union, 56
Theme and Variations (P. I. Tchaikovsky — George Balanchine), 128
Thomashevsky, Boris, 96
Throckmorton, Cleon, 24
Too Much Johnson (William Gillette), 23
Tosca (Giacomo Puccini), 90, 94
TPS (Theatre Production Service), 24-25, 37
Trueman, Paula, 14
Tsarouchis, Yanni, 102
Tudor, Antony, 128, 129

Variety, 113
Venice Theatre (New Century), 18, 20-21
Verdi, Giuseppe, 95. See also specific operas
Verdon, Gwen, 33
Victor, Lucia, 3, 124, 131
Vienna State Opera, 102

Wagner, Richard, 54, 91, 125
Walker, David, 112
Wallace, Mr. and Mrs. DeWitt, 111
Waltz (La Valse) (Maurice Ravel — George Balanchine), 126
Warfield, David, 55
Welles, Orson, 16, 17, 18-23, 24, 31, 32, 56, 119
Wertenbaker, Lael, 68, 70, 111-112
West, Christopher, 125
West Side Story (Arthur Laurents — Jerome Robbins — Leonard Bernstein), 25, 63
White Peacock, The (Charles Griffes — Irene Lewisohn), 14
Williams, Tennessee, 70. See also specific plays
Windust, Bretaigne, 33
Winesburg, Ohio (Christopher Sergal — Sherwood Anderson), 63
Wintzler, F. A., 52
Wise, Eleanor, 24, 36
Wittop, Freddie, 76, 81

Yale University, 15-16, 24, 47

Zeffirelli, Franco, 33, 95, 101

About the Authors

Jean Rosenthal was the award-winning designer of about 4000 productions in all aspects of theater, including such shows as *West Side Story; Plaza Suite; Becket; Hello, Dolly!, Hamlet* (with Richard Burton), *The Odd Couple, Cabaret,* and *Fiddler on the Roof.*

Lael Wertenbaker has written seventeen works of fiction, nonfiction, drama, and juvenile literature, including *Death of a Man, Festival, The World of Picasso, The Eye of the Lion, To Mend the Heart, The Afternoon Women,* and *Unbidden Guests.*